Financial Accounting

Second Edition

Jae K. Shim, Ph.D.
Professor of Accountancy and Finance
California State University at Long Beach

Joel G. Siegel, Ph.D., CPA
Professor of Accounting and Information Systems
Queens College, City University of New York

Schaum's Outline Series

New York   Chicago   San Francisco   Lisbon   London   Madrid
Mexico City   Milan   New Delhi   San Juan   Seoul
Singapore   Sydney   Toronto

The **McGraw·Hill** Companies

JAE K. SHIM is currently professor of Accountancy and Finance at California State University at Long Beach. He received his M.B.A. and Ph.D. from the University of California at Berkeley. Professor Shim has published over 40 articles in accounting, finance, economics, and operations research journals. He is a coeditor of *Readings in Cost and Managerial Accounting*. He is also a coauthor of the Schaum's Outlines in *Financial Accounting, Personal Finance,* and *Managerial Finance,* and of the AICPA's *Variance Analysis for Cost Control and Profit Maximization* and *Account for and Evaluation of Process Cost Systems*. Dr. Shim was the recipient of the 1982 Credit Research Foundation award.

JOEL G. SIEGEL is professor of Accounting and Information Systems at Queens College of the City University of New York. He received his Ph.D. in accounting from the Bernard M. Baruch College of the City University of New York and a CPA certificate from New York. In 1972, Dr. Siegel was the recipient of the Outstanding Educator of America Award. He was employed as a staff accountant with Coopers and Lybrand, CPAs. Professor Siegel is a coauthor of the Schaum's Outlines of *Financial Accounting* and *Managerial Finance*. He has also written *How to Analyze Businesses, Financial Statements and the Quality of Earnings,* published by Prentice-Hall. Dr. Siegel is the author of five publications in continuing professional education published by the AICPA.

2 3 4 5 6 7 8 9 10   CUS/CUS   1 9 8 7 6 5 4 3

ISBN   978-0-07-176250-2
MHID   0-07-176250-7

McGraw-Hill books are available at special quantity discounts to use as premiums and sales promotions or for use in corporate training programs. To contact a representative, please e-mail us at bulksales@mcgraw-hill.com.

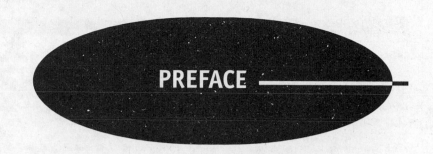

PREFACE

Schaum's Outline of Theory and Problems of Financial Accounting presents all important financial accounting topics in a clear, concise manner, thereby enabling students to enhance their understanding of this discipline. Intended primarily for students enrolled in an introductory financial accounting course at the undergraduate or graduate level, the book is also highly recommended for individuals in private study, those seeking college credit by examination, and students requiring a review of the subject before proceeding to more advanced accounting courses. Because the emphasis of the Outline is on developing the student's ability to solve problems, this book is useful for those individuals who are preparing to take the CPA (Certified Public Accountant), CIA (Certified Internal Auditor), CMA (Certified Management Accountant), CFM (Certified in Financial Management), and CFA (Chartered Financial Analyst) examinations.

This Outline should prove invaluable to students of financial accounting for the following reasons:

1. The presentation of financial accounting theory is straightforward, logical, and intelligible, permitting students to comprehend the subject.

2. Examples are used to illustrate all important procedures and concepts.

3. Solved problems, with detailed step-by-step solutions, enable students to succeed in the practical application of the concepts learned.

4. Review questions and answers are provided so that students can check their comprehension of the material.

5. Examination questions and their solutions are given for each three or four chapters covered, so that students can measure their progress.

We wish to acknowledge our gratitude to several colleagues who provided valuable suggestions for the book's content, especially Professors David Davidson and Michael Constas. Professor Loc Nyuen contributed Chapter 16.

Most of all we would like to thank our graduate assistants, Cher Ragge and Allison Shim, for their assistance with the word processing of the manuscript.

JAE K. SHIM
JOEL G. SIEGEL

CONTENTS

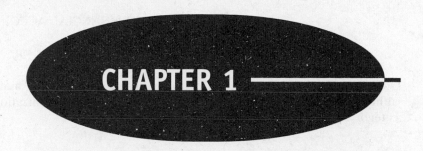

CHAPTER 1

Introduction to Financial Accounting

1.1 SCOPE AND PURPOSE OF ACCOUNTING

Financial accounting is the language of business. It is concerned with assisting individuals, businesses, and nonprofit organizations in recording financial transactions (events which have occurred), in preparing performance reports and reports that reflect the current financial position, and in assisting in the decision-making processes of financial statement users. Thus, *financial accounting may be defined as the recording, classifying, summarizing, and reporting of transactions with the aim of showing the financial health of an entity.*

Financial information generated by the accounting process is used by many diverse parties. Business owners use it primarily in evaluating the return they are receiving on their investment, while management's interest is in determining the financial strengths and weaknesses of the business so that performance may be improved. Potential investors and their advisors are concerned with whether a firm represents a sound avenue for investment, while creditors use financial information to determine a firm's financial capacity to meet its obligations when they become due. The Internal Revenue Service is interested in determining tax revenues based on an entity's profitability, while customers are concerned with a firm's continuing ability to supply their needs, and employees need to evaluate the firm's financial ability to meet wage demands. Other users of financial information are attorneys, security exchanges, regulatory agencies, and trade associations.

1.2 BRANCHES OF ACCOUNTING

The major branches of accounting are private, public, and governmental accounting.

Private accounting refers primarily to the private business sector, either sole proprietors, partnerships, or corporations. Private accountants generally work for the controller's (the chief accounting officer) office and prepare budget reports and departmental performance reports, among others, that management uses for evaluation and decision making.

Public accounting refers to work done by independent firms that audit the books of companies to ensure that corporate financial data are properly stated. To work as a public accountant a license, called the "Certified Public Accountant," is required. The license is given to those who pass an examination and meet specified minimum experience requirements.

Governmental accounting refers primarily to federal, state, and local governmental institutions, although some nonprofit organizations, such as charitable organizations and hospitals, also fall into this category.

1.3 PURPOSES OF A BUSINESS ENTITY

There are different types of business entities, such as a sole proprietorship, a partnership, and a corporation. In the *sole proprietorship* there is only *one* owner. In the event the business fails, the owner is *personally* liable for all debts incurred. A *partnership* has more than one owner. The partnership contract spells out the rights of each partner in such matters as profit distribution and withdrawal of funds; personal liability exists in partnerships. In a *corporation*, the equity interest belongs to investors who have purchased shares of stock in the business. Only *limited* liability exists for stockholders if the corporation fails, in that they will lose only what they have invested. No personal liability exists.

A business entity provides goods or services or both to customers in order to generate a profit (net income) for its owners. *Profit* is the excess of *revenue* (resources received for the goods or services) over *expenses* (resources used to produce the goods or services). For a manufacturing or retail business revenue consists of the sales price charged, while for a service business (e.g., an accountant) revenue is the fee charged for services rendered. Expenses are incurred in order to obtain that revenue. Examples of expenses are wages, rent, and telephone. The profit-generating activities of a business over a period of time are shown in the *income statement*.

An entity must be financially sound in order to satisfy its debts at maturity. A measure of financial health is the degree to which assets (economic resources) exceed liabilities (obligations due). A picture of a company's financial status at the end of an accounting period is shown in the *balance sheet* (statement of financial position).

A business entity is also expected to have sufficient funds in order to carry out its business activities. The flow of funds into and out of the entity is described in the statement of changes in financial position (funds statement).

1.4 PRINCIPLES AND ASSUMPTIONS OF FINANCIAL ACCOUNTING

Financial accounting requirements are promulgated by the Financial Accounting Standards Board (FASB), which is the principal rule-making body. The requirements are in the form of FASB *Statements* and *Interpretations*. Also, the Securities and Exchange Commission (SEC) issues *Accounting Series Releases*, which dictate accounting requirements for companies required to file with the SEC because they issue stock. The American Institute of Certified Public Accountants (AICPA) issues *Statements on Auditing Standards* to be followed by independent CPAs who audit their clients' accounting records.

In order for financial data generated to be useful in economic decision making, financial accounting is based on the following principles, assumptions, and definitions:

Relevance. Information provided by the accounting system must be pertinent to the financial status and performance of the entity.

Understandability. To be useful, accounting data must be understandable to users. Proper means of communication, including use of appropriate, standard terminology, must be employed.

Verifiability. Accounting data must be verifiable. A report is verifiable when two accountants arrive at *close* answers when given the same financial data.

Objectivity. Accounting information provided should be *neutral* in the sense that data are not manipulated to favor one party over another. It should satisfy the common needs of diverse users.

Matching. For any period in which revenue is recognized, expenses incurred in obtaining that revenue should also be recognized. An example is the sales price of merchandise being matched with its cost.

Timeliness. For information generated by the accounting system to be useful for decision making, it must be received *shortly* after the entity's accounting period.

Consistency. This principle refers to the use of the *same accounting method* from reporting period to reporting period so that proper evaluation can be made of an entity's progress over time.

Comparability. Financial reports must be in a form that permits comparison of one company with other companies in the industry. Comparability is facilitated when companies use similar accounting methods, terminology, and financial statement format.

Disclosure. All data which would *influence* the assessment of the company's health by outsiders should be disclosed in the financial statements.

Conservatism. It is better to *understate* rather than overstate a company's financial position in order to reduce the possibility of outsiders being hurt by viewing the company as being better than it really is. Thus, it is better to understate assets than overstate them.

Entity. This is an *accounting unit* that is separate and apart from the owner or owners.

Continuity (going concern). The business is assumed to continue in operation *indefinitely*.

Stable dollar. It is assumed that prices remain *constant* over time. Thus, historical cost (the price originally paid for an item) is used to value assets. Rapid inflation in recent years makes this once generally accepted assumption dubious, however. Many now advocate the use of current values to record assets.

Accounting period. This concept refers to the time span over which accounting data are recorded and reported in the financial statements. Although any time period may be used to assemble data, *quarterly* (interim) and *annual* financial statements are the ones most commonly prepared for external parties.

1.5 THE ACCOUNTING EQUATION

An entity's financial position is reflected by the relationship between its assets and its liabilities and capital.

Assets are resources which are *owned* by the business and which can be expressed in monetary terms. Assets which will be converted into cash within one year are classified as *current*. Examples are cash, receivables (amounts owed to the business by customers), and inventory. Assets having a life exceeding one year are classified as *noncurrent*. Examples are land, buildings, and machinery.

Liabilities are obligations in the form of money to be paid or services to be rendered by the business to outside parties. Liabilities payable within one year are classified as *current*, such as accounts payable (amounts owed to creditors and suppliers), notes payable (maturity of one year or less), and taxes payable. Obligations payable in a period longer than one year, for example, bonds payable, are termed *noncurrent*.

Capital is the *equity interest* of the owner in the business which constitutes the difference between assets and liabilities. In a sole proprietorship, there is only one capital account since there is only one owner. In a partnership, a capital account exists for each owner. In a corporation, capital represents the *stockholders' equity*, which equals the capital stock issued plus the accumulated earnings of the business (called retained earnings). There are two types of capital stock—*common stock* and *preferred stock*. Common stock entitles its owners to voting rights, while preferred stock does not. Preferred stock entitles its owners to priority in the receipt of dividends and in repayment of capital in the event of corporate dissolution.

The *accounting equation* reflects these elements by expressing the equality of assets to creditors' claims and owners' equity as follows:

$$\text{Assets} = \text{Liabilities} + \text{Capital}$$

The equation in effect says that a company's assets are subject to the rights of debt holders and owners.

The accounting equation is the basis for *double entry accounting*, which means that each transaction has a dual effect. A transaction affects either both sides of the equation by the same amount or one side of the equation only, by both increasing and decreasing it by identical amounts and thus netting to zero.

EXAMPLE 1   If a business has assets of $500,000, obligations of $300,000, and owners' equity of $200,000, the accounting equation is

$$\text{ASSETS} \quad = \quad \text{LIABILITIES} \quad + \quad \text{CAPITAL}$$
$$\$500,000 \quad = \quad \$300,000 \quad + \quad \$200,000$$

If at the end of the reporting period, the business derived net income of $50,000, the accounting equation becomes

$$\text{ASSETS} \quad = \quad \text{LIABILITIES} \quad + \quad \text{CAPITAL}$$
$$\$550,000 \quad = \quad \$300,000 \quad + \quad \$250,000$$

If $10,000 was then used to pay creditors, the accounting equation becomes

$$\text{ASSETS} \quad = \quad \text{LIABILITIES} \quad + \quad \text{CAPITAL}$$
$$\$540,000 \quad = \quad \$290,000 \quad + \quad \$250,000$$

In the next example, we will illustrate how the *transactions* of a business are recorded and what effect they have on the accounting equation.

EXAMPLE 2   Mark Jones, an accountant, experienced the following events in the month of September 20XX:

1. Started his accounting practice with a cash investment of $10,000 and office equipment worth $5,000
2. Purchased office supplies of $800 by paying cash
3. Bought a word processor for $500 on account from IBM
4. Paid $400 in salary to his staff
5. Received an electric bill for $300
6. Earned professional fees of $20,000, of which $12,000 was received in cash and $8,000 was owed by clients
7. Paid $300 to IBM
8. Withdrew $100 from the business for personal use
9. Received $1,000 from one of the clients who owed him money
10. Worth of office supplies on hand at month's end, $600

The transactions will now be analyzed.

Transaction 1. Jones started his practice by investing $10,000 in cash and $5,000 in office equipment.
The assets Cash and Office Equipment are increased, and the capital is also increased for the total investment of the owner.

ASSETS (A)		=	LIABILITIES (L)	+	CAPITAL (C)
Cash	Office Equipment (OE)				M. Jones, Capital (C)
$10,000	$5,000				$15,000

Transaction 2. Acquired office supplies for cash, $800.
The asset Office Supplies goes up by $800 with a corresponding reduction in the asset Cash. This is an example of one asset being used to acquire another one.

	A		=	L	+	C
			Office			
Cash	OE	Supplies (OS)				
$10,000	$5,000				$15,000	
−800		$800				
$ 9,200	$5,000	$800			$15,000	

Transaction 3. Purchased a word processor on account, $500.

An asset, Office Equipment, is being acquired on credit, thereby creating a *liability* for future payment called Accounts Payable. Accounts payable is defined as the amount owed to suppliers.

	A		=	L	+	C
Cash	OE	OS		Accounts Payable (AP)		
$9,200	$5,000	$800			$15,000	
	+500			$500		
$9,200	$5,500	$800		$500	$15,000	

Transaction 4. Paid salary, $400.

Cash and capital are both being reduced because of the wage expense. Capital is reduced because expenses of the business decrease the equity of the owner.

	A		=	L	+	C
Cash	OE	OS		AP		
$9,200	$5,500	$800		$500	$15,000	
−400					−400	
$8,800	$5,500	$800		$500	$14,600	

Transaction 5. Received an electric bill for $300 (not paid).

Liabilities are increased by $300 since the business *owes* the utility money for electricity supplied. Capital is reduced for the expense.

	A		=	L	+	C
Cash	OE	OS		AP		
$8,800	$5,500	$800		$ 500	$14,600	
				+300	−300	
$8,800	$5,500	$800		$ 800	$14,300	

Transaction 6. Earned fees of $20,000, of which $12,000 was received in cash and $8,000 was owed by clients.

Cash goes up by $12,000 and the account Accounts Receivable (amounts owed to the business from customers) is created. Professional fees earned is *revenue* to the business and hence increases the owner's equity. Thus, capital is increased by $20,000.

	A			=	L	+	C
			Accounts				
Cash	OE	OS	Receivable (AR)		AP		
$ 8,800	$5,500	$800			$800	$ 14,300	
+12,000			$8,000			+20,000	
$ 20,800	$5,500	$800	$8,000		$800	$ 34,300	

Transaction 7. Paid $300 to IBM (in partial payment of the amount owed to them).

The payment lowers the asset Cash and reduces the liability Accounts Payable.

	A			=	L	+	C
Cash	OE	OS	AR		AP		
$20,800	$5,500	$800	$8,000		$ 800	$34,300	
−300					−300		
$20,500	$5,500	$800	$8,000		$ 500	$34,300	

Transaction 8. Withdrew $100 for *personal* use.

Cash is reduced and so is capital. The personal withdrawal is, in effect, a disinvestment in the business and hence reduces capital. It is *not* an expense in running the business.

	A			=	L	+	C
Cash	OE	OS	AR		AP		
$20,500	$5,500	$800	$8,000		$500		$34,300
−100							−100
$20,400	$5,500	$800	$8,000		$500		$34,200

Transaction 9. Received $1,000 from one of the clients who owed him money.

This increases Cash and reduces Accounts Receivable since the client now owes the business less money. One asset is being substituted for another one.

	A			=	L	+	C
Cash	OE	OS	AR		AP		
$20,400	$5,500	$800	$ 8,000		$500		$34,200
+1,000			−1,000				
$21,400	$5,500	$800	$ 7,000		$500		$34,200

Transaction 10. Worth (determined by an inventory count) of office supplies on hand at month's end, $600.

Since the worth of office supplies originally acquired was $800 and $600 is left on hand, the business used $200 in supplies. This reduces the asset Office Supplies and correspondingly reduces capital. The supplies used up represent office supplies expense.

	A			=	L	+	C
Cash	OE	OS	AR		AP		
$21,400	$5,500	$ 800	$ 7,000		$500		$34,200
		−200					−200
$21,400	$5,500	$ 600	$ 7,000		$500		$34,000

Summary of Transactions
September 20XX

		A			=	L	+	C	
	Cash	OE	OS	AR		AP			
1.	$10,000	$5,000						$15,000	
2.	−800		$800						
	$ 9,200	$5,000	$800					$15,000	
3.		+500				$ 500			
	$ 9,200	$5,500	$800			$ 500		$15,000	
4.	−400							−400	Wage Expense
	$ 8,800	$5,500	$800			$ 500		$14,600	
5.						+300		−300	Utilities Expense
	$ 8,800	$5,500	$800			$ 800		$14,300	
6.	+12,000			$8,000				+20,000	Professional Fee Revenue
	$20,800	$5,500	$800	$8,000		$ 800		$34,300	
7.	−300					−300			
	$20,500	$5,500	$800	$8,000		$ 500		$34,300	
8.	−100							−100	Drawing
	$20,400	$5,500	$800	$8,000		$ 500		$34,200	
9.	+1,000			−1,000					
	$21,400	$5,500	$800	$7,000		$ 500		$34,200	
10.			−200					−200	Office Supplies Expense
	$21,400	$5,500	$600	$7,000		$ 500		$34,000	

By looking at the capital column, we can determine the firm's *net income*, which is equal to revenue less expenses.

EXAMPLE 3

Income Statement

Professional Fee Revenue		$20,000
Less: Expenses		
Wage Expense	$400	
Utilities Expense	300	
Office Supplies Expense	200	
Total Expenses		900
Net Income		$19,100

Note: As mentioned earlier, the Drawing account is not an expense, but rather a withdrawal of money for personal use by the owner and therefore a disinvestment in the business.

Summary

(1) _____ accounting refers to working for an independent firm that audits the books of companies.

(2) Economic resources owned by a business are referred to as _____ .

(3) _____ are obligations of a business to others.

(4) According to the accounting equation, assets equal liabilities plus _____ .

(5) Resources received for goods or services are referred to as _____ .

(6) Resources used up in producing goods or services are called _____ .

(7) If revenue exceeds expenses, the difference is called _____ .

(8) Rent is an example of _____ .

(9) Using the same accounting method over a period of years is referred to as the _____ principle.

(10) Understating assets rather than overstating them is an example of the _____ principle.

(11) The purchase of an auto on account increases _____ and _____ .

(12) The payment of telephone expense reduces _____ and _____ .

(13) Receiving cash for professional fees rendered increases _____ and _____ .

(14) Paying a creditor reduces _____ and _____ .

(15) Assets which will be converted into cash within one year are classified as _____ .

(16) The principal rule-making body in financial accounting is the _____ .

(17) The accumulated earnings of a corporation are called _____ .

(18) The two types of stock that a corporation can issue are _____ and _____ .

Answers: (1) public; (2) assets; (3) liabilities; (4) capital; (5) revenue; (6) expenses; (7) net income (or profit); (8) an expense; (9) consistency; (10) conservatism; (11) assets, liabilities; (12) assets, capital; (13) assets, capital; (14) liabilities, assets; (15) current; (16) Financial Accounting Standards Board (FASB); (17) retained earnings; (18) common stock, preferred stock

Solved Problems

1.1 For each of the items listed below, place the symbol in the space provided to indicate the major category of the item in the accounting equation. *Symbols:* Asset, A; Liability, L; Capital, C.

	Answers
Example: Cash	A
(a) Taxes Payable	_____
(b) Smith, Capital	_____
(c) Land	_____
(d) Accounts Receivable	_____
(e) Supplies	_____
(f) Bonds Payable	_____
(g) Merchandise Inventory	_____
(h) Accounts Payable	_____
(i) Smith, Withdrawal	_____
(j) Salaries	_____
(k) Professional Fees	_____

SOLUTION

(a) L; (b) C; (c) A; (d) A; (e) A; (f) L; (g) A; (h) L; (i) C; (j) C; (k) C

1.2 Answer in the space provided whether each of the following represents a *recordable transaction.*

	Yes or No
(a) Collected cash for services	_____
(b) Paid salaries	_____
(c) Paid off a note plus interest	_____
(d) Hired an employee who will start next month	_____
(e) Used up part of supplies	_____

(f) Purchased delivery truck, payment to be made next year   _____

(g) Withdrawal of cash by owner for personal use   _____

(h) Agreed to supply a company with a product for the next few years   _____

SOLUTION

(a) Yes; (b) Yes; (c) Yes; (d) No; (e) Yes; (f) Yes; (g) Yes; (h) No

1.3   Show the effect (increase = +; decrease = −; no effect = 0) on assets of the following transactions.

		+, −, 0
(a)	Owner withdraws cash.	_____
(b)	Business purchases land on credit.	_____
(c)	There is a cash sale.	_____
(d)	Business purchases delivery truck for cash.	_____
(e)	Business pays for telephone bill.	_____
(f)	Business pays off a note to the bank.	_____
(g)	Business sells merchandise on account.	_____
(h)	Business enters into an agreement with the bank for a future loan.	_____

SOLUTION

(a) −; (b) +; (c) +; (d) +, − [One asset (cash) is exchanged for another (equipment); see also Transaction 2 of Example 2]; (e) −; (f) −; (g) +, − [Accounts receivable is increased, while merchandise is decreased; unless the merchandise was sold at or below cost, the total effect of this transaction would be to increase assets (and capital) by the excess of sales price over the cost of the merchandise]; (h) 0.

1.4   Supply the missing amount for each of the following cases:

	ASSETS	LIABILITIES	CAPITAL
(a)	$ 4,000	$ 2,500	$ _____
(b)	12,800	_____	5,700
(c)	_____	2,800	3,900
(d)	5,560	_____	2,820
(e)	57,000	28,000	_____

SOLUTION

Calculations are based on the accounting equation:

$$\text{Assets} = \text{Liabilities} + \text{Capital}$$

(a) $1,500 ($4,000 − $2,500)

(b) $7,100 ($12,800 − $5,700)

(c) $6,700 ($2,800 + $3,900)

(d) $2,740 ($5,560 − $2,820)

(e) $29,000 ($57,000 − $28,000)

1.5   Compute the missing amount for each of the following cases:

	A	B	C
Accounts Payable	$ _____	$ 5,000	$ 2,000
Accounts Receivable	15,500	30,000	13,000
Office Supplies	2,700	5,000	2,500
Cash	5,970	5,500	8,000
Capital	49,000	57,500	_____
Office Equipment	30,000	_____	12,000
Land	14,000	2,500	10,000

SOLUTION

We can list the entries in the accounting equation according to category as follows:

ASSETS	=	LIABILITIES	+	CAPITAL

Cash + Accounts Receivable + Office Supplies
+ Office Equipment + Land   =   Accounts Payable   +   Capital

By inserting the amounts for each entry, we can solve for the missing element.

Case A

$$\$5,970 + \$15,500 + \$2,700 + \$30,000 + \$14,000 = \text{Accounts Payable} + \$49,000$$
$$\$68,170 = \text{Accounts Payable} + \$49,000$$
$$\text{Accounts Payable} = \underline{\$19,170}$$

Case B

$$\$5,500 + \$30,000 + \$5,000 + \text{Office Equipment} + \$2,500 = \$5,000 + \$57,500$$
$$\$43,000 + \text{Office Equipment} = \$62,500$$
$$\text{Office Equipment} = \underline{\$19,500}$$

Case C

$$\$8,000 + \$13,000 + \$2,500 + \$12,000 + \$10,000 = \$2,000 + \text{Capital}$$
$$\$45,500 = \$2,000 + \text{Capital}$$
$$\text{Capital} = \underline{\$43,500}$$

1.6   Transactions completed by Brian Koppelman, CPA, appear below. In the following table, indicate the effects of the transactions on each part of the accounting equation by writing +, −, or 0 to denote increase, decrease, or no effect, respectively.

	Transactions	ASSETS	=	LIABILITIES	+	CAPITAL
(a)	Invested cash in business					
(b)	Paid rental expenses					
(c)	Received professional fees in cash					
(d)	Bought supplies for cash					
(e)	Bought equipment on credit					
(f)	Withdrew cash					
(g)	Bought supplies on account					
(h)	Lost equipment in fire					

SOLUTION

	Explanations	ASSETS	=	LIABILITIES	+	CAPITAL
(a)	Increase in cash and capital	+		0		+
(b)	Decrease in cash and capital	−		0		−
(c)	Increase in cash and capital	+		0		+
(d)	Increase in supplies and decrease in cash	+, −		0		0
(e)	Increase in equipment and in accounts payable	+		+		0
(f)	Decrease in cash and capital	−		0		−
(g)	Increase in supplies and in accounts payable	+		+		0
(h)	Decrease in equipment and in capital	−		0		−

1.7   On July 1, Margaret Johnson opened a business by investing $10,000 in a liquor store. During the month of July, she purchased office equipment costing $5,000, of which one-half was paid in cash and the remainder was on credit. Record the transaction in the space provided.

	ASSETS			=	LIABILITIES	+	CAPITAL
	Cash	+	Office Equipment	=	Accounts Payable	+	M. Johnson, Capital
Balance							
July 1	$10,000						$10,000
Entry							
During							
July	_____		_____		_____		_____
Balance	══════		══════		══════		══════

SOLUTION

	ASSETS		=	LIABILITIES	+	CAPITAL
	Cash	+ Office Equipment	=	Accounts Payable	+	M. Johnson, Capital
Balance July 1	$10,000					$10,000
Entry During July	−2,500	$5,000		$2,500		
Balance	$ 7,500 +	$5,000	=	$2,500	+	$10,000

1.8 Guy Benjamin invested his savings in a small cleaning shop. Record the transactions listed below in the form provided; then total and prove the results.

(*a*) Opened the shop by investing $15,000 in cash
(*b*) Bought $1,500 of supplies on account from Steve Dil Co.
(*c*) Bought cleaning equipment for $8,500 cash
(*d*) Received cash for cleaning services, $1,550
(*e*) Paid salaries and other expenses of $450
(*f*) Bought additional $2,500 of supplies from Steve Dil Co.; paid $1,500 cash, remainder on account
(*g*) Withdrew $500 for personal use

	ASSETS			=	LIABILITIES	+	CAPITAL
	Cash	+ Supplies	+ Equipment	=	Accounts Payable	+	G. Benjamin, Capital
(*a*)	_____	_____	_____		_____		_____
(*b*)	_____	_____	_____		_____		_____
Balance							
(*c*)	_____	_____	_____		_____		_____
Balance							
(*d*)	_____	_____	_____		_____		_____
Balance							
(*e*)	_____	_____	_____		_____		_____
Balance							
(*f*)	_____	_____	_____		_____		_____
Balance							
(*g*)	_____	_____	_____		_____		_____
Balance							

SOLUTION

	ASSETS			=	LIABILITIES	+	CAPITAL
	Cash	+ Supplies	+ Equipment	=	Accounts Payable	+	G. Benjamin, Capital
(*a*)	$15,000						$15,000
(*b*)		$ 1,500			$ 1,500		
Balance	$15,000	$ 1,500		=	$ 1,500	+	$15,000
(*c*)	−8,500		$8,500				
Balance	$ 6,500	$ 1,500	$8,500	=	$ 1,500	+	$15,000
(*d*)	+1,550						+1,550
Balance	$ 8,050	$ 1,500	$8,500	=	$ 1,500	+	$16,550

	Cash +	ASSETS Supplies +	Equipment	=	= LIABILITIES Accounts Payable	+	+ CAPITAL G. Benjamin, Capital
(e)	−450						−450
Balance	$ 7,600	$ 1,500	$8,500	=	$ 1,500	+	$16,100
(f)	−1,500	+2,500			+1,000		
Balance	$ 6,100	$ 4,000	$8,500	=	$ 2,500	+	$16,100
(g)	−500						−500
Balance	$ 5,600	$ 4,000	$8,500	=	$ 2,500	+	$15,600

1.9 Based on the information in the Capital column in Problem 1.8, determine the net income.

SOLUTION

Income Statement

Revenue from cleaning	$1,550
Less: Salaries and Other Expenses	450
Net Income	$1,100

Note that a withdrawal of money for personal use by the owner is not included because such a withdrawal is *not* an expense.

1.10 J. Winfield opened a small antique shop by investing $5,000 cash on the first day of May. The following transactions occurred during the month of May.

(a)   Purchased $2,000 of merchandise on account from a supplier
(b)   Purchased store equipment for $1,500 cash
(c)   Sold merchandise for cash: cost, $1,200; selling price, $1,600
(d)   Paid salary expense for the month, $500
(e)   Paid rental expense for the month, $350
(f)   Sold merchandise for cash: cost, $700; selling price, $1,200
(g)   Purchased merchandise for $2,500; paid $1,100, the remainder on account
(h)   Withdrew $1,000 for personal use

Record the transactions and running balances in the form provided below.

	Cash +	Merchandise +	Equipment	=	Accounts Payable	+	J. Winfield, Capital
	$5,000						$5,000
(a)	____	____	____		____		____
Balance							
(b)	____	____	____		____		____
Balance							
(c)	____	____	____		____		____
Balance							
(d)	____	____	____		____		____
Balance							
(e)	____	____	____		____		____
Balance							
(f)	____	____	____		____		____
Balance							
(g)	____	____	____		____		____
Balance							
(h)	____	____	____		____		____
Balance							

SOLUTION

	Cash	+	Merchandise	+	Equipment	=	Accounts Payable	+	J. Winfield, Capital
	$5,000								$5,000
(a)			$2,000				$2,000		
Balance	$5,000	+	$2,000			=	$2,000	+	$5,000
(b)	−1,500				$1,500				
Balance	$3,500	+	$2,000	+	$1,500	=	$2,000	+	$5,000
(c)	+1,600		−1,200						+400
Balance	$5,100	+	$ 800	+	$1,500	=	$2,000	+	$5,400
(d)	−500								−500
Balance	$4,600	+	$ 800	+	$1,500	=	$2,000	+	$4,900
(e)	−350								−350
Balance	$4,250	+	$ 800	+	$1,500	=	$2,000	+	$4,550
(f)	+1,200		−700						+500
Balance	$5,450	+	$ 100	+	$1,500	=	$2,000	+	$5,050
(g)	−1,100		+2,500				+1,400		
Balance	$4,350	+	$2,600	+	$1,500	=	$3,400	+	$5,050
(h)	−1,000								−1,000
Balance	$3,350	+	$2,600	+	$1,500	=	$3,400	+	$4,050

1.11 Based on the information in the Capital column in Problem 1.10, determine the net income.

SOLUTION

Income Statement

Sales Revenue*		$900
Less: Expenses		
Salaries	$500	
Rent	350	
Total Expenses		850
Net income		$ 50

---

*Sum of (c) and (f) in Capital column of Problem 1.10. Alternatively, we can determine net sales revenue by subtracting the cost of merchandise from the selling price as follows:

Transaction (c)   Transaction (f)
($1,600 selling price − $1,200 cost) + ($1,200 selling price − $700 cost) = Sales revenue
$400 + $500 = $900

Note that withdrawal of money for personal use is not an expense.

1.12 The summary data of the Geller Real Estate Agency are presented below in equation form. Describe the possible transactions for entries (a) to (g).

	Cash	+	Accounts Receivable	+	Office Furniture	=	Accounts Payable	+	Geller, Capital
(a)	$4,000								$4,000
(b)					$820		$820		
(c)	+120		30		−150				
(d)	30		−30						
(e)	−260						−260		
(f)	+650								+650
(g)	−35								−35

SOLUTION

(a) Geller invested $4,000 to open the Geller Real Estate Agency.

(b) Office furniture costing $820 was purchased on credit.

(c) An item of office furniture was sold for $150, of which $120 was paid in cash with $30 on account.

(d) The $30 due from the customer in (c) was received.

(e) Geller paid $260 toward the amount owed in (b) for office furniture purchased.

(f) Sale of a client's house resulted in a commission payment of $650 to the agency.

(g) An expense of $35 (such as a telephone bill) was paid, or Geller withdrew that amount for personal use.

1.13 The summary data of Smith Company are given below in equation form. Describe the possible transactions for entries (a) to (g).

	Cash	+	Merchandise	+	Equipment	=	Accounts Payable	+	Smith Co., Capital
Beginning Balance	$ 3,000		$ 4,000		$1,000		$ 2,000		$6,000
(a)	+400		−300						+100
(b)	+500				−700				−200
(c)	−1,500						+1,500		
(d)	+2,100		−1,700						+400
(e)	−900		+2,500				+1,600		
(f)	−600								−600
(g)			+3,000				+3,000		

SOLUTION

(a) Merchandise costing $300 was sold for $400, netting a profit of $100.

(b) Equipment which cost $700 was sold for $500, which resulted in a net loss of $200.

(c) The company paid an outstanding liability in the amount of $1,500.

(d) Merchandise costing $1,700 was sold for $2,100, resulting in a net profit of $400.

(e) The company purchased merchandise costing $2,500 by paying $900 in cash with the remainder on account.

(f) The owner withdrew cash ($600) for personal use, representing a disinvestment in the business; or the company paid an expense of $600.

(g) Merchandise costing $3,000 was purchased on account.

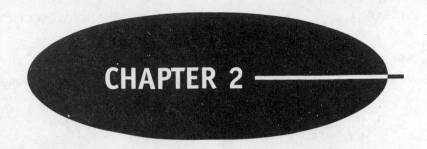

CHAPTER 2

Financial Statements

2.1 INTRODUCTION

The owner of a business is concerned with how well he or she is doing financially. One measure of performance is the net income (profit) earned for the reporting period. This is shown in the *income statement*, also called the statement of operations or profit-and-loss (P&L) statement. Another measure is the owner's capital (the difference between the entity's total assets and total liabilities) at the end of the period. *Assets*, *liabilities*, and *capital* are reported in the *balance sheet* (statement of financial position). The income statement and balance sheet summarize the voluminous data contained in the detailed accounting records of the business.

The profit as shown in the income statement is derived by subtracting *total expenses* from *total revenue* (income). A detailed listing showing the source and amount of revenue and expenses is provided in the income statement. This breakdown is needed, among other reasons, so that the owner can determine the trend in revenue and expense items. For example, the owner would like to know if a given expense item (e.g., telephone) is disproportionately great so that he or she can determine the reasons why and possibly control that expense item.

The balance sheet lists the type and amount of each asset, liability, and the capital account existing as of the *last day* of the reporting period. This listing is necessary so that the proprietor knows the specific items he or she owns (i.e., cash, inventory, machinery), what is owed (accounts payable, loans payable), and the amount of ending equity in the business (capital account). The equity at the end of the period consists of the capital investments made plus the profits earned less any withdrawals.

EXAMPLE 1 As of the end of September 20XX the business of Mark Jones shows the following account balances (see bottom row of Summary of Transactions in Example 2 of Chapter 1):

ACCOUNTS	ASSETS	LIABILITIES AND CAPITAL
Cash	$21,400	
Accounts Receivable	7,000	
Office Supplies	600	
Office Equipment	5,500	
Accounts Payable		$ 500
M. Jones, Capital		34,000
Total	$34,500	$34,500

16

Jones's assets went up from the original investment of $15,000 (Transaction 1 in Example 2 of Chapter 1) to the ending balance of $34,500. However, the increase of $19,500 does *not* reflect the net income for the period because consideration must be given to any change in liabilities as well as any withdrawals (representing a disinvestment in the business) made by the owner.

The initial *net* assets (assets minus liabilities) were $15,000, the original investment. The net assets at month's end were $34,000 (total assets of $34,500 less liabilities of $500). The net assets for the month thus went up by $19,000. However, there was a withdrawal of $100 during the month. Hence, Jones must have made a net profit of $19,100, which is the increase of $19,000 in net assets for the period plus the $100 disinvestment in the business. (See Net Income in Example 3 of Chapter 1.)

2.2   CASH BASIS VERSUS ACCRUAL BASIS OF ACCOUNTING

The income statement reports the profitability of a business over a specified *time period*. Thus, it is necessary to reflect revenue and expense items applicable to that period.

The *cash basis* of accounting recognizes revenue and expenses only when the related cash is received and disbursed. Thus, income statement recognition of transactions is tied to cash flow. Individuals and professionals (e.g., doctors) generally use the cash basis as a measure of what they earned for a given time period. However, the cash basis is an inappropriate accounting method when considerable inventory exists.

Under *accrual* accounting, revenue is recognized when *earned* and expenses are recorded when *incurred*. Most companies account under the accrual basis in accordance with generally accepted accounting principles.

Inherent in the accrual method of accounting is the *matching* principle, which states that expenses should be deducted against the revenue to which they are directly related. For example, the monthly rent paid for a store should be matched against the sales made by the owner for that month. The accrual concept also requires the *adjustment* of income statement accounts at the end of a period to appropriately reflect the revenue earned and expenses incurred for that period. For example, assume that for the month of January, employees were last paid on January 28. They have since worked three additional days (January 29–January 31) but will not be paid until the next pay period, which is in early February. Assuming that the pay for the three days totals $200, we should *accrue* for an additional salary expense of $200 for the month of January to properly reflect the total salary expense for that month.

2.3   INCOME STATEMENT

The income statement shows the *revenue, expenses, and net income (or net loss) for a period of time*. A definition of each element follows.

Revenue is the increase in capital arising from the sale of merchandise (as by a retail business) or the performance of services (as by a doctor). When revenue is earned it results in an increase in either Cash or Accounts Receivable.

Expenses decrease capital and result from performing those functions necessary to generate revenue. The amount of an expense is either equal to the cost of the inventory sold, the value of the services rendered (e.g., salary expense), or the expenditures necessary for conducting business operations (e.g., rent expense) during the period.

Net income is the amount by which total revenue exceeds total expenses for the reporting period. The resulting profit is added to the owner's capital account. However, if total expenses are greater than total revenue, a net loss ensues and decreases the capital account.

It should be noted that revenue does not necessarily mean receipt of cash and expense does not automatically imply a cash payment. Net income and net cash flow (cash receipts less cash payments) are different. For example, taking out a bank loan will generate cash but this is not revenue since merchandise has not been sold nor have services been provided. Further, capital has not been altered because of the loan.

EXAMPLE 2 Charlene Drake is a self-employed engineer. For the month of October 20XX, she earned income of $10,000 from services rendered. Her business expenses were: telephone $1,000, electricity $500, rent $2,000, secretarial salary $300, and office supplies used, $400. Her income statement for the period is as follows:

Charlene Drake
Income Statement
For the Month Ended October 31, 20XX

Revenue from professional services		$10,000
Less: Operating Expenses		
Telephone	$1,000	
Electricity	500	
Rent	2,000	
Secretarial Salary	300	
Office Supplies	400	
Total Operating Expenses		4,200
Net Income		$ 5,800

Note that each revenue and expense item has its own account. This specificity enables one to better evaluate and control revenue and expense sources and to examine relationships among account categories. For instance, the ratio of telephone expense to revenue is 10 percent ($1,000/$10,000). If in the previous month the relationship was 3 percent, Charlene Drake would, no doubt, attempt to determine the cause for this significant increase.

Income statement accounts are of a *temporary* nature and are closed out at the end of the period with the net difference being transferred to the capital account. In the above case, for example, the net income of $5,800 would be credited to the capital account.

2.4 BALANCE SHEET

The balance sheet portrays the financial position of the entity by listing the balances of assets, liabilities, and capital at the *end* of the reporting period. For the case presented in Example 2, the end of the reporting period is October 31, 20XX. The balance sheet is subject to the accounting equation (see Chapter 1).

$$\text{Assets} - \text{Liabilities} = \text{Capital}$$

The balance sheet is cumulative and thereby differs from the income statement, which shows the profit earned for a given time interval only (for example, October 1–October 31, 20XX).

The balance sheet is useful to management for evaluation and planning because it indicates what resources the entity has and what it owes.

The balance sheet may be prepared either in *report form* or *account form*. In the report form, assets, liabilities, and capital are listed vertically. In the account form, assets are listed on the left side and liabilities and capital on the right side.

EXAMPLE 3 Report Form

Charlene Drake
Balance Sheet
October 31, 20XX

ASSETS

Cash	$10,000
Accounts Receivable	20,500
Office Supplies	10,500
Office Equipment	30,000
Total Assets	$71,000

LIABILITIES AND CAPITAL

Liabilities			
Accounts Payable			$30,000
Capital			
Balance, October 1, 20XX		$35,600	
Net Income for October	$5,800		
Less: Withdrawals	400		
Increase in Capital		5,400	
Total Capital			41,000
Total Liabilities and Capital			$71,000

From the examples given, it is evident that a tie-in exists between the income statement and the balance sheet. Drake's net income of $5,800 (last item in her income statement from Example 2) is added to capital in her balance sheet in the above example. In effect, the income statement serves as the bridge between two consecutive balance sheets. Further, the net balance of the income statement accounts is used to adjust the capital account.

EXAMPLE 4   Account Form

Charlene Drake
Balance Sheet
October 31, 20XX

ASSETS		**LIABILITIES AND CAPITAL**			
Cash	$10,000	*Liabilities*			
Accounts Receivable	20,500	Accounts Payable			$30,000
Office Supplies	10,500	*Capital*			
Office Equipment	30,000	Balance, Oct. 1, 20XX		$35,600	
		Net income for Oct.	$5,800		
		Less: Withdrawals	400		
		Increase in Capital		5,400	
		Total Capital			
Total Assets	$71,000	Total Liabilities and Capital			41,000
					$71,000

2.5   CLASSIFIED FINANCIAL STATEMENTS

Businesses differ in nature, and therefore the specific entries differ from business to business. Hence, to facilitate financial analysis and evaluation of trends and productivity, it is useful to classify the entries in financial statements into major categories. Financial statements organized in such a fashion are called classified.

CLASSIFIED INCOME STATEMENT

In a classified income statement the dollar amounts for each major revenue and expense function are listed to facilitate analysis of the statement by management and other financial statement users (e.g., bank loan officers). The entries in classified income statements covering different time periods are easily compared; the comparison over time of revenue sources, expense items, and the relationship between them might reveal areas requiring attention and corrective action. For example, if revenue from services has been sharply declining over the past several months, management will want to take action to reverse this negative trend.

The entries in an income statement are usually classified into four major functions; revenue, cost of goods sold, operating expenses, and other revenue or expenses.

Revenue comprises the gross income generated by selling goods (sales) or performing services (professional fees, commission income). To determine *net* sales, gross sales are reduced by sales returns and allowances as well as sales discounts. For example, if a retail store sells ten television sets at $100 each in the month of January 20XX, gross sales are $1,000. If there were sales returns of $100 during the month, net sales for the period would be $900.

Cost of goods sold is the cost of the merchandise or services sold. In a retail store, it is the cost of buying goods from the manufacturer (e.g., cost of a television set from RCA). In a service business, it is the cost of the employee services rendered. For a manufacturing company, determining the cost of goods sold is considerably more complex, and students interested in pursuing this topic are referred to *Schaum's Outline of Managerial Accounting*.

Operating expenses consists of all expenses incurred or resources used in generating revenue. Two types of operating expenses exist—selling expenses and general and administrative expenses. *Selling expenses* are those incurred in obtaining the sale of goods or services (e.g., advertising, salespeople's salaries) and in distributing the merchandise to the customer (e.g., freight paid on a shipment). They relate solely to the selling function. In a large business, there is usually a sales manager who is responsible for generating sales, and his or her performance is judged on the relationship between promotion costs incurred and sales obtained. *General and administrative expenses* apply to the costs of running the business as a whole and do not relate to the selling function. Examples are the salaries of the general office clerical staff, administrative executive salaries, and depreciation on office equipment.

Other revenue (expense) applies to incidental sources of revenue and expense that are of a *nonoperating* nature. These revenue (expense) sources do not relate to the major purpose of the business. Examples are interest income, dividend income, and interest expense. Such revenue and expenses are *netted* to arrive at the total for this category.

Example 5 shows a classified income statement.

EXAMPLE 5

Mr. John Weston
Classified Income Statement
For the Year Ended December 31, 20XX

Revenue			
Gross Sales		$40,000	
Less: Sales Returns and Allowances	$1,000		
Sales Discounts	500	1,500	
Net Sales			$38,500
Cost of Goods Sold			
Inventory, January 1		$ 1,000	
Add: Purchases		15,000	
Cost of Goods Available for Sale		$16,000	
Less: Inventory, December 31		5,000	
Cost of Goods Sold			11,000
Gross Profit			$27,500
Operating Expenses			
Selling Expenses			
Advertising	$3,000		
Salespeople's Salaries	2,000		
Travel and Entertainment	1,000		
Depreciation on Delivery Truck	500	$ 6,500	

General and Administrative Expenses			
Officers' Salaries			
Rent	$5,000		
Insurance	2,000		
Total Operating Expenses	1,000	8,000	14,500
Operating Income			$13,000
Other Expenses (net)			
Interest Expense			
Less: Interest Income		$ 2,000	
Dividend Income	$ 500		
Other Expenses (net)	1,000	1,500	500
Net Income			$12,500

CLASSIFIED BALANCE SHEET

The balance sheet is classified into major groups of assets and liabilities in order to facilitate analysis of the entity's financial health. For example, a company's liquidity (its short-term ability to meet current debts with current assets) can be evaluated by looking at the *current ratio*, which is current assets divided by current liabilities. Another useful ratio which can be derived is total liabilities to capital; the greater the ratio, the more debt there is in the business, and hence the more risk. Surely, an owner would rather have less of liabilities and more of his or her own capital in a business.

A classified balance sheet generally breaks down assets into five categories: current assets; long-term (short-term) investments; property, plant, and equipment (fixed assets); intangible assets; and deferred charges.

Current assets are those assets which are expected to be converted into cash or used up within one year or the normal operating cycle of the business, whichever is greater. The operating cycle is the time period between the purchase of inventory to transfer of inventory through sales, listed as accounts receivable, and receipt of cash. In effect, the firm is going from paying cash to receiving cash. *In most cases, the current asset classification is based upon a life of one year or less.* Examples of current assets are cash, accounts receivable, inventory, and prepaid expenses. Prepaid expenses refer to expenditures made which will expire within one year from the balance sheet date; they represent a prepayment for an expense which has not yet been incurred. For instance, if there was the entry Prepaid Insurance of $1,000 as of December 31, 20XX on a policy which had eight months to run, the account would be listed under current assets.

Short-term investments in debt and equity securities are grouped into three separate portfolios for valuation and reporting purposes. These portfolios are categorized as follows:

1. *Held-to-maturity:* Debt securities that the enterprise has the positive intent and ability to hold to maturity.
2. *Trading:* Debt and equity securities bought and held primarily for sale in the near term to generate income on short-term price differences.
3. *Available-for-sale:* Debt and equity securities not classified as held-to-maturity or trading securities.

Trading securities (whether debt or equity) should be reported at market value as current assets. Available-for-sale securities (whether debt or equity) are presented at market value and are typically classified as a noncurrent asset. Held-to-maturity securities can only be debt (not equity), because only debt has a maturity date. Held-to-maturity securities are presented at amortized cost under Noncurrent Assets.

Long-term investments refer to investments in other companies' stocks (common or preferred) or bonds where the *intent* is to hold them for a period greater than one year (which is often the case). Securities are usually reported in the balance sheet at the original purchase cost. Such cost includes the market price of the securities and brokerage fees. Note that if the intent is to hold given securities for one year or less, they would be included in the current asset category and listed as short-term investments (marketable securities).

Property, plant, and equipment are assets employed in the production of goods or rendering of services and have a life greater than one year. They are *tangible* in nature, which means that they have physical substance (i.e., you can physically see and touch them). These assets are actually being used. Examples are land, buildings, machinery, and automobiles. Unlike inventory, these assets are not being held for sale in the normal course of business.

Intangible assets are assets with a long-term life that *lack* physical substance, such as goodwill, or arise from a right granted by the government, such as patents, copyrights, and trademarks, or by another company, such as franchise fees. An example of the latter is the right (acquired by paying a fee) to open a fast-food franchise and use the name of McDonald's.

Deferred charges are certain expenditures already incurred which are deferred to the future either because they are expected to benefit future revenues or because they represent an appropriate allocation of costs to future operations. Examples are plant rearrangement costs and moving costs. No cash can be realized from such assets because they represent past expenditures that are being written off in the future. For example, you cannot sell deferred moving costs to anyone because no one will buy them.

It should be noted that when one or more of these categories is immaterial in amount relative to total assets, such categories can be listed under one caption called Other Assets.

Liabilities may be classed as either current or noncurrent. As noted in Chapter 1, one year is the demarcation line. *Current liabilities* will be satisfied out of current assets. Examples are accounts payable, short-term notes payable, and accrued liabilities. *Accrued liabilities* are defined as obligations from expenses incurred but not paid at the end of the reporting period. Salaries payable and telephone payable are examples. Examples of *long-term liabilities*, which have a majority of greater than a year, are a two-year note payable, bonds payable, and mortgage payable. It should be noted, however, that the current portion of a long-term liability (which is to be paid within one year) is to be shown under current liabilities. For example, if $1,000 of a $10,000 mortgage is to be paid within the year, that $1,000 would be listed as a current liability; the remaining $9,000 would be shown under noncurrent liabilities.

EXAMPLE 6

Mr. John Weston
Statement of Capital
For the Year Ended December 31, 20XX

Capital, January 1		$27,500
Net Income for the year	$12,500	
Less: Withdrawals	1,000	
Increase in Capital		11,500
Capital, December 31		$39,000

A classified balance sheet is shown in Example 7. Although in prior examples adjustments to the capital account were shown in the balance sheet itself, the more common treatment is to show only the ending capital account balance and have a supporting schedule for the capital account. Example 6 shows the supporting schedule for the balance sheet in Example 7.

EXAMPLE 7

Mr. John Weston
Classified Balance Sheet
December 31, 20XX

ASSETS

Current Assets

Cash	$ 3,000	
Accounts Receivable	6,000	
Inventory	5,000	
Office Supplies	1,000	
Total Current Assets		$15,000

Long-Term Investments

Investment in X Company Stock		2,000

Property, Plant, and Equipment

Land	$20,000	
Building	30,000	
Machinery	7,000	
Delivery Truck	5,000	
Total Property, Plant, and Equipment		62,000

Intangible Assets

Patents		$ 3,000

Deferred Charges

Deferred Moving Costs		1,000
Total Assets		$83,000

LIABILITIES AND CAPITAL

Current Liabilities

Accounts Payable	$ 8,000	
Notes Payable (9 months)	4,000	
Accrued Liabilities	2,000	
Total Current Liabilities		$14,000

Noncurrent Liabilities

Mortgage Payable		30,000
Total Liabilities		$44,000
Capital, December 31 (see Example 6)		39,000
Total Liabilities and Capital		$83,000

Up to this point, we have assumed the existence of a sole proprietorship or a partnership. The principles are basically the same for a corporation with one major exception. As discussed in Chapter 1, when we are accounting for a corporation, we list the ownership section in the balance sheet as *stockholders' equity* (owners' equity), which consists of the capital stock issued and the retained earnings. Any dividends to stockholders come out of retained earnings. Dividends are a distribution of assets (typically cash) by a corporation to its stockholders; payment of dividends is a reduction in owners' equity and *not* an expense.

The stockholders' equity section of a balance sheet follows.

EXAMPLE 8

ABC Corporation
Stockholders' Equity
For the Year Ended December 31, 20XX

Capital Stock	$1,000,000
Retained Earnings	30,000
Total Stockholders' Equity	$1,030,000

A statement of retained earnings can be prepared to show the activities in that account category during the period.

EXAMPLE 9

ABC Corporation
Statement of Retained Earnings
For the Year Ended December 31, 20XX

Retained Earnings, January 1	$10,000
Net Income for the year	25,000
Subtotal	$35,000
Dividends	5,000
Retained Earnings, December 31	$30,000

Example 10 shows a classified balance sheet for a corporation.

EXAMPLE 10

XYZ Corporation
Classified Balance Sheet
December 31, 20XX

ASSETS

Current Assets		
Cash	$10,000	
Accounts Receivable	14,000	
Inventory	30,000	
Total Current Assets		$ 54,000
Property, Plant, and Equipment		
Land	$20,000	
Building	40,000	
Machinery	18,000	
Total Property, Plant, and Equipment		78,000
Total Assets		$132,000

LIABILITIES AND CAPITAL

Current Liabilities

Accounts Payable	$10,000	
Income Taxes Payable*	14,000	
Total Current Liabilities		$ 24,000

Long-term Liabilities

Bonds Payable		30,000
Total Liabilities		$ 54,000

Stockholders' Equity

Capital Stock	$50,000	
Retained Earnings (see Example 11)	28,000	
Total Stockholders' Equity		$ 78,000
Total Liabilities and Stockholders' Equity		$132,000

---

*Income Taxes Payable is shown as a liability only on a corporation's books. It is not shown as a liability for a sole proprietorship or a partnership because an unincorporated business is not a taxable entity under the Internal Revenue Code.

EXAMPLE 11

XYZ Corporation
Statement of Retained Earnings
For the Year Ended December 31, 20XX

Retained Earnings, January 1	$12,000
Net Income for the year	20,000
Subtotal	$32,000
Dividends	4,000
Retained Earnings, December 31	$28,000

Summary

(1) The net income for an entity for a period of time is shown in the _____ statement.

(2) Net income is equal to the difference between _____ and _____ .

(3) An increase in capital arising from the sale of merchandise is called _____ .

(4) A decrease in capital due to performing a function necessary for obtaining revenue is termed a(n) _____ .

(5) Income statement accounts are of a(n) _____ nature since they are eventually closed out to the capital account.

(6) Under accrual accounting, revenue is recognized when _____ and expenses are recognized when _____ .

(7) When the owner of a business withdraws money for personal use the _____ account is reduced.

(8) Listed in the balance sheet are the _____ , _____ , and _____ .

(9) The balance sheet is prepared as of the _____ of the reporting period.

(10) Two types of format for the preparation of the balance sheet are the _____ form and the _____ form.

(11) The connecting link between two successive balance sheets is the _____ statement.

(12) Advertising is an example of a(n) _____ expense.

(13) The salary of a company's president is a(n) _____ expense.

(14) Current assets divided by current liabilities is termed the _____ ratio.

(15) A patent is an example of a(n) _____ asset.

(16) Dividends reduce _____ .

(17) Income taxes payable is shown only on a(n) _____ books.

Answers: (1) income; (2) revenue, expenses; (3) revenue; (4) expense; (5) temporary; (6) earned, incurred; (7) capital; (8) assets, liabilities, capital; (9) end; (10) report, account; (11) income; (12) selling; (13) administrative; (14) current; (15) intangible; (16) retained earnings; (17) corporation's

Solved Problems

2.1 Decatur B. Smith's capital as of January 1, 20XX was $10,000. During the year, the net income was $18,000 and he withdrew $5,000. What is Smith's capital as of December 31, 20XX?

SOLUTION

Statement of Capital

Capital, January 1		$10,000
Net Income	$18,000	
Drawing	5,000	
Increase in Capital		13,000
Capital, December 31		$23,000

2.2 If, in Problem 2.1, Smith had withdrawn $20,000 rather than $5,000, what would be his ending capital?

SOLUTION

Statement of Capital

Capital, January 1		$10,000
Net Income	$18,000	
Drawing	20,000	
Decrease in Capital		2,000
Capital, December 31		$ 8,000

2.3 From the following information, determine the capital balance as of December 31, 20XX: capital–January 1, $40,000; net loss for year, $8,000; drawing, $3,000.

SOLUTION

Statement of Capital

Capital, January 1		$40,000
Net Loss	$8,000	
Drawing	3,000	
Decrease in Capital		11,000
Capital, December 31		$29,000

2.4 Income statement data for Jane Prince is as follows: professional fee income, $20,000; advertising expense, $4,000; salaries expense, $6,000; electricity expense, $2,000. If $3,000 was withdrawn by the owner from the business, what was the increase or decrease in capital?

SOLUTION

First, an income statement must be prepared to determine the net income or net loss.

Income Statement

Professional Fee Income		$20,000
Less: Expenses		
Advertising Expense	$4,000	
Salaries Expense	6,000	
Electricity Expense	2,000	
Total Expenses		12,000
Net Income		$ 8,000

Second, the change in the capital account is determined by deducting the owner's withdrawal from the net income for the period.

Statement of Capital

Net Income	$8,000
Less: Withdrawal	3,000
Increase in Capital	$5,000

2.5 If the withdrawal in Problem 2.4 was $10,000 rather than $3,000, how did capital change?

SOLUTION

Statement of Capital

Net Income	$ 8,000
Less: Withdrawal	10,000
Decrease in Capital	$ 2,000

Since the withdrawal exceeds the net income, there is a *decrease* in capital of $2,000.

2.6 If a company's total assets are $25,000 and total liabilities are $12,000, how much capital does the company have?

SOLUTION

From the accounting equation (see Chapter 1) we know that

$$\text{Assets} = \text{Liabilities} + \text{Capital}$$

By inserting the amounts for assets and liabilities into this equation, we can solve for the unknown, capital:

$$\$25,000 = \$12,000 + \text{Capital}$$
$$\$25,000 - \$12,000 = \text{Capital}$$
$$\$13,000 = \text{Capital}$$

2.7 Given the following account balances at year's end, determine the ending capital.

Cash	$8,000
Accounts Receivable	4,000
Machinery	6,000
Accounts Payable	2,000
Income Taxes Payable	5,000

SOLUTION

Organizing the entries into a balance sheet is one way of solving this problem. In preparing the balance sheet, we determine total assets and total liabilities from the data given and then calculate the capital by using the accounting equation. We then complete the balance sheet, which serves as a proof of the solution.

Balance Sheet

ASSETS		LIABILITIES AND CAPITAL	
Cash	$ 8,000	*Liabilities*	
Accounts Receivable	4,000	Accounts Payable	$ 2,000
Machinery	6,000	Income Taxes Payable	5,000
Total Assets	$18,000	Total Liabilities	$ 7,000
		Capital	11,000*
		Total Liabilities and Capital	$18,000

---

*Using the accounting equation (Assets = Liabilities + Capital), we calculated capital as follows:

Total Assets	$18,000
Less: Total Liabilities	7,000
Capital	$11,000

2.8   The assets and liabilities for Ginger Bakers in 20XX were:

	January 1	December 31
Assets	$31,000	$44,000
Liabilities	12,000	17,000

The owner withdrew $4,000 during the year. What was the net income for the year?

SOLUTION

Capital, December 31	$27,000	($44,000 − $17,000)
Capital, January 1	19,000	($31,000 − $12,000)
Increase in Capital	$12,000	

Net income less withdrawal equals change in capital (see explanation in Example 1). In this case, the change in capital is an increase, so we can write

$$\text{Net Income} - \text{Drawing} = \text{Increase in Capital}$$
$$\text{Net Income} - \$4,000 = \$12,000$$
$$\text{Net Income} = \$12,000 + \$4,000$$
$$\text{Net Income} = \$16,000$$

2.9   Prepare an income statement from the following data: professional fee income, $50,000; telephone expense, $5,000; salaries expense, $10,000; rent expense, $12,000.

SOLUTION

Income Statement

Professional Fee Income		$50,000
Less: Expenses		
Telephone Expense	$ 5,000	
Salaries Expense	10,000	
Rent Expense	12,000	
Total Expenses		27,000
Net Income		$23,000

2.10   If the professional fee income in Problem 2.9 was $26,000 instead of $50,000, what was the net income or net loss?

SOLUTION

Income Statement

Professional Fee Income		$26,000
Less: Expenses		
Telephone Expense	$ 5,000	
Salaries Expense	10,000	
Rent Expense	12,000	
Total Expenses		27,000
Net Income (Net Loss)		($ 1,000)

2.11 Classify the following income statement accounts by placing an **X** in the appropriate column.

	Revenue	Cost of Goods Sold	Selling Expenses	General and Admin. Expenses	Other Expenses
Sales					
Advertising Expense					
Rent Expense					
Professional Fee Income					
Purchases					
Interest Expense					
Insurance Expense					

SOLUTION

	Revenue	Cost of Goods Sold	Selling Expenses	General and Admin. Expenses	Other Expenses
Sales	X				
Advertising Expense			X		
Rent Expense				X	
Professional Fee Income	X				
Purchases		X			
Interest Expense					X
Insurance Expense				X	

2.12 Prepare a classified income statement from the following information: sales, $30,000; sales returns, $5,000; cost of goods sold, $7,000; operating expenses, $8,000; interest income, $4,000.

SOLUTION

Classified Income Statement

Revenue		
Sales	$30,000	
Less: Sales Returns	5,000	
Net Sales		$25,000
Cost of Goods Sold		7,000
Gross Profit		$18,000
Operating Expenses		8,000
Operating Income		$10,000
Other Income		
Interest Income		4,000
Net Income		$14,000

2.13 In the previous problem, we assumed no income tax expense. However, a company must pay an income tax expense on its profit. Assuming that the tax rate for the company in Problem 2.12 is 30 percent, determine the income tax expense as well as the after-tax net income.

SOLUTION

Income before Tax	$14,000
Income Tax Expense	
($14,000 × 30%)	4,200
Net Income	$ 9,800

2.14 The following are accounts of Ian Henry's business as of September 30, 20XX: notes payable, $5,000; accounts receivable, $1,500; cash, $2,500; land, $11,000; accounts payable, $400; building, $7,500; equipment, $3,100; truck, $2,800; mortgage payable $____; Mr. Henry, Capital, $18,000. Prepare a balance sheet (in account form) as of September 30, 20XX.

SOLUTION

Ian Henry
Balance Sheet
September 30, 20XX

ASSETS

Current Assets		
Cash	$ 2,500	
Accounts Receivable	1,500	
Total Current Assets		$ 4,000
Fixed Assets		
Land	$11,000	
Building	7,500	
Equipment	3,100	
Truck	2,800	
Total Fixed Assets		24,400
Total Assets		$28,400

LIABILITIES AND CAPITAL

Current Liabilities		
Accounts Payable	$ 400	
Notes Payable	5,000	
Total Current Liabilities		$ 5,400
Noncurrent Liabilities		
Mortgage Payable		5,000
Total Liabilities		$10,400
Capital		
I. Henry, Capital		18,000
Total Liabilities and Capital		$28,400

The Mortgage Payable of $5,000 is computed as follows:

To balance the accounting equation, liabilities must total $10,400 ($28,400 in assets − $18,000 in capital). Since total liabilities are $10,400 and we know that total current liabilities are $5,400, noncurrent liabilities must be the balance of $5,000. Since the only noncurrent liability is mortgage payable, it must be $5,000. The mathematical process is:

ASSETS	**=**	**LIABILITIES**	**+**	**CAPITAL**
$28,400	=	$5,400 (Current Liabilities) + Mortgage Payable	+	$18,000
$28,400 − $5,400 − $18,000	=	Mortgage Payable		
$5,000	=	Mortgage Payable		

2.15 On April 1, 20XX, Holly Johnson decided to start a business. During the month, she invested $10,000 in cash and $500 in office equipment. She also bought for a note payable a small building and a lot, for $8,500 and $10,000, respectively. Johnson then purchased a used truck for $1,000 cash. Prepare a classified balance sheet (in account form) for Holly Johnson as of April 30, 20XX.

SOLUTION

Holly Johnson
Classified Balance Sheet
April 30, 20XX

ASSETS			LIABILITIES AND CAPITAL		
Current Assets			*Current Liabilities*		
Cash		$ 9,000*	Notes Payable		$18,500**
Fixed Assets			*Capital*		
Land	$10,000		H. Johnson, Capital		10,500†
Building	8,500		Total Liabilities and Capital		29,000
Office Equipment	500				
Truck	1,000				
Total Fixed Assets		20,000			
Total Assets		$29,000			

*Invested cash	$10,000
Paid cash for truck	1,000
Cash balance	$ 9,000

**Notes payable here consists of $8,500 for the building and $10,000 for the land.

†Capital here consists of the original cash investment of $10,000 plus the $500 investment in office equipment. For further explanation, see Example 2 in Chapter 1.

2.16 Prepare a statement of retained earnings and a classified balance sheet (account form) as of December 31, 20XX, based upon the following data: cash, $10,000; supplies, $1,000; auto, $17,000; notes payable, $6,000; capital stock, $10,000; retained earnings (January 1, 20XX), $8,000; dividends, $2,000; net income $6,000.

SOLUTION

Statement of Retained Earnings

Retained Earnings, January 1, 20XX	$ 8,000
Net Income	6,000
Subtotal	$14,000
Dividends	2,000
Retained Earnings, December 31, 20XX	$12,000

Classified Balance Sheet

ASSETS			LIABILITIES AND STOCKHOLDERS' EQUITY		
Current Assets			*Current Liabilities*		
Cash	$10,000		Notes Payable		$ 6,000
Supplies	1,000		*Stockholders' Equity*		
Total Current Assets		$11,000	Capital Stock	$10,000	
Fixed Assets			Retained Earnings	12,000	22,000
Auto		17,000	Total Liabilities and		
Total Assets		$28,000	Stockholders' Equity		$28,000

2.17 Classify the following assets by putting an **X** in the correct column.

Asset	Current Assets	Long-Term Investments	Fixed Assets	Intangible Assets	Deferred Charges
Auto					
Accounts Receivable					
Trademark					
Prepaid Insurance					
Land					
Patent					
Investment in Stock					
Moving Cost					
Franchise Fee					

SOLUTION

Asset	Current Assets	Long-Term Investments	Fixed Assets	Intangible Assets	Deferred Charges
Auto			X		
Accounts Receivable	X				
Trademark				X	
Prepaid Insurance	X				
Land			X		
Patent				X	
Investment in Stock		X			
Moving Cost					X
Franchise Fee				X	

2.18 Classify the following liability and stockholders' equity accounts by placing an **X** in the appropriate column.

Account	Current Liabilities	Noncurrent Liabilities	Stockholders' Equity
Capital Stock			
Accounts Payable			
Mortgage Payable			
Retained Earnings			
Salaries Payable			
Bonds Payable			
Taxes Payable			

SOLUTION

Account	Current Liabilities	Noncurrent Liabilities	Stockholders' Equity
Capital Stock			X
Accounts Payable	X		
Mortgage Payable		X	
Retained Earnings			X
Salaries Payable	X		
Bonds Payable		X	
Taxes Payable	X		

2.19 Prepare a classified balance sheet (in report form) as of December 31 based upon the following data: cash, $2,000; patents, $1,000; accounts payable, $3,000; accounts receivable, $4,000; taxes payable, $1,000; machinery, $17,000; mortgage payable, $7,000; retained earnings (December 31), $3,000; capital stock, $10,000.

SOLUTION

Classified Balance Sheet

ASSETS

Current Assets

Cash	$2,000	
Accounts Receivable	4,000	
Total Current Assets		$ 6,000

Fixed Assets

Machinery		17,000

Intangible Assets

Patents		1,000
Total Assets		$24,000

LIABILITIES AND STOCKHOLDERS' EQUITY

Current Liabilities

Accounts Payable	$ 3,000	
Taxes Payable	1,000	
Total Current Liabilities		$ 4,000

Noncurrent Liabilities

Mortgage Payable		7,000
Total Liabilities		$11,000

Stockholders' Equity

Capital Stock	$10,000	
Retained Earnings	3,000	
Total Stockholders' Equity		13,000
Total Liabilities and Stockholders' Equity		$24,000

2.20 Determine the current ratio from the data given in the preceding problem and explain the result.

SOLUTION

$$\text{Current Ratio} = \frac{\text{Total Current Assets}}{\text{Total Current Liabilities}} = \frac{\$6,000}{\$4,000} = 1.5:1$$

This means that for every $1 in current liabilities, the company has $1.50 in current assets.

2.21 Westside Corporation had the following account balances as of December 31, 20XX: equipment, $15,000; cash, $10,000; sales, $30,000; capital stock, $10,000; accounts payable, $9,000; retained earnings (January 1, 20XX), $4,000; advertising expense, $2,000; dividends, $3,000; cost of goods sold, $18,000; sales commissions, $5,000.

Prepare (*a*) a classified income statement, (*b*) a statement of retained earnings, and (*c*) a classified balance sheet (in report form).

SOLUTION

(*a*)
Westside Corporation
Classified Income Statement
For the Year Ended December 31, 20XX

Revenue		
Sales		$30,000
Cost of Goods Sold		18,000
Gross Profit		$12,000
Operating Expenses		
Advertising Expense	$2,000	
Sales Commissions	5,000	
Total Operating Expenses		7,000
Net Income		$ 5,000

(*b*)
Westside Corporation
Statement of Retained Earnings
For the Year Ended December 31, 20XX

Retained Earnings, January 1	$4,000
Net Income	5,000
Subtotal	$9,000
Dividends	3,000
Retained Earnings, December 31	$6,000

(*c*)
Westside Corporation
Classified Balance Sheet
December 31, 20XX

ASSETS

Current Assets	
Cash	$10,000
Fixed Assets	
Equipment	15,000
Total Assets	$25,000

LIABILITIES AND STOCKHOLDERS' EQUITY

Current Liabilities

Accounts Payable		$ 9,000
Stockholders' Equity		
Capital Stock	$10,000	
Retained Earnings	6,000	
Total Stockholders' Equity		16,000
Total Liabilities and Stockholders' Equity		$25,000

2.22 The following are the account balances for Harris Corporation as of December 31, 20XX: investment in General Motors stock, $9,000; auto, $22,000; cash, $10,000; accounts payable, $2,000; notes receivable, $6,000; trademark, $4,000; capital stock, $20,000; taxes payable, $1,000; retained earnings (January 1, 20XX), $7,000; professional fee income, $30,000; mortgage payable, $10,000; telephone expense, $8,000; advertising expense, $11,000.

Prepare (*a*) an income statement, (*b*) a statement of retained earnings, and (*c*) a classified balance sheet (report form).

SOLUTION

(*a*)
Harris Corporation
Income Statement
For the Year Ended December 31, 20XX

Professional Fee Income		$30,000
Less: Expenses		
Telephone Expense	$ 8,000	
Advertising Expense	11,000	
Total Expenses		19,000
Net Income		$11,000

(*b*)
Harris Corporation
Statement of Retained Earnings
For the Year Ended December 31, 20XX

Retained Earnings, January 1	$ 7,000
Net Income	11,000
Retained Earnings, December 31	$18,000

(c)

Harris Corporation
Classified Balance Sheet
December 31, 20XX

ASSETS

Current Assets
Cash	$10,000	
Notes Receivable	6,000	
Total Current Assets		$16,000

Long-Term Investments
Investment in General Motors Stock	9,000

Fixed Assets
Auto	22,000

Intangible Assets
Trademark	4,000
Total Assets	$51,000

LIABILITIES AND STOCKHOLDERS' EQUITY

Current Liabilities
Accounts Payable	$ 2,000	
Taxes Payable	1,000	
Total Current Liabilities		$ 3,000

Noncurrent Liabilities
Mortgage Payable	10,000
Total Liabilities	$13,000

Stockholders' Equity
Capital Stock	$20,000	
Retained Earnings	18,000	
Total Stockholders' Equity		38,000
Total Liabilities and Stockholders' Equity		$51,000

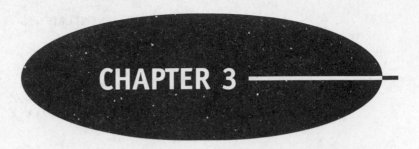

CHAPTER 3

Analyzing and Recording Financial Transactions

3.1 INTRODUCTION

To prepare an equation of Assets = Liabilities + Stockholders' Equity for each transaction would be extremely time consuming. Also, information about a specific item (e.g., accounts receivable) would be lost through this process. Rather, there should be an *account* established for each type of item. At the end of the reporting period, the financial statements can then be prepared based upon the balances in these accounts.

3.2 ACCOUNTS FOR RECORDING TRANSACTIONS

A *separate* account exists for each item shown on the financial statements. Thus, balance sheet accounts consist of assets, liabilities, and stockholders' equity. Income statement accounts are either expenses or revenue. The increases, decreases, and balance are shown for each account. For example, an increase in the cash account arises from receiving cash while a decrease ensues when a cash payment is made.

The "T" account, shown in Fig. 3-1, is the simplest form of account. It consists of a name and number, a debit side (left side), and a credit side (right side).

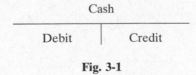

Fig. 3-1

Increases and decreases in an item are entered in the account. The side in which the increase or decrease of an item is placed depends upon the nature of the item. This is discussed further in Section

3.5. The account balance at the end of the period is inserted on the side having the greater dollar amount.

Although the "T" account form is usually the most convenient to use, an account form that permits the listing of more detailed information, including a *running* balance, may be used. Such an account form is shown in Fig. 3-2.

Cash   *Account No. 1*

Date	Explanation	Reference	Debit	Credit	Balance

Fig. 3-2

The *Date* column is for transaction dates. Although seldom used, the *Explanation* column is for recording any important particulars of the transaction. The *Reference* column is used to indicate the journal page number in which the transaction was originally recorded. (The journal is explained in Section 3.6.) The *Balance* column is used to reflect the new balance after each debit or credit.

3.3 LEDGER

All accounts of an entity are kept in a separate book called the *ledger*. The ledger, in effect, is a classification and summarization of financial transactions and is the basis for the preparation of the balance sheet and income statement. It is also useful for decision making because it provides the manager with the balance in a given account at a particular time. For example, if business seems poor, the manager can determine the sales for the reporting period. Similarly, the manager will want to know the cash balance at the end of the reporting period in order to determine whether adequate funds are on hand to meet operating requirements.

For businesses that utilize computers, the accounts may be stored on magnetic tapes or disks rather than in a ledger binder. If so, the accounting principles are still the same.

3.4 A CHART OF ACCOUNTS

The sequence and numbering of ledger accounts is customarily in the order in which they will appear in the financial statements. Listed first are the balance sheet accounts—assets, liabilities, and stockholders' equity, in that order. The income statement accounts—revenue and expenses—follow. Of course, the more complex the organization, the greater the number of ledger accounts required. Each account has its own number. A listing of the account names and numbers is called the *chart of accounts*. The chart serves as a useful source for locating a given account within the ledger.

The numbering system for the chart of accounts must leave room for new accounts. A range of numbers is assigned to each financial statement category. For example, asset accounts may be assigned the numbers 1–39, liabilities 40–59, stockholders' equity 60–69, revenue 70–89, and expenses 90–120. A partial chart of accounts is shown in the following example.

EXAMPLE 1

Chart of Accounts (partial)

Account Title	Account Number
ASSETS	
Current Assets	
Cash	1
Accounts Receivable	2
Inventory	6
Property, Plant, and Equipment	
Land	15
Machinery	18
LIABILITIES	
Current Liabilities	
Accounts Payable	40

For large businesses, a wider range of numbers would be required for each financial statement grouping. In fact, some companies employ a three-digit numbering system for each account. In such a case, the first digit identifies the financial statement category and the remaining digits apply to the position of that account within that category. For example, 1 may be the first digit for Assets, and Cash, being the first asset account, would be identified as 101.

3.5   REFLECTING DEBITS AND CREDITS IN THE ACCOUNTS

As previously mentioned, a debit (Dr.) is reflected in the left side of an account form and a credit (Cr.) in the right side. Debits are sometimes called charges. By convention, increases in certain account categories, namely assets and expenses, are debits. Hence, decreases in these accounts must be credits. On the other hand, increases in liabilities, stockholders' equity, and revenue are regarded as credits. Thus, decreases in these accounts are recorded as debits. This rule is illustrated in Fig. 3-3.

Assets and Expenses		Liabilities, Stockholders' Equity, and Revenue	
Dr. Increase	Cr. Decrease	Dr. Decrease	Cr. Increase

Fig. 3-3

For each business transaction, two or more accounts are always involved. In recording a transaction, *debits always equal credits*. This is referred to as the *double-entry system* (see also Section 1.5 in Chapter 1). For example, if cash is used to buy an auto, the auto account is debited (since an increase in an asset is a debit) and the cash account is credited (since a decrease in an asset is a credit).

A single account has a debit balance when the sum of its debits exceeds the sum of its credits. A credit balance ensues when total credits exceed total debits.

Dollar signs are not shown in ledger accounts.

EXAMPLE 2 Recording of Transactions in Ledger Accounts

Transaction 1. On March 1, the Westside Corporation received $50,000 in cash from the sale of 5,000 shares of capital stock.

The asset Cash is increased. An increase in an asset is a debit and is therefore listed on the left side of the account form. The stockholders' equity account Capital Stock is increased. An increase in stockholders' equity is a credit and is listed on the right side.

Cash			Capital Stock	
3/1 50,000				3/1 50,000

Transaction 2. On March 5, an auto was acquired by paying cash of $6,000.

Two asset accounts are involved. The asset Auto is increased and hence is a debit, while the asset Cash is decreased and thus is a credit.

Cash			Auto	
3/1 50,000	3/5 6,000		3/5 6,000	

Transaction 3. On March 8, furniture was purchased, on credit, $1,000.

The receipt of the asset Furniture requires a debit. The increase in the liability Accounts Payable requires a credit.

Furniture			Accounts Payable	
3/8 1,000				3/8 1,000

Transaction 4. On March 10, rent of $1,500 was paid.

An expense is recorded as a debit. Thus, Rent is charged. The decrease in the asset account Cash requires a credit.

Cash			Rent Expense	
3/1 50,000	3/5 6,000		3/10 1,500	
	3/10 1,500			

Transaction 5. On March 15, creditors were paid $300.

The asset Cash is reduced and thus requires a credit. A reduction in the liability Accounts Payable necessitates a debit.

Cash			Accounts Payable	
3/1 50,000	3/5 6,000	3/15 300		3/8 1,000
	3/10 1,500			
	3/15 300			

Transaction 6. On March 20, professional services were rendered to clients on account, $15,000.

This represents a receivable from clients. Thus, the asset Accounts Receivable increases and is therefore a debit. The professional services rendered involve fees which represent revenue to the company. Revenue is a credit.

Accounts Receivable			Professional Fee Income	
3/20 15,000				3/20 15,000

Transaction 7. On March 26, salaries of $2,000 were paid to employees.

Since an expense is a debit, salary expense is charged. The payment of cash involves a reduction in the asset Cash, which is credited.

Cash				Salary Expense	
3/1 50,000	3/5	6,000		3/26 2,000	
	3/10	1,500			
	3/15	300			
	3/26	2,000			

Transaction 8. On March 29, land was purchased for $8,000 with a down payment of $2,000 cash and the balance on account.

The asset Land is increased and must be debited. The asset Cash is decreased and therefore requires a credit. The liability Accounts Payable increases and thus must be credited for $6,000, the balance. In this case, more than two accounts are involved. This is called a *compound entry*. Of course, the total debits still equal the total credits.

Cash			Accounts Payable				Land	
3/1 50,000	3/5	6,000	3/15 300	3/8	1,000		3/29 8,000	
	3/10	1,500		3/29	6,000			
	3/15	300						
	3/26	2,000						
	3/29	2,000						

Transaction 9. On March 31, $5,000 was collected from customers.

Since the asset Cash is increased, it is debited. The reduction in the asset Accounts Receivable requires a credit.

Cash				Accounts Receivable			
3/1	50,000	3/5	6,000	3/20 15,000	3/31	5,000	
3/31	5,000	3/10	1,500				
		3/15	300				
		3/26	2,000				

3.6 THE JOURNAL

Up to this point, we have discussed the manner in which transactions are analyzed and classified in the accounts. The purpose was to gain an understanding of why an entry is made in a particular manner. However, the entries made in the "T" accounts do not furnish the data required about a given transaction nor is listing of transactions in chronological order possible on "T" accounts. These deficiencies are overcome through the use of a *journal*.

In actual accounting practice, business transactions are first recorded in the journal from information in the source documents (e.g., telephone bill). The data are then transferred from the journal to the ledger by debiting and crediting the particular accounts involved. This process is called *posting*.

The journal is the book of original entry in which transactions are entered on a daily basis in chronological order. This process is called *journalizing*. Debits and credits are listed along with the appropriate explanations. Thus, the journal reflects in one place all information about a transaction.

Different types of journals exist which may be grouped into the categories of (1) general journals and (2) specialized journals. The latter is used when there are many repetitive transactions (e.g., sales). The headings used in a general journal are shown in Fig. 3-4.

General Journal

Page No.

Date	Accounts	Posting Reference	Debit	Credit

Fig. 3-4

The *Date* column contains the year, month, and day of the initial transaction. The year and month is not repeated for later transactions unless there is a new page or new month. The *Accounts* column shows the account debited, the name of which is entered close to the left margin. The dollar amount of the debit is listed in the *Debit* column. The account credited is listed indented and directly underneath the account debited in the *Accounts* column, and the amount credited is entered in the *Credit* column. Immediately after the credit entry, an explanation for the transaction is given in the *Accounts* column. If there is a compound entry, all debits are listed before the credits. The *Posting Reference* (P.R.) column is used for the ledger account number after the posting from the journal to the ledger takes place. This provides a cross-reference between journal and ledger.

A blank line is left after each journal entry.

3.7 JOURNAL ENTRIES

The process of making journal entries is best described by showing an example. The journalized transactions of Westside Corporation for the month of March 20XX are shown in Example 3. Note that dollar signs are not used in a journal. The account numbers assigned in the P.R. column are based upon the chart of accounts numbering system presented in Section 3.4.

EXAMPLE 3

General Journal

Date	Accounts	P.R.	Debit	Credit
20XX				
March 1	Cash	1	50,000	
	Capital Stock	60		50,000
	Issued 5,000 shares of stock			
5	Auto	10	6,000	
	Cash	1		6,000
	Bought an auto			
8	Furniture	12	1,000	
	Accounts Payable	40		1,000
	Acquired furniture on credit			
10	Rent Expense	90	1,500	
	Cash	1		1,500
	Paid the monthly rent			

General Journal (continued)

Date	Accounts	P.R.	Debit	Credit
15	Accounts Payable	40	300	
	Cash	1		300
	Partial payment to creditors			
20	Accounts Receivable	2	15,000	
	Professional Fee Income	70		15,000
	Performed services			
26	Salary Expense	91	2,000	
	Cash	1		2,000
	Paid employee salaries			
29	Land	9	8,000	
	Cash	1		2,000
	Accounts Payable	40		6,000
	Acquired land			
31	Cash	1	5,000	
	Accounts Receivable	2		5,000
	Received partial collection from clients			

3.8 POSTING

Posting was defined earlier as the transferring of information from the journal to the ledger. Posting involves the following steps:

1. The date and amount of the debits and credits are entered in the ledger accounts (solid arrows).
2. The journal page numbers of the accounts are listed (dashed arrows).
3. The account number, which serves as a cross reference, is transferred from the ledger to the P.R. column of the journal (dotted arrows).

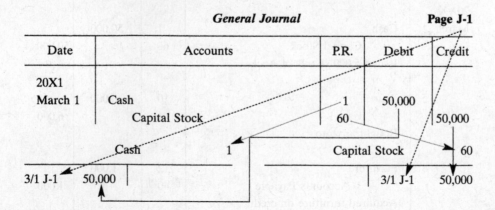

The posting of the Westside Corporation's March transactions from the journal to the ledger is shown in Example 4. The accounts are arranged in financial statement order (assets, liabilities, stockholders' equity, revenue, and expenses). Although several accounts are listed on the same page here in order to conserve space, in real life each account has its own page in the ledger book.

EXAMPLE 4

The Ledger

ASSETS				=	LIABILITIES				+	STOCKHOLDERS' EQUITY		
Cash			1		Accounts Payable			40		Capital Stock		60
3/1	50,000	3/5	6,000	3/15	300	3/8	1,000			3/1	50,000
3/31	5,000	3/10	1,500			3/29	6,000				
		3/15	300								
		3/26	2,000								
		3/29	2,000								

Accounts Receivable			2		Professional Fee Income		70
3/20	15,000	3/31	5,000			3/20	15,000

Land		9		Rent Expense		90
3/29	8,000			3/10	1,500	

Auto		10		Salary Expense		91
3/5	6,000			3/26	2,000	

Furniture		12
3/8	1,000	

3.9   PREPARING THE TRIAL BALANCE

In the process of posting to the ledger accounts, debits must equal credits; therefore the total debits in the ledger must be in agreement with the total credits. A *trial balance* is prepared which shows this equality in a schedule containing two columns—debit and credit. All accounts are listed in the order in which they appear in the ledger, and their balances are placed under the appropriate columns. When all accounts have been listed, the total in the debit column must prove to the total in the credit column. If so, there is an equality of debits and credits for the transactions entered into the ledger. If not, an error has been made.

Even though the trial balance furnishes arithmetical proof that debits equal credits, it does not guard against all errors. Postings to the wrong accounts may occur. For example, if a debit was incorrectly entered into the rent expense account rather than the auto account, the total in the columns of the trial balance would agree but incorrect balances would exist in Rent Expense and Auto. Also, if a transaction was omitted from the ledger, the accounts involved would be misstated.

The trial balance is a worksheet and *not* a formal financial statement. It serves as a convenient basis for the preparation of the balance sheet and income statement.

EXAMPLE 5

Westside Corporation
Trial Balance
March 31, 20XX

	Debit	Credit
Cash	$43,200	
Accounts Receivable	10,000	
Land	8,000	
Auto	6,000	
Furniture	1,000	
Accounts Payable		$ 6,700
Capital Stock		50,000
Professional Fee Income		15,000
Rent Expense	1,500	
Salary Expense	2,000	
	$71,700	$71,700

3.10 FINANCIAL STATEMENT PREPARATION

Using the trial balance, we will now construct the income statement and balance sheet for Westside Corporation.

EXAMPLE 6

Westside Corporation
Income Statement
For the Month Ended March 31, 20XX

Professional Fee Income		$15,000
Less: Expenses		
Rent Expense	$1,500	
Salary Expense	2,000	
Total Expenses		3,500
Net Income		$11,500

Westside Corporation
Balance Sheet
March 31, 20XX

ASSETS

Current Assets		
Cash	$43,200	
Accounts Receivable	10,000	
Total Current Assets		$53,200
Fixed Assets		
Land	$ 8,000	
Auto	6,000	
Furniture	1,000	
Total Fixed Assets		15,000
Total Assets		$68,200

LIABILITIES AND STOCKHOLDERS' EQUITY

Current Liabilities

Accounts Payable		$ 6,700
Stockholders' Equity		
Capital Stock	$50,000	
Retained Earnings	11,500	
Total Stockholders' Equity		61,500
Total Liabilities and Stockholders' Equity		$68,200

Summary

(1) A(n) _____ classifies and summarizes a single item.

(2) All accounts of the company appear in the _____.

(3) The simplest format for an account is called the _____ account.

(4) The right side of an account is called a(n) _____.

(5) An increase in an asset or expense requires a(n) _____.

(6) An increase in a liability, stockholders' equity, or revenue account involves a(n) _____.

(7) Debits are sometimes called _____.

(8) The essence of the double-entry system is the equality of _____ and _____.

(9) The list of numbers for all accounts appears in the _____.

(10) In the chart of accounts, the first general financial statement account category is _____.

(11) Transactions are initially recorded in the _____.

(12) _____ is the procedure of transferring data from the journal to the ledger.

(13) When more than two accounts are involved in a transaction we have a(n) _____ entry.

(14) After each journal entry there is a(n) _____ line.

(15) Not shown in the ledger or journal are _____.

(16) A listing of all accounts in the ledger along with their balances to prove that the total debits equal the total credits appears in the _____.

Solved Problems

3.1 List the following in the sequence in which they are done in the accounting cycle:

Trial balance
Posting
Financial statements
Journalizing

SOLUTION

1. Journalizing
2. Posting
3. Trial balance
4. Financial statements

3.2 For the "T" accounts listed below, state which side represents an increase and which represents a decrease.

Assets and Expenses		Liabilities, Stockholders' Equity, and Revenue	
Dr.	Cr.	Dr.	Cr.

SOLUTION

Assets and Expenses		Liabilities, Stockholders' Equity, and Revenue	
Dr.	Cr.	Dr.	Cr.
Increase	Decrease	Decrease	Increase

3.3 For each account listed below, indicate with an **X** whether a debit or credit is involved.

	Debit	Credit
1. Cash is decreased.		
2. Revenue is increased.		
3. Advertising Expense is increased.		
4. Capital Stock is increased.		
5. Notes Payable is decreased.		
6. Accounts Receivable is decreased.		

SOLUTION

		Debit	Credit
1.	Cash is decreased.		X
2.	Revenue is increased.		X
3.	Advertising Expense is increased.	X	
4.	Capital Stock is increased.		X
5.	Notes Payable is decreased.	X	
6.	Accounts Receivable is decreased.		X

3.4 For each transaction noted below, write in the appropriate column the names of the accounts to be debited and credited.

		Debit	Credit
1.	Issued capital stock for cash		
2.	Paid salary expense		
3.	Purchased an auto on credit		
4.	Received cash for professional services rendered		
5.	Paid a creditor		
6.	Borrowed money from a bank issuing a note		

SOLUTION

		Debit	Credit
1.	Issued capital stock for cash	Cash	Capital Stock
2.	Paid salary expense	Salary Expense	Cash
3.	Purchased an auto on credit	Auto	Accounts Payable
4.	Received cash for professional services rendered	Cash	Fee Income
5.	Paid a creditor	Accounts Payable	Cash
6.	Borrowed money from a bank issuing a note	Cash	Notes Payable

3.5 Record the following transactions in the accounts listed below.

1. Received cash from professional services rendered, $2,500
2. Purchased furniture for $1,000, making a down payment of 30%
3. Incurred telephone expense on account, $100
4. Paid $400 to creditors

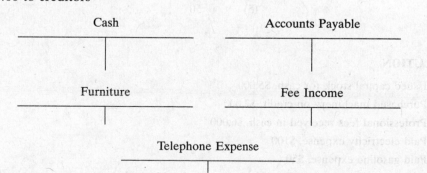

SOLUTION

	Cash					Accounts Payable		
(1)	2,500	(2)	300		(4)	400	(2)	700
		(4)	400				(3)	100

	Furniture				Fee Income	
(2)	1,000				(1)	2,500

	Telephone Expense	
(3)	100	

3.6 Provide an explanation for each transaction shown in the following ledger accounts:

	Cash					Accounts Payable	
(1)	5,000	(4)	100			(2)	2,000
(3)	6,000	(5)	50			(6)	5,000
		(6)	2,000				

	Machinery				Capital Stock	
(2)	2,000				(1)	5,000

	Furniture				Professional Fee Income	
(6)	7,000				(3)	6,000

	Electricity Expense	
(4)	100	

	Gasoline Expense	
(5)	50	

SOLUTION

1. Issued capital stock for cash, $5,000
2. Purchased machinery on credit, $2,000
3. Professional fees received in cash, $6,000
4. Paid electricity expense, $100
5. Paid gasoline expense, $50
6. Bought furniture of $7,000; paid $2,000 in cash with the balance on account

3.7   What is the proper sequence for accounts listed in the chart of accounts?

SOLUTION

Assets
Liabilities
Stockholders' Equity
Revenue
Expenses

3.8   A company's chart of accounts provides the following numbering system:

Assets		101–199
Current Assets	101–120	
Fixed Assets	121–150	
Liabilities		201–299
Current Liabilities	201–220	
Noncurrent Liabilities	221–250	
Stockholders' Equity		301–399
Revenue		401–499
Expenses		501–599

Arrange the following accounts as they should appear in the ledger and assign an appropriate ledger account number.

Advertising Expense	Auto
Capital Stock	Mortgage Payable
Professional Fee Income	Accounts Payable
Rent Expense	Interest Income
Cash	

SOLUTION

Account	Number
Cash	101
Auto	121
Accounts Payable	201
Mortgage Payable	221
Capital Stock	301
Professional Fee Income	401
Interest Income	402
Advertising Expense	501
Rent Expense	502

3.9   Arrange the following accounts in proper order and prepare a trial balance.

Accounts Receivable	$10,000
Postage Expense	6,000
Cleaning Expense	8,000
Professional Fee Income	30,000
Retained Earnings	12,000
Capital Stock	20,000
Notes Payable	7,000
Equipment	25,000
Copyright	9,000
Cash	11,000

SOLUTION

Trial Balance

Cash	$11,000	
Accounts Receivable	10,000	
Equipment	25,000	
Copyright	9,000	
Notes Payable		$ 7,000
Capital Stock		20,000
Retained Earnings		12,000
Professional Fee Income		30,000
Postage Expense	6,000	
Cleaning Expense	8,000	
	$69,000	$69,000

3.10   The following trial balance for Loretta Company was prepared by the owner, who has little knowledge of accounting. It therefore didn't balance. Prepare a corrected trial balance.

Trial Balance

Cash	$ 50,000	
Notes Receivable	10,000	
Accounts Payable	10,000	
Building	65,000	
Notes Payable		$ 50,000
Accounts Receivable		5,000
Capital Stock		70,000
	$135,000	$125,000

SOLUTION

The Loretta Company
Trial Balance

Cash	$ 50,000	
Accounts Receivable	5,000	
Notes Receivable	10,000	
Building	65,000	
Accounts Payable		$ 10,000
Notes Payable		50,000
Capital Stock		70,000
	$130,000	$130,000

3.11 The following trial balance of Hardy Corporation does not balance:

Hardy Corporation
Trial Balance

Cash	$10,000	
Accounts Receivable	12,500	
Machinery	7,000	
Accounts Payable		$ 5,000
Capital Stock		8,100
Professional Fee Income		30,000
Salary Expense	9,000	
Rent Expense	4,000	
	$42,500	$43,100

After reviewing the ledger account balances, it was found that: (1) Accounts Receivable has total debits of $20,000 and total credits of $6,500, (2) cash paid of $600 for a machine was not posted to the Machinery account, (3) the balance for Professional Fee Income should be $1,000 more than stated, and (4) a payment to a creditor of $700 was not posted to any account. Prepare a corrected trial balance.

SOLUTION

Hardy Corporation
Trial Balance

Cash	$ 9,300	
Accounts Receivable	13,500	
Machinery	7,600	
Accounts Payable		$ 4,300
Capital Stock		8,100
Professional Fee Income		31,000
Salary Expense	9,000	
Rent Expense	4,000	
	$43,400	$43,400

3.12 If a $1,000 credit is incorrectly posted as a debit, will the trial balance balance?

SOLUTION

No. The total debits and total credits of the trial balance will not prove. The total debits will be greater because they include an extra $1,000 debit that should have been a credit. The trial balance will be out of balance by $2,000, which is double the amount that was erroneously posted. The $2,000 is computed as follows:

Overstatement of debits	$1,000
Understatement of credits	1,000
Total difference	$2,000

3.13 Enter the following transactions in the ledger accounts listed below.

1. Received $20,000 cash from the issuance of common stock
2. Bought equipment of $8,000 on account
3. Paid travel expense, $1,000
4. Rendered professional services of $30,000, receiving $10,000 in cash with the balance on account
5. Paid $5,000 to creditors
6. Sold for $3,000 cash equipment having a value per books of $3,000 (therefore, experienced no gain or loss)

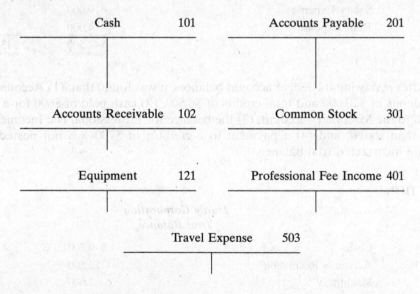

```
        Cash              101              Accounts Payable      201
   _____|_____                      _____|_____
          |                                     |
          |                                     |
          |                                     |



   Accounts Receivable   102              Common Stock          301
   _____|_____                      _____|_____
          |                                     |
          |                                     |



        Equipment         121          Professional Fee Income  401
   _____|_____                      _____|_____
          |                                     |
          |                                     |



                    Travel Expense       503
               _____|_____
                      |
```

SOLUTION

	Cash		101		Accounts Payable		201
(1)	20,000	(3)	1,000	(5)	5,000	(2)	8,000
(4)	10,000	(5)	5,000				
(6)	3,000						

Accounts Receivable 102			Common Stock 301	
(4)	20,000			(1) 20,000

Equipment 121			Professional Fee Income 401	
(2)	8,000	(6) 3,000		(4) 30,000

Travel Expense 503	
(3)	1,000

3.14 From the ledger accounts of Problem 3.13, prepare a trial balance.

SOLUTION

Trial Balance

Cash	$27,000	
Accounts Receivable	20,000	
Equipment	5,000	
Accounts Payable		$ 3,000
Common Stock		20,000
Professional Fee Income		30,000
Travel Expense	1,000	
	$53,000	$53,000

3.15 Give a brief explanation for each of the following entries:

General Journal

Account	Debit	Credit
1. Cash	10,000	
Notes Payable		10,000
2. Cash	5,000	
Accounts Receivable		5,000
3. Accounts Payable	2,000	
Notes Payable		2,000
4. Prepaid Insurance	1,000	
Cash		1,000
5. Cash	500	
Interest Income		500

SOLUTION

1. Issued a note payable for cash of $10,000
2. Received a payment from a customer, $5,000
3. A note payable of $2,000 was given in settlement of an account payable
4. Paid $1,000 cash for an insurance policy providing future protection
5. Received interest income of $500 on a bank account

3.16 Drake Corporation started its business by issuing $25,000 in capital stock in exchange for the following assets: Cash, $10,000; Land, $6,000; Building, $9,000. Prepare the opening journal entry.

SOLUTION

General Journal

Account	Debit	Credit
Cash	10,000	
Land	6,000	
Building	9,000	
Capital Stock		25,000

3.17 Simonson Corporation bought the following assets: office equipment, $2,000; auto, $7,000; and land, $3,000. It gave a note payable of $5,000 and paid the balance in cash. Prepare the required compound journal entry.

SOLUTION

General Journal

Account	Debit	Credit
Office Equipment	2,000	
Auto	7,000	
Land	3,000	
Note Payable		5,000
Cash		7,000

3.18 Prepare the journal entries, including explanations, for the following transactions, which occurred during the month of September 20XX:

Sept. 1. Issued capital stock for cash, $20,000

Sept. 11. Bought a building for $10,000 with a down payment of $3,500 and a note payable for the balance

Sept. 23. Purchased a truck for $3,000 on account

Sept. 28. Bought supplies on account, $800

SOLUTION

General Journal

Date	Account	Debit	Credit
20XX			
Sept. 1	Cash	20,000	
	Capital Stock		20,000
	Issuance of capital stock		
11	Building	10,000	
	Cash		3,500
	Note Payable		6,500
	Purchased a building for cash and a		
	note payable		
23	Truck	3,000	
	Accounts Payable		3,000
	Bought a truck on account		
28	Supplies	800	
	Accounts Payable		800
	Acquired supplies on account		

3.19 Dr. Smith is an allergy doctor. On May 6, 20XX, he rendered professional services to his patients for $1,000. He received cash of $400 for the day, and the remaining amount was billed to his patients. Prepare the appropriate journal entry.

SOLUTION

General Journal

Date	Account	Debit	Credit
20XX			
May 6	Cash	400	
	Accounts Receivable	600	
	Professional Fee Income		1,000

3.20 With regard to the prior problem, on June 8, 20XX, Dr. Smith received $350 in cash from the patients he billed on May 6, 20XX. What is the appropriate journal entry?

SOLUTION

Date	Account	Debit	Credit
20XX			
June 8	Cash	350	
	Accounts Receivable		350

3.21 Why did we not credit the professional fee income account for $350 in Problem 3.20?

SOLUTION

The reason we did not credit the professional fee income account is that it was already credited on May 6, 20XX, when the doctor performed the services. Under the accrual basis of accounting, revenue is recorded when the services are rendered, not when cash is received.

3.22 Catherine Ackerman started her own business. Based upon the following transactions, (a) prepare journal entries, (b) post to the ledger accounts, and (c) prepare a trial balance (report form).

Jan. 1.   Opened a bank account by depositing $15,000 cash
Jan. 15. Purchased equipment on account, $1,000
Jan. 24. Issued a note payable of $5,000 for a franchise to operate the business

SOLUTION

(a)   *General Journal*

Date	Account	Debit	Credit
Jan. 1	Cash	15,000	
	C. Ackerman, Capital		15,000
15	Equipment	1,000	
	Accounts Payable		1,000
24	*Franchise Fee	5,000	
	Note Payable		5,000

*Note: A franchise fee is an intangible asset.

(b)   *Ledger*

Cash 101*		Accounts Payable 201	
Jan. 1 15,000			Jan. 15 1,000

Equipment 121		Notes Payable 202	
Jan. 15 1,000			Jan. 24 5,000

Franchise 153		Ackerman, Capital 301	
Jan. 24 5,000			Jan. 1 15,000

*For chart of accounts, see Section 3.4 and Problem 3.8.

(c)   **Catherine Ackerman**
Trial Balance
January 31, 20XX

	Debit	Credit
Cash	$15,000	
Equipment	1,000	
Franchise	5,000	
Accounts Payable		$ 1,000
Notes Payable		5,000
C. Ackerman, Capital		15,000
	$21,000	$21,000

3.23 Prepare the journal entries for the following transactions of Apex Corporation.

1. Paid $3,000 for office equipment
2. Received professional fees of $12,000 for services rendered
3. Bought an auto for $10,000, paying 20 percent down and the balance with a note payable
4. Purchased a machine for $6,000 on credit from Lawrence Machine Company
5. Paid 30 percent of the amount owed Lawrence Machine Company
6. Paid maintenance expenses of $300

SOLUTION

General Journal

	Account	Debit	Credit
1.	Office Equipment	3,000	
	Cash		3,000
2.	Cash	12,000	
	Professional Fee Income		12,000
3.	Auto	10,000	
	Cash		2,000
	Notes Payable		8,000
4.	Machinery	6,000	
	Accounts Payable		6,000
5.	Accounts Payable	1,800	
	Cash		1,800
6.	Maintenance Expense	300	
	Cash		300

3.24 Post the journal entries in Problem 3.23 to the appropriate "T" accounts.

SOLUTION

Cash					Accounts Payable		
(2)	12,000	(1)	3,000		(5) 1,800	(4)	6,000
		(3)	2,000				
		(5)	1,800				
		(6)	300				

Auto			Notes Payable		
(3)	10,000			(3)	8,000

Machinery			Professional Fee Income		
(4)	6,000			(2)	12,000

Office Equipment		Maintenance Expense	
(1) 3,000		(6) 300	

3.25 Prepare a trial balance based upon the "T" account balances from Problem 3.24.

SOLUTION

Trial Balance

	Debit	Credit
Cash	$ 4,900	
Auto	10,000	
Machinery	6,000	
Office Equipment	3,000	
Accounts Payable		$ 4,200
Notes Payable		8,000
Professional Fee Income		12,000
Maintenance Expense	300	
	$24,200	$24,200

3.26 Larkin Corporation's trial balance on March 31, 20XX, was as follows:

Larkin Corporation
Trial Balance
March 31, 20XX

	Debit	Credit
Cash	$ 4,000	
Accounts Receivable	7,000	
Auto	9,000	
Building	10,000	
Accounts Payable		$ 7,000
Common Stock		20,000
Retained Earnings		3,000
	$30,000	$30,000

The following transactions occurred in April 20XX:

April 5. Paid creditors, $1,000

April 17. Received collections from customers, $2,000

April 19. Professional fees earned received in cash, $7,000

April 30. Paid rent expense, $2,000

The account numbers are: Cash, 101; Accounts Receivable, 102; Auto, 120; Building, 121; Accounts Payable, 201; Capital Stock, 301; Retained Earnings, 302; Professional Fee Income, 401; Rent Expense, 502.

Based on these data, (a) prepare appropriate April entries on page 4 of the journal, and (b) fill in the balances as of April 1, 20XX, in the ledger accounts ("T" account form) and post April entries from the journal to the ledger. Make the journal and ledger complete in all respects.

SOLUTION

(a)

Date 20XX	Account	P.R.	Debit	Credit
Apr. 5	Accounts Payable	201	1,000	
	Cash	101		1,000
	Payment to creditors			
Apr. 17	Cash	101	2,000	
	Accounts Receivable	102		2,000
	Remittance from customers			
19	Cash	101	7,000	
	Professional Fee Income	401		7,000
	Professional services rendered			
30	Rent Expense	502	2,000	
	Cash	101		2,000

General Journal   **J-4**

(b)

Cash			101		Accounts Payable			201
4/1	4,000	4/5 J-4	1,000	4/5 J-4	1,000	4/1	7,000	
4/17 J-4	2,000	4/30 J-4	2,000					
4/19 J-4	7,000							

Accounts Receivable			102		Capital Stock			301
4/1	7,000	4/17 J-4	2,000			4/1	20,000	

Auto			120		Retained Earnings			302
4/1	9,000					4/1	3,000	

Building			121		Professional Fee Income			401
4/1	10,000					4/19 J-4	7,000	

Rent Expense			502
4/30 J-4	2,000		

Note that the beginning balances dated 4/1 are the same as the ending balances as of March 31.

3.27 Based upon the ledger account balances from Problem 3.26, prepare a trial balance for April 30, 20XX.

SOLUTION

Larkin Corporation
Trial Balance
April 30, 20XX

	Debit	Credit
Cash	$10,000	
Accounts Receivable	5,000	
Auto	9,000	
Building	10,000	
Accounts Payable		$ 6,000
Capital Stock		20,000
Retained Earnings		3,000
Professional Fee Income		7,000
Rent Expense	2,000	
	$36,000	$36,000

3.28   Based upon the trial balance in Problem 3.27, prepare the income statement, statement of retained earnings, and the balance sheet (account form) for Larkin Corporation.

SOLUTION

Larkin Corporation
Income Statement
For the Month Ended April 30, 20XX

Professional Fee Income	$7,000
Less: Rent Expense	2,000
Net Income	$5,000

Larkin Corporation
Statement of Retained Earnings
For the Month Ended April 30, 20XX

Retained Earnings, April 1, 20XX	$3,000
Net Income	5,000
Retained Earnings, April 30, 20XX	$8,000

Larkin Corporation
Balance Sheet
For the Month Ended April 30, 20XX

ASSETS			**LIABILITIES AND STOCKHOLDERS' EQUITY**		
Current Assets			*Current Liabilities*		
Cash	$10,000		Accounts Payable		$ 6,000
Accounts Receivable	5,000		*Stockholders' Equity*		
Total Current Assets		$15,000	Capital Stock	$20,000	
Fixed Assets			Retained Earnings	8,000	
Auto	$ 9,000		Total Stockholders'		
Building	10,000		Equity		28,000
Total Fixed Assets		19,000	Total Liabilities and		
Total Assets		$34,000	Stockholders' Equity		$34,000

EXAMINATION I

Chapters 1–3

1. What is financial accounting?

2. What is the name of the major rule-making body that formulates financial accounting requirements?

3. What does the accounting principle of consistency mean?

4. What are the two types of financial statements and what do they show about a business?

5. Define the following financial statement categories:

   (*a*) Current Assets
   (*b*) Fixed Assets
   (*c*) Long-Term Investments
   (*d*) Noncurrent Liabilities
   (*e*) Stockholders' Equity
   (*f*) Revenue
   (*g*) Selling Expenses

6. What is the accrual basis of accounting?

7. What are dividends?

8. What is a ledger?

9. What is meant by posting?

10. What is the double-entry accounting system?

11. What are temporary accounts?

12. Based upon the following information, prepare a statement of retained earnings for Charles Corporation for the year ended December 31, 20XX.

Retained Earnings—January 1, 20XX	$10,000
Net Income	2,000
Dividends	500

13. Westec Corporation shows the following income statement accounts for the year ended December 31, 20XX:

Professional Fee Income	$31,000	Rent Expense	$7,000
Advertising Expense	10,000	Insurance Expense	6,000
Salespeople Commission Expense	4,000	Interest Expense	1,000

Prepare an income statement.

14. Larkin Corporation shows the following balance sheet accounts as of December 31, 20XX:

Investment in Ford Co. Bonds	$ 8,000	Accounts Receivable	$ 5,000
Cash	10,000	Retained Earnings	3,000
Copyright	6,000	Capital Stock	15,000
Auto	4,000	Accounts Payable	9,000
Machinery	7,000	Mortgage Payable	10,000
Taxes Payable	3,000		

Prepare a classified balance sheet in report form.

15. Below are the account balances for Ajax Corporation as of December 31, 20XX.

Salaries Payable	$ 2,000	Franchise Fee	$ 4,000
Professional Fee Income	20,000	Retained Earnings	5,000
Cash	5,000	Office Furniture	10,000
Capital Stock	8,000	Salaries Expense	13,000
Repair Expense	3,000		

Prepare (a) a trial balance, (b) an income statement, (c) a statement of retained earnings, and (d) a balance sheet in report form.

16. Swift Company entered into the following transactions for the month of January 20XX:

Jan. 1. Issued $30,000 of capital stock

4. Purchased equipment on account, $6,000

7. Paid salaries of $4,000

9. Borrowed $5,000 from the bank, issuing a note payable

14. Paid creditors, $4,000

18. Rendered professional services to clients of $10,000, of which $3,000 was received in cash with the balance on account

20. Paid a telephone bill of $500

27. Received $5,000 from clients for amounts owed and previously billed to them

31. Purchased an auto for cash, $7,000

Prepare (a) journal entries, (b) ledger "T" accounts, and (c) a trial balance.

Answers to Examination I

1. Financial accounting is the recording, classifying, summarizing, and reporting of transactions to show the financial health of a business.

2. Financial Accounting Standards Board.

3. Consistency means using the same accounting method from reporting period to reporting period.

4. The two financial statements are the balance sheet and income statement. The balance sheet provides a picture of an entity's financial health at the end of the reporting period. It shows the assets, liabilities, and stockholders' equity. Assets represent the resources owned. Liabilities are what is owed. Stockholders' equity is the ownership interest of investors in the company. Assets minus liabilities equal stockholders' equity. The income statement shows the operating performance of the business for the reporting period. Net income or net loss is the difference between total revenue and total expenses.

5. (*a*) Assets having a life less than one year
    (*b*) Assets having a life greater than one year and possessing physical substance
    (*c*) Investments in other companies where the intent is to hold the stock or bond for more than one year
    (*d*) Amounts owed to others which are payable in a period greater than one year
    (*e*) The ownership interest of stockholders in the corporation
    (*f*) The gross income derived from the business either by selling merchandise or rendering services
    (*g*) Expenses related either to obtaining the sale or service or to the distribution of the merchandise

6. The accrual basis of accounting is the recognition of revenue when earned and expenses when incurred.

7. Dividends are a distribution of assets (typically cash) by a corporation to its stockholders.

8. A ledger is a listing of the accounts of a business and their balances.

9. Posting is the process of going from the journal to the ledger.

10. In the double-entry system, the total debits and total credits for a transaction equal. Usually, there is only one debit and one credit to a transaction. When more than one debit or one credit is required for a transaction, the entry is referred to as a compound entry.

11. Temporary, or nominal, accounts are income statement accounts. Revenue and expenses are closed out at the end of the fiscal year and the resulting net income or net loss is transferred to retained earnings. Thus at the beginning of the next fiscal year, these accounts have a zero balance.

12.
Charles Corporation
Statement of Retained Earnings
For the Year Ended December 31, 20XX

Retained Earnings—January 1	$10,000
Net Income	2,000
Subtotal	$12,000
Dividends	500
Retained Earnings—December 31	$11,500

13.

Westec Corporation
Income Statement
For the Year Ended December 31, 20XX

Professional Fee Income		$31,000
Less: Operating Expenses		
Advertising	$10,000	
Salespeople Commissions	4,000	
Rent	7,000	
Insurance	6,000	
Total Operating Expenses		27,000
Operating Income		$ 4,000
Less: Other Expenses		
Interest Expense		1,000
Net Income		$ 3,000

14.

Larkin Corporation
Balance Sheet
December 31, 20XX

ASSETS

Current Assets		
Cash	$10,000	
Accounts Receivable	5,000	
Total Current Assets		$15,000
Long-Term Investments		
Investment in Ford Co. Bonds		8,000
Fixed Assets		
Machinery	$ 7,000	
Auto	4,000	
Total Fixed Assets		11,000
Intangible Assets		
Copyright		6,000
Total Assets		$40,000

LIABILITIES AND STOCKHOLDERS' EQUITY

Current Liabilities		
Accounts Payable	$ 9,000	
Taxes Payable	3,000	
Total Current Liabilities		$12,000
Noncurrent Liabilities		
Mortgage Payable		10,000
Total Liabilities		$22,000
Stockholders' Equity		
Capital Stock	$15,000	
Retained Earnings	3,000	
Total Stockholders' Equity		18,000
Total Liabilities and Stockholders' Equity		$40,000

15. *(a)*

Ajax Corporation
Trial Balance
December 31, 20XX

Cash	$ 5,000	
Office Furniture	10,000	
Franchise Fee	4,000	
Salaries Payable		$ 2,000
Capital Stock		8,000
Retained Earnings		5,000
Professional Fee Income		20,000
Salaries Expense	13,000	
Repair Expense	3,000	
	$35,000	$35,000

(b)

Ajax Corporation
Income Statement
For the Year Ended December 31, 20XX

Professional Fee Income		$20,000
Less: Operating Expenses		
Salaries Expense	$13,000	
Repair Expense	3,000	
Total Operating Expenses		16,000
Net Income		$ 4,000

(c)

Ajax Corporation
Statement of Retained Earnings
For the Year Ended December 31, 20XX

Retained Earnings—January 1	$5,000
Net Income	4,000
Retained Earnings—December 31	$9,000

(d)

Ajax Corporation
Balance Sheet
December 31, 20XX

ASSETS

Current Assets	
Cash	$ 5,000
Fixed Assets	
Office Furniture	10,000
Intangible Assets	
Franchise Fee	4,000
Total Assets	$19,000

LIABILITIES AND STOCKHOLDERS' EQUITY

Current Liabilities

Salaries Payable		$ 2,000

Stockholders' Equity

Capital Stock	$8,000	
Retained Earnings	9,000	
Total Stockholders' Equity		17,000
Total Liabilities and Stockholders' Equity		$19,000

16. *(a)*

General Journal

Date	Account	Debit	Credit
20XX			
Jan. 1	Cash	30,000	
	Capital Stock		30,000
4	Equipment	6,000	
	Accounts Payable		6,000
7	Salaries Expense	4,000	
	Cash		4,000
9	Cash	5,000	
	Notes Payable		5,000
14	Accounts Payable	4,000	
	Cash		4,000
18	Cash	3,000	
	Accounts Receivable	7,000	
	Professional Fee Income		10,000
20	Telephone Expense	500	
	Cash		500
27	Cash	5,000	
	Accounts Receivable		5,000
31	Auto	7,000	
	Cash		7,000

(b)

Ledger

Cash					Accounts Payable			
1/1	30,000	1/7	4,000		1/14	4,000	1/4	6,000
1/9	5,000	1/14	4,000					
1/18	3,000	1/20	500					
1/27	5,000	1/31	7,000					

Accounts Receivable					Notes Payable			
1/18	7,000	1/27	5,000				1/9	5,000

Equipment				Capital Stock			
1/4	6,000					1/1	30,000

Auto				Professional Fee Income			
1/31	7,000					1/18	10,000

Salaries Expense		
1/7	4,000	

Telephone Expense		
1/20	500	

(c)

Swift Company
Trial Balance
January 31, 20XX

Cash	$27,500	
Accounts Receivable	2,000	
Equipment	6,000	
Auto	7,000	
Accounts Payable		$ 2,000
Notes Payable		5,000
Common Stock		30,000
Professional Fee Income		10,000
Salaries Expense	4,000	
Telephone Expense	500	
	$47,000	$47,000

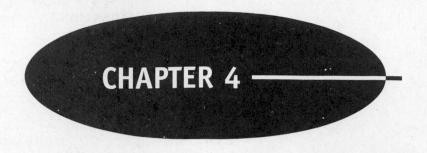

CHAPTER 4

Adjusting and Closing Entries

4.1 INTRODUCTION

As discussed in Chapter 2, companies use the *accrual basis* of accounting in keeping their records. This means that *revenue is recognized when earned* irrespective of when cash is received, and *expenses are recognized when incurred* regardless of when cash is paid. Revenue is customarily earned when goods or services have been *provided*, since at that time a legal obligation exists for customer payment. Some revenue is recognized based on time, such as interest income on a bank account that is earned when the reporting period elapses.

When a transaction is started in one accounting period and concluded in a later one, *adjusting journal entries* are necessary. Adjusting journal entries are entered at the *end of the reporting period* to record revenue and expenses applicable to that period. An adjusting entry always involves an income statement account (revenue or expense) and a balance sheet account (asset or liability).

The four basic types of adjusting entries relate to prepaid (unexpired) expenses, unearned (deferred) revenue, accrued expenses, and accrued revenue. They will be explained in the following sections.

4.2 PREPAID EXPENSES

Prepaid expenses are assets because they relate to expenditures made which have future economic benefit. Examples are prepaid insurance and prepaid rent. When a prepayment expires in a given accounting period we are required to record that expiration as an *expense*. Thus, *prepaid expenses are items which have been prepaid but not as yet incurred*.

The journal entry to reclassify a prepaid expense to an actual expense for the period takes the following form:

Expense

Prepaid Expense

EXAMPLE 1 Prepaid Insurance

On January 1, Drake Company paid $3,000 for a one-year insurance policy. This transaction is recorded as an increase in the asset Prepaid Insurance and a reduction in the asset Cash. The journal entry is

Jan. 1	Prepaid Insurance	3,000	
	Cash		3,000

At the end of January, 1/12 of the premium, or $250 ($3,000/12) has expired. The adjusting entry requires a decrease in the account Prepaid Insurance, which thus must be credited, and the recognition of an insurance expense which must be debited. This journal entry is

Jan. 31	Insurance Expense	250	
	Prepaid Insurance		250

Insurance expense of $250 would be shown in the income statement for January. The January 31 balance sheet would show prepaid insurance of $2,750.

EXAMPLE 2 Prepaid Income Taxes

On January 1, Drake Company prepaid $900 of its estimated corporate tax for the first quarter (January 1–March 31). The prepayment requires a debit to the asset Prepaid Corporate Taxes and a reduction to the asset Cash. The income tax expense for the first month is $300 ($900/3). The appropriate journal entries are

Jan. 1	Prepaid Corporate Taxes	900	
	Cash		900
31	Income Tax Expense	300	
	Prepaid Corporate Taxes		300

The income statement would show income tax expense of $300. The balance sheet would reflect as of January 31 prepaid corporate taxes of $600.

EXAMPLE 3 Office Supplies

A slightly different type of prepayment is that for office supplies. Assume that on January 1 office supplies of $700 were acquired on credit. On January 31, a count of office supplies reveals that $600 are on hand. Hence, $100 of supplies were used during the month. Applicable journal entries are

Jan. 1	Office Supplies	700	
	Accounts Payable		700
31	Office Supplies Expense	100	
	Office Supplies		100

4.3 UNEARNED REVENUE

Unearned revenue refers to *revenue received in advance*. Since a future obligation exists on the part of the company to perform the services for which the advance payment was received, unearned revenue constitutes a *liability*. (Although a liability is usually thought of as an obligation requiring a future monetary payment, it can also relate to the rendering of future services.) *When the services are performed revenue is then earned* and the following journal entry is required:

Unearned Revenue	
Revenue	

EXAMPLE 4   Unearned Professional Fees

On January 1, a client made an advance payment of $1,000 for professional fees to be rendered over the next four months. *After* performance of the first month's services, the liability Unearned Professional Fee Income would be decreased and hence debited for $250 and the revenue account Professional Fee Income would be credited. The necessary journal entries are

Jan.	1	Cash	1,000	
		Unearned Professional Fee Income		1,000
	31	Unearned Professional Fee Income	250	
		Professional Fee Income		250

EXAMPLE 5   Unearned Rental Income

On January 1, a landlord receives $500 from a tenant as an advance for the month's rent. The journal entries are

Jan.	1	Cash	500	
		Unearned Rental Income		500
	31	Unearned Rental Income	500	
		Rental Income		500

4.4   ACCRUED EXPENSES

To accrue means to accumulate. An accrued (unrecorded) expense is an *expense that has been incurred at the end of the reporting period but has not been paid.* An example would be unpaid interest incurred on a loan for, say, the month of January. An accrued expense requires an adjusting entry in the journal as follows:

Expense

Payable

EXAMPLE 6   Accrued Interest Payable

On January 1, a one-year loan with 15 percent interest rate was taken out for $10,000. The interest for one year is $1,500 ($10,000 × 15%). For the month of January, accrued interest on the loan comes to $125 ($1,500/12). The appropriate adjusting entry is

Jan.	31	Interest Expense	125	
		Interest Payable		125

EXAMPLE 7   Accrued Salaries Payable

The last payroll date was January 28. The next payroll date is February 11. For the last few days of the month (January 29–January 31) the company owes its employees $500 in salaries. The appropriate journal entry for accrued salaries is

Jan.	31	Salary Expense	500	
		Salary Payable		500

4.5 ACCRUED REVENUE

Accrued or unrecorded revenue represents *revenue which has been earned but has not been received as of the end of the reporting period.* An example is interest earned on customer notes. The appropriate journal entry is

Receivable

Income

EXAMPLE 8 Rent Receivable

A landlord has not received January rent of $300 from a tenant. The adjusting entry at the end of January is

Jan. 31	Rent Receivable	300	
	Rental Income		300

4.6 DEPRECIATION

Some assets (e.g., a car) depreciate in value over time due to use and obsolescence. The depreciation expense as well as the decline in value of the asset for each period requires a journal entry. To show the decline in value, an offset (contra) account is set up to reduce the asset's original cost. Thus, the asset's cost less the related accumulated depreciation (contra account) gives us the *book value* (carrying value) of the asset at a given time. As time goes on, the book value of the asset diminishes. Depreciation expense is, of course, an income statement account. The book value of the asset is shown in the balance sheet.

Methods for determining the depreciation expense for a period are numerous. The one we will discuss in this chapter is the easiest. It is called *straight-line depreciation*, and provides for equal depreciation charges for each period. For example, assume an auto having a five-year life expectancy was acquired on January 1 for $12,000. Each year the depreciation would be $2,400 ($12,000/5 years). For the month of January, depreciation expense is $200 ($2,400/12). The appropriate journal entry on January 31 is

Jan. 31	Depreciation Expense	200	
	Accumulated Depreciation		200

The book value of the auto on January 31 is $11,800 ($12,000 − $200). The auto would be shown in the balance sheet in the following manner:

Auto	$12,000
Less: Accumulated Depreciation	200
Book Value	$11,800

The appropriate journal entry on February 28 is the same, namely

Feb. 28	Depreciation Expense	200	
	Accumulated Depreciation		200

As of February 28, the book value of the asset has decreased to $11,600, as evidenced in the February balance sheet below.

Auto	$12,000
Less: Accumulated Depreciation	400
Book Value	$11,600

4.7 DIVIDENDS

Dividends are a distribution to stockholders by the corporation and come out of retained earnings. Dividends may be either in the form of cash or stock. When a cash dividend is declared, it becomes a legal liability of the business. Hence, the stockholders' equity account Retained Earnings is reduced and thus must be debited, and the liability account Cash Dividends Payable comes into being and therefore must be credited. Assuming a cash dividend of $0.10 per share is declared and there are 1,000 shares outstanding, the dividend would be $100 ($0.10 × 1,000). The appropriate journal entry is

Retained Earnings	100	
Cash Dividends Payable		100

When the cash dividend is paid, the journal entry is

Cash Dividends Payable	100	
Cash		100

4.8 CLOSING ENTRIES

After the financial statements have been prepared from a worksheet (to be fully discussed in the next chapter) at the end of the fiscal year, an income summary account (Revenue and Expense Summary) is established. *Closing entries* are then prepared in which all expense accounts are credited so that *zero balances* are left in them, and the total is debited to the income summary account. The journal entry is

Dec. 31	Income Summary	
	Expense	

In a similar manner, all revenue accounts are debited to arrive at *zero balances* and the total is credited to Income Summary. The journal entry is

Dec. 31	Revenue	
	Income Summary	

After the closing entries have been made, all revenue and expense accounts will balance to zero. Hence, for the new fiscal year we will be starting fresh in that no income statement account balances will exist. Thus, revenue and expenses applicable to the next fiscal year can be recorded.

Income Summary is a temporary account. It reflects in it the net income or net loss for the year since total revenue and total expenses have been closed to it. The net income or net loss which exists in the account is then transferred to retained earnings. As previously mentioned in Chapter 1, retained earnings is the accumulated earnings of the company since inception less any dividends paid out. The retained earnings account customarily has a credit balance since in most cases a company is profitable over the years. It is possible, however, for the retained earnings account to have a debit balance (deficit) when the company has been operating at net losses. The journal entry to transfer profit is

Income Summary
Retained Earnings

If a net loss occurred, the above entry would be reversed.

Retained Earnings
Income Summary

Since the purpose of closing entries is to determine and transfer the net income or net loss to stockholders' equity, they affect *only* income statement accounts. Balance sheet accounts are *not* closed out. They remain intact because assets, liabilities, and stockholders' equity continue to the next fiscal year.

EXAMPLE 9   Assume Lakeside Corporation has the following trial balance as of December 31, 20XX.

Lakeside Corporation
Trial Balance
December 31, 20XX

Cash	$ 4,000	
Accounts Receivable	5,000	
Machinery	12,000	
Accounts Payable		$ 5,000
Capital Stock		10,000
Retained Earnings		2,000
Professional Fee Income		12,000
Salary Expense	3,000	
Telephone Expense	1,000	
Rent Expense	4,000	
	$29,000	$29,000

The closing entries in the journal as of December 31, 20XX, are as follows:

Professional Fee Income	12,000	
Income Summary		12,000
To close revenue		

Income Summary	8,000	
Salary Expense		3,000
Telephone Expense		1,000
Rent Expense		4,000
To close expenses		

The balance in Income Summary is now $4,000 ($12,000 less $8,000), which represents the net income for the period since revenue exceeds expenses. The profit must now be transferred to the Retained Earnings account as follows:

Income Summary	4,000	
Retained Earnings		4,000

After this entry, Income Summary is now closed out—that is, there is a zero balance in it.

After the closing entries, no income statement accounts exist. The net effect has been to increase retained earnings by $4,000, the profit for the year. Hence, the Retained Earnings account has an ending balance of $6,000 ($2,000 + $4,000).

4.9   POST-CLOSING TRIAL BALANCE

After the closing entries have been prepared, a post-closing trial balance is made in order to ensure that the balance sheet accounts (income statement accounts have all been closed) are in balance. If the accounts are not in balance, an error in recording or posting the closing entries is indicated. The post-closing trial balance shows only assets, liabilities, and stockholders' equity accounts.

EXAMPLE 10

Lakeside Corporation
Post-closing Trial Balance
December 31, 20XX

Cash	$ 4,000	
Accounts Receivable	5,000	
Machinery	12,000	
Accounts Payable		$ 5,000
Capital Stock		10,000
Retained Earnings		6,000
	$21,000	$21,000

Summary

(1) The _____ principle recognizes revenue when earned and expenses when incurred.

(2) Expenses paid in advance but not yet incurred are called _____ .

(3) The adjusting entry at the end of the period for prepaid taxes is to debit _____ and credit _____ .

(4) Prepaid expenses are shown in the _____ .

(5) If office supplies at the beginning of a period are $100 and at the end of the period are $80, office supplies expense will be _____ .

(6) Revenue received in advance but not yet earned is called _____ .

(7)   Unearned Revenue is a(n) _____ account.

(8)   If unearned rent of $600 for three months is received in advance at the beginning of the first month, the amount of rental income for the first month is _____ .

(9)   Expenses incurred but not paid are referred to as _____ expenses.

(10) An adjusting entry at the end of the reporting period to record accrued salaries debits the _____ account and credits the _____ account.

(11) Accrued Salaries is reported in the balance sheet as a(n) _____ .

(12) Interest income earned but not received at the end of the period requires a debit to the _____ account and a credit to the _____ account.

(13) Interest Receivable is a(n) _____ account.

(14) Each adjusting entry involves a(n) _____ account and a(n) _____ account.

(15) In preparing closing entries, revenue and expenses are transferred to the _____ account.

(16) Net Income for the year requires a debit to _____ and a credit to _____ .

(17) The entry to record the depreciation of an asset is to debit the _____ account and credit the _____ account.

(18) To obtain the book value of an asset, the cost of the asset should be reduced by the _____ .

(19) Cash Dividends Payable is a(n) _____ account.

(20) _____ represent the accumulated earnings of a company less any dividends paid out.

(21) Closing entries only affect _____ accounts.

(22) After the closing entries have been prepared, each income statement account will have a(n) _____ balance in it.

(23) The only accounts involved in a post-closing trial balance are _____ , _____ , and _____ .

Answers: (1) accrual; (2) prepaid expenses; (3) tax expense, prepaid taxes; (4) balance sheet; (5) $20; (6) unearned revenue; (7) liability; (8) $200; (9) accrued or unrecorded; (10) salary expense, salaries payable; (11) liability; (12) Interest Receivable, Interest Income; (13) asset; (14) income statement, balance sheet; (15) Income Summary; (16) Income Summary, Retained Earnings; (17) Depreciation Expense, Accumulated Depreciation; (18) accumulated depreciation; (19) liability; (20) retained earnings; (21) income statement; (22) zero; (23) assets, liabilities, stockholders' equity

Solved Problems

4.1   What do the four types of adjusting entries relate to?

SOLUTION

They relate to prepaid expenses, unearned revenue, accrued expenses, and accrued revenue.

4.2   For each account listed below, put an **X** in the appropriate column.

Account	Assets	Liabilities	Revenue	Expenses
Unearned Rental Income				
Income Tax Expense				
Prepaid Taxes				
Interest Income				

SOLUTION

Account	Assets	Liabilities	Revenue	Expenses
Unearned Rental Income		X		
Income Tax Expense				X
Prepaid Taxes	X			
Interest Income			X	

4.3   On July 1, Company C prepaid advertising of $500 for a two-year period. Give the journal entry required on July 1 for the prepayment.

SOLUTION

July 1	Prepaid Advertising	500	
	Cash		500

4.4   With regard to Problem 4.3, what should the adjusting entry be on December 31?

SOLUTION

Dec. 31	Advertising Expense	125	
	Prepaid Advertising		125

The calculations are

$$\frac{\$500}{2 \text{ years}} = \$250 \text{ per year} \times \frac{6}{12} = \$125$$

Note that the yearly amount is multiplied by $\frac{6}{12}$ because six of the twelve months in a year have elapsed from July 1 to December 31.

4.5   On October 1, the company prepaid insurance of $100 for a six-month policy. What adjusting entry is required on December 31? What should be reported on the balance sheet as of December 31?

SOLUTION

Dec. 31	Insurance Expense	50	
	Prepaid Insurance		50

Since $100 is for six months, three months must be $\frac{1}{2}$ of $100 or $50.

Prepaid insurance should be listed as a current asset since as of December 31 $50 remains, representing future payments for three months of the following year (January, February, and March).

4.6   On December 1, a payment of $3,000 is made for prepaid rent for one year. What is the adjusting entry on December 31?

SOLUTION

Dec. 31	Rent Expense	250	
	Prepaid Rent		250

The calculations are

$$\$3,000 \text{ per year} \times \frac{1}{12} = \$250 \text{ per month}$$

4.7   With regard to Problem 4.6, what would be reported on the balance sheet as of December 31 and on the income statement for the month of December?

SOLUTION

On the balance sheet, under current assets, we would enter prepaid rent of $2,750 ($3,000 − $250). On the income statement, under general and administrative expenses, we would list rent expense of $250 for the month.

4.8   At the beginning of the year office supplies were $1,000. At the end of the year, $400 of the original office supplies were on hand. What is the adjusting entry on December 31?

SOLUTION

Dec. 31	Office Supplies Expense	600	
	Office Supplies		600

4.9   With regard to Problem 4.8, the beginning balance of office supplies is indicated in the "T" account below. Post the above (end-of-year) entry to the ledger accounts.

Office Supplies		Office Supplies Expense	
Bal. 1,000			

SOLUTION

Office Supplies		Office Supplies Expense	
Bal. 1,000	Dec. 31 600	Dec. 31 600	

4.10 What type of account is Office Supplies? Why?

SOLUTION

Office Supplies is a current asset since it represents supplies on hand which will be used up in the next year.

4.11 The consecutive balance sheets of Altman Corporation show the following amounts for prepaid insurance:

	Dec. 31, 20X0	Dec. 31, 20X1
Prepaid Insurance	0	$400

The income statement shows an insurance expense of $500. What was the amount paid for prepaid insurance during 20X1? You may find it helpful to fill in the "T" account below.

Prepaid Insurance

Beginning Prepaid during year Ending	Insurance expired

SOLUTION

Prepaid Insurance

Beginning	0	Insurance expired 500
Prepaid during year	900	
Ending	400	

The ending balance is $400 and the insurance expired is $500; therefore, the amount paid for prepaid insurance for the year must have been $900.

4.12 On October 1, 20XX, $5,000 was received by J. Forker, Inc., as an advance payment for future work to be performed over the next year. Prepare the appropriate journal entry on October 1, 20XX.

SOLUTION

Oct. 1	Cash	5,000	
	Unearned Service Income		5,000

4.13 With regard to Problem 4.12, what is the adjusting entry required on December 31, 20XX?

SOLUTION

Dec. 31	Unearned Service Income	1,250	
	Service Income		1,250

The calculation is

$$\$5,000 \times \frac{3}{12} = \$1,250$$

4.14 How would the balance sheet and income statement for J. Forker, Inc., reflect the above cited prepayment as of December 31, 20XX?

SOLUTION

The balance sheet would show unearned service income of \$3,750 (\$5,000 − \$1,250) as a current liability, since nine months of future service are required.

The income statement would show service income of \$1,250.

4.15 On January 1, 20X5, a company received rental income of \$40,000 in advance covering a four-year period. Unearned Rental Income was originally credited for \$40,000. What is the adjusting entry required as of December 31, 20X5?

SOLUTION

Dec. 31	Unearned Rental Income	10,000	
	Rental Income		10,000

The calculation is

$$\$40,000 \div 4 \text{ years} = \$10,000 \text{ per year}$$

4.16 With regard to Problem 4.15, how would unearned rental income be reported in the balance sheet as of December 31, 20X5?

SOLUTION

Balance Sheet
December 31, 20X5

Current Liabilities	
Unearned Rental Income	\$10,000
Noncurrent Liabilities	
Unearned Rental Income	\$20,000

Under Current Liabilities is shown the unearned rental income to be recognized over the next year (January 1, 20X6–December 31, 20X6).

Under Noncurrent Liabilities is shown the unearned rental income of \$20,000 for the period due greater than one year from the balance sheet date (January 1, 20X7–December 31, 20X8).

4.17 Preston Corporation shows the following amounts for unearned commission income in two consecutive balance sheets:

	Dec. 31, 20X0	Dec. 31, 20X1
Unearned Commission Income	\$300	\$800

The income statement for 20X1 shows earned commission income of \$600.

What was the amount of unearned commission income received for the year? You may find it helpful to fill in the "T" account below.

Unearned Commission Income

Earned during year	Beginning
	Received during year
	Ending

SOLUTION

Unearned Commission Income

Earned during		Beginning	300
year	600	Received during	
		year	1,100
		Ending	800

Because the advance payment received during 20X1 is the balancing figure in the above account, we know that the ending unearned commission income must equal the total prepayment (beginning amount + amount received during the year) less the portion earned during the year. If we let X be the unearned commission income received during the year, we can write

Total unearned income − Income earned = Ending unearned income

$300 + X$	−	$600	=	$800
		X	=	$1,100

4.18 During December, Trans Plumbing Company performed maintenance work amounting to $600 on TKM company's building. However, as of December 31, TKM had not yet received a bill. What is the appropriate entry in TKM's journal on December 31?

SOLUTION

Dec. 31	Repair Expense	600	
	Accounts Payable		600

4.19 On May 1, 20X5, the company took out a $10,000, one-year bank note at 12 percent interest. What is the adjusting entry on December 31, 20X5, for the accrual of interest?

SOLUTION

Dec. 31	Interest Expense	800	
	Interest Payable		800

Because accrued interest is for eight months (May 1 to December 31), the above amount is calculated as follows:

$$\$10,000 \times 12\% \times \frac{8}{12} = \$800$$

4.20 On November 1, 20X5, the company issued a $6,000, six-month, 10 percent note. What is the adjusting entry on December 31, 20X5, for the accrued interest?

SOLUTION

Dec. 31	Interest Expense	100	
	Interest Payable		100

There is two months of accrued interest from November 1 to December 31; hence the calculation is

$$\$6,000 \times 10\% \times \frac{2}{12} = \$100$$

4.21 A company pays salaries bi-weekly (every two weeks) on Fridays. The next bi-weekly payroll will be $8,000. Therefore since there are 10 working days, the salary per day will be $800

($8,000/10). Since the last pay date (December 28), there have been three additional working days (December 29, 30, 31). (*a*) What adjusting entry is required on December 31? (*b*) What should be reported in the balance sheet?

SOLUTION

(*a*)

| | Dec. 31 | Salaries Expense | 2,400 | |
| | | Salaries Payable | | 2,400 |

The amount is calculated as follows:

$$\$800 \times 3 = \$2,400$$

(*b*) Salaries payable of $2,400 would be listed under current liabilities in the balance sheet.

4.22   As of December 31, all work for a customer has been furnished amounting to $500. However, a bill for professional services has not as yet been made. What is the appropriate adjusting entry?

SOLUTION

| Dec. 31 | Accounts Receivable | 500 | |
| | Professional Fee Income | | 500 |

4.23   Rental income of $300 was due from a tenant on December 31 but has not been received. What adjusting entry is required as of December 31?

SOLUTION

| Dec. 31 | Rent Receivable | 300 | |
| | Rental Income | | 300 |

4.24   On August 1, 20X5, a customer gave the company a $12,000, 10 percent, nine-month note. What adjusting entry is required to accrue interest on this note on December 31?

SOLUTION

| Dec. 31 | Interest Receivable | 500 | |
| | Interest Income | | 500 |

The accrued interest is for five months (August 1 to December 31), and the calculation is

$$12,000 \times 10\% \times \frac{5}{12} = \$500$$

4.25   With regard to Problem 4.24, what is to be reported in the balance sheet and income statement?

SOLUTION

Interest Receivable of $500 is shown as a current asset in the balance sheet.
Interest Income of $500 is shown as Other Income in the income statement.

4.26   On January 1, 20XX, the company purchased an auto for $10,000. The company decides to depreciate the car based on miles driven. The estimated total miles to be driven are 10,000. In the first year, 2,000 miles are actually driven. What is the appropriate journal entry on December 31, 20XX?

SOLUTION

Dec. 31	Depreciation Expense	2,000	
	Accumulated Depreciation		2,000

The calculation is as follows:

$$\text{Original cost} \times \frac{\text{Miles driven in year}}{\text{Estimated total miles}} = \text{Depreciation for year}$$

$$\$10{,}000 \times \frac{2{,}000}{10{,}000} = \$2{,}000$$

This type of depreciation is called *unit depreciation*, and yearly amounts are not necessarily the same.

4.27   On February 1, 20X5, an auto was purchased for $12,000. It has a five-year life. Straight-line depreciation is used. What journal entry should be prepared on December 31, 20X5?

SOLUTION

Dec. 31	Depreciation Expense	2,200	
	Accumulated Depreciation		2,200

The calculations are

$$\frac{\$12{,}000}{5 \text{ years}} = \$2{,}400 \text{ depreciation per year}$$

The depreciation is for 11 months (February 1–December 31 = 11 months)

$$\frac{11}{12} \times \$2{,}400 = \$2{,}200 \text{ depreciation for 20X5}$$

4.28   With regard to Problem 4.27, how should the auto account be reported in the balance sheet as of December 31, 20X5?

SOLUTION

Fixed Assets		
Auto	$12,000	
Less: Accumulated Depreciation	2,200	
Book Value		$9,800

4.29   How should the auto account of the previous problem be reported in the balance sheet as of December 31, 20X6?

SOLUTION

Fixed Assets		
Auto	$12,000	
Less: Accumulated Depreciation	4,600*	
Book Value		$7,400

*Prior year balance	$2,200
Depreciation for current year	2,400 (full year's depreciation)
Accumulated depreciation	$4,600

4.30 For each of the following transactions, make the necessary adjusting journal entries for the M.R. Corporation at December 31, 20X8.

(a) Received cash of $9,000 on September 1, 20X8, for a half-year's rent in advance. On this date the unearned rental income account was credited for the amount received.

(b) On November 1, 20X8, M.R. Corporation loaned another party $4,000 on an 8 percent, six-month note.

(c) The company stocks a large amount of supplies in the administrative department. The supplies account showed a balance of $2,000. At year's end the supplies on hand amounted to $500.

(d) On July 1, 20X8, the company paid $850 for a five-year insurance policy. The transaction was initially recorded as a debit to Prepaid Insurance.

(e) Interest accrued on bonds owned by the company as of the end of the year was $200.

(f) On December 1, the company signed a lease to rent an auto for six months at $0.20 per mile. During December, 1,000 miles were driven. No recognition has been given yet to the rental charge on such auto.

(g) On December 18, the company signed an agreement to buy a new auto on March 2, 20X9, from a car dealer. No down payment was given.

SOLUTION

General Journal

(a)	Dec. 31	Unearned Rental Income	6,000*	
		Rental Income		6,000
(b)		Interest Receivable	53**	
		Interest Income		53
(c)		Supplies Expense	1,500	
		Supplies		1,500
(d)		Insurance Expense	85†	
		Prepaid Insurance		85
(e)		Interest Receivable	200	
		Interest Income		200
(f)		Rent Expense	200	
		Rent Payable		200

$*\$9,000 \times \dfrac{4 \text{ months}}{6 \text{ months}} = \$6,000$

$**\$4,000 \times 0.08 \times \dfrac{2}{12} = \$53$

†$850/5$ years $= \$170$ per year

$\$170 \times \dfrac{6 \text{ months}}{12 \text{ months}} = \$85$

(g) No journal entry is required since the asset has not been bought nor has any cash been paid. All that is needed is to keep a record of the agreement in the file.

4.31 On October 1, 20XX, land was purchased for $1,000 cash. In error, Repair Expense was debited. What adjusting entry is necessary at December 31, 20XX, to correct for this error?

SOLUTION

Dec. 31	Land	1,000	
	Repair Expense		1,000

4.32 On December 31, 20XX, you are looking over the year-end entries made by the company's bookkeeper and discover that the entry made to record depreciation expense on autos was

Dec. 31	Depreciation Expense	300	
	Auto		300

What correcting entry is required on December 31?

SOLUTION

Dec. 31	Auto	300	
	Accumulated Depreciation		300

The accumulated depreciation on an asset is recognized in a separate account called Accumulated Depreciation to keep track of the asset's book value to date. To credit the auto account for the accumulated depreciation is wrong since a credit to Auto is only made upon disposal of a car.

4.33 Place an **X** in the appropriate column to indicate whether the accounts listed below would be debited or credited when making closing entries. If the account is not involved in the closing entry process, put an **X** in the Not Applicable column.

Account	Debit	Credit	Not Applicable
Salary Expense			
Dividend Income			
Rent Expense			
Accounts Payable			
Unearned Service Income			
Machinery			
Sales			

SOLUTION

Account	Debit	Credit	Not Applicable
Salary Expense		X	
Dividend Income	X		
Rent Expense		X	
Accounts Payable			X
Unearned Service Income			X
Machinery			X
Sales	X		

4.34 Western's before-closing trial balance shows the following accounts: Professional Fee Income, $10,000; Rental Income, $2,000; Promotion and Entertainment Expense, $3,000; Interest Expense, $1,000; Contribution Expense, $500; Retained Earnings, $5,000. Prepare closing entries for (a) revenue, (b) expenses, and (c) transfer of profit or loss to stockholders' equity.

SOLUTION

General Journal

(a)	Professional Fee Income	10,000	
	Rental Income	2,000	
	Income Summary		12,000
(b)	Income Summary	4,500	
	Promotion and Entertainment		3,000
	Interest Expense		1,000
	Contribution Expense		500
(c)	Income Summary	7,500	
	Retained Earnings		7,500

The net income of $7,500 transferred to Retained Earnings is the difference between total revenue of $12,000 from (a) and total expenses of $4,500 from (b).

4.35 With regard to Problem 4.34, fill in the postings to the Income Summary and Retained Earnings accounts. After doing that, indicate what would be reported on the year-end balance sheet.

Income Summary		Retained Earnings	
		Beginning	5,000

SOLUTION

Income Summary				Retained Earnings		
(b)	4,500	(a)	12,000		Beginning	5,000
(c)	7,500				(c)	7,500

The balance sheet would show under stockholders' equity retained earnings of $12,500.

4.36 The following is an income summary account of Childs Corporation on December 31, 20X5, after all revenue and expenses have been closed to the account.

Income Summary	
97,000	90,000

(a) What do the figures in the account represent?

(b) What is the net income or net loss?

(c) Close out the income summary account to Retained Earnings.

SOLUTION

(*a*) The credit amount of $90,000 represents the total revenue for 20X5. The debit figure of $97,000 represents the total expenses for the year.

(*b*) Since expenses exceed revenue, there is a net loss for the year of $7,000.

(*c*) The entry to transfer the net loss is

Dec. 31	Retained Earnings	7,000	
	Income Summary		7,000

4.37 From the before-closing trial balance listed below, prepare all necessary closing entries for the journal.

Trial Balance

Cash	$10,000	
Accounts Receivable	13,000	
Auto	9,000	
Common Stock		$15,000
Retained Earnings		12,000
Professional Fee Income		18,000
Interest Income		2,000
Salary Expense	6,000	
Rent Expense	5,000	
Cleaning Expense	4,000	
	$47,000	$47,000

SOLUTION

General Journal

(*a*)	Professional Fee Income	18,000	
	Interest Income	2,000	
	Income Summary		20,000
(*b*)	Income Summary	15,000	
	Salary Expense		6,000
	Rent Expense		5,000
	Cleaning Expense		4,000
(*c*)	Income Summary	5,000	
	Retained Earnings		5,000

4.38 Post the journal entries indicated in the preceding problem to the following ledger accounts:

Cash		Common Stock	
Bal. 10,000		Bal. 15,000	

Accounts Receivable		Retained Earnings	
Bal. 13,000		Bal. 12,000	

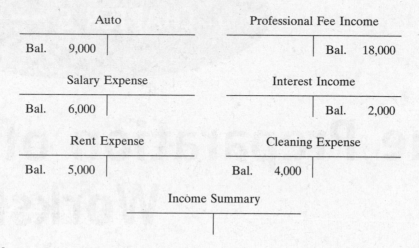

Auto			Professional Fee Income		
Bal.	9,000			Bal.	18,000

Salary Expense			Interest Income		
Bal.	6,000			Bal.	2,000

Rent Expense			Cleaning Expense		
Bal.	5,000		Bal.	4,000	

Income Summary	

SOLUTION

Cash			Common Stock		
Bal.	10,000			Bal.	15,000

Accounts Receivable			Retained Earnings		
Bal.	13,000			Bal.	12,000
				(c)	5,000

Auto			Professional Fee Income		
Bal.	9,000		(a)	18,000	Bal. 18,000

Salary Expense			Interest Income		
Bal.	6,000	(b) 6,000	(a)	2,000	Bal. 2,000

Rent Expense			Cleaning Expense		
Bal.	5,000	(b) 5,000	Bal.	4,000	(b) 4,000

Income Summary			
(b)	15,000	(a)	20,000
(c)	5,000		

4.39 From the ledger account balances of Problem 4.38 prepare a post-closing trial balance.

SOLUTION

Post-closing Trial Balance

Cash	$10,000	
Accounts Receivable	13,000	
Auto	9,000	
Common Stock		$15,000
Retained Earnings		17,000
	$32,000	$32,000

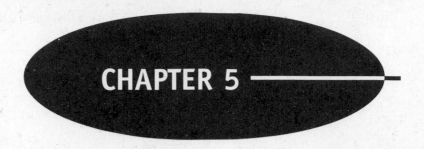

The Preparation of the Worksheet

5.1 INTRODUCTION

Chapters 3 and 4 discussed the recording of transactions, adjusting entries, and closing entries. Errors in the accounting process, such as posting a wrong amount from the journal to the ledger, are to be anticipated. A key means of avoiding errors is the preparation of an informal schedule called a *worksheet* at the end of the reporting period. The worksheet is *not* a permanent accounting record but rather is used to put the detailed accounting data in *one place*, and hence to save time and effort in correcting errors. Of course, it is easier to make corrections in an informal schedule than in the formal accounting records. Errors are reduced because the worksheet helps identify discrepancies which may exist in the journal, errors made in posting, or miscalculations made in determining account balances.

5.2 WORKSHEET FOR A SERVICE-ORIENTED BUSINESS

A service-oriented business is one in which revenue is derived from rendering services as, for example, the professional fees earned by a doctor or lawyer.

The worksheet is customarily prepared in pencil on a multicolumn sheet called analysis paper. The columns of a typical worksheet appear in the following order: trial balance, adjustments, income statement, and balance sheet. After the trial balance is copied onto the worksheet, adjusting entries are reflected so that adjusted account balances may then be derived and the appropriate figures placed under the financial statement columns to which they relate. From these financial statement columns, the income statement and balance sheet are prepared.

Preparation of the worksheet provides for quick review of ledger account balances as well as the adjusting entries affecting the accounts. A worksheet also serves as a source for making the adjusting and closing entries for the journal. Further, it facilitates financial statement preparation since we prove in the worksheet that the income statement and balance sheet accounts reconcile.

A typical worksheet takes the form shown in Fig. 5-1.

X Company
Worksheet
For the Year Ended December 31, 20XX

Account	Trial Balance		Adjustments		Income Statement		Balance Sheet	
	Dr.	Cr.	Dr.	Cr.	Dr.	Cr.	Dr.	Cr.

Fig. 5-1

Note that the four groups each have two columns (Dr. and Cr.). Hence, eight money columns exist. To complete the worksheet, the following steps are necessary:

1. Transfer the account balances from the ledger to the Trial Balance columns. Make sure that the total debits equal the total credits.

2. Fill in the adjusting entries in the Adjustments columns. For cross-referencing, the debit and credit for each entry should be *keyed* (starting with entry *a*). If an adjusting entry is for an account not listed on the trial balance, it should be *added* on the next available line below the trial balance totals. The total debits and credits in the Adjustment columns must prove before proceeding further.

3. Extend the adjusted account figures (ledger balances after adjusting entries) to either an Income Statement column or a Balance Sheet column. Each account is extended to only *one* column.

4. Total the debit and credit columns for the income statement and the balance sheet.

5. Determine the net income or net loss, which is the balancing figure in the Income Statement and Balance Sheet columns. Net income or net loss is written under the Account column, and if, for example, there is a net income (the Credit column total exceeds the Debit column total of Income Statement), then the net income will be shown in the Debit column of Income Statement and, on the same line, in the Credit column of Balance Sheet (representing an increase in owners' equity) to balance it. Assets must, of course, prove to liabilities plus stockholders' equity. If the Balance Sheet columns do not agree, an error is indicated.

Dollar signs are not used in worksheets.

EXAMPLE 1 Based on the following ledger accounts and information for Quick Service Corporation, prepare a worksheet:

Quick Service Corporation
Trial Balance
December 31, 20X4

Cash	$ 6,000	
Accounts Receivable	12,000	
Supplies	500	
Prepaid Insurance	2,000	
Machinery	10,000	
Accumulated Depreciation		$ 3,000
Accounts Payable		4,000
Notes Payable		2,000
Unearned Service Fees		1,000
Capital Stock		10,000
Retained Earnings		3,000
Service Fee Income		15,000
Salary Expense	5,000	
Telephone Expense	2,500	
	$38,000	$38,000

Step 1. *Enter the trial balance amounts onto the worksheet.* In Fig. 5-2, note that the amount of each ledger account is reflected in the appropriate Trial Balance column. The account balances reflect all transactions for the accounting period prior to making any necessary adjusting entries. The total debits and total credits in the Trial Balance columns must agree.

Quick Service Corporation
Worksheet
Year Ending December 31, 20X4

Account	Trial Balance Debit	Trial Balance Credit	Adjustments Debit	Adjustments Credit	Income Statement Debit	Income Statement Credit	Balance Sheet Debit	Balance Sheet Credit
Cash	6,000						6,000	
Accounts Receivable	12,000						12,000	
Supplies	500			(a) 300			200	
Prepaid Insurance	2,000			(b) 500			1,500	
Machinery	10,000						10,000	
Accumulated Depreciation		3,000		(c) 1,000				4,000
Accounts Payable		4,000						4,000
Notes Payable		2,000						2,000
Unearned Service Fees		1,000	(d) 500					500
Capital Stock		10,000						10,000
Retained Earnings		3,000						3,000
Service Fee Income		15,000		(d) 500		15,500		
Salaries Expense	5,000		(f) 150		5,150			
Telephone Expense	2,500				2,500			
	38,000	38,000						
Supplies Expense			(a) 300		300			
Insurance Expense			(b) 500		500			
Depreciation Expense			(c) 1,000		1,000			
Interest Expense			(e) 50		50			
Interest Payable				(e) 50				50
Salaries Payable				(f) 150				150
			2,500	2,500	9,500	15,500	29,700	23,700
Net Income					6,000			6,000
					15,500	15,500	29,700	29,700

Fig. 5-2

Step 2. *Reflect the adjusting entries in the Adjustments columns* (see Fig. 5-2). After the adjusting entries have been reflected on the worksheet, the total debit column must agree with the total credit column.

(a) *Supplies.* A count of supplies at year's end revealed that $200 was on hand. Since the beginning balance was $500, $300 must have been used and thus represents the supplies expense for the period. Because no supply expense account exists, one must be established on the next available line of the worksheet. The adjusting entry is

Supplies Expense	300	
Supplies		300

(b) *Insurance.* Prepaid insurance of $2,000 at the beginning of the year was for a four-year policy commencing January 1, 20X4. Thus, the amount of insurance expense for 20X4 is $500 ($2,000/4 years). Since no account for insurance expense exists, one must be set up. The adjusting entry is

Insurance Expense	500	
Prepaid Insurance		500

(c) *Depreciation.* The machine was acquired on January 1, 20X1, and has a 10-year life. Hence, the depreciation expense for 20X4, using the straight-line method, would be $1,000 ($10,000/10 years). The account Depreciation Expense must be entered on the bottom of the worksheet. The entry is

Depreciation Expense	1,000	
Accumulated Depreciation		1,000

(d) *Service fee income.* At the beginning of the year, there was a liability for unearned service fee income of $1,000. The advance payment for future services was made on January 1, 20X4, for a two-year period. Therefore, $500 of the advance service fee had been earned as of December 31, 20X4. The appropriate adjusting entry is

Unearned Service Fees	500	
Service Fee Income		500

(e) *Interest.* The note payable of $2,000 was issued on October 1, 20X4. It bears an annual interest rate of 10 percent. The note is for a one-year period. The accrued interest for three months (October 1, 20X4, to December 31, 20X4) is $50 ($2,000 × 10% × 3/12). The accrual entry is

Interest Expense	50	
Interest Payable		50

(f) *Salaries.* The salaries expense shown in the trial balance constitutes payroll payments made for the year. Not included is $150 for salaries earned in the latter part of December to be paid in the next payroll period, which is the first week of January 20X5. The following entry reflects the accrual:

Salaries Expense	150	
Salaries Payable		150

Step 3. Extend the adjusted account balances to the Income Statement or Balance Sheet columns. Revenue and expenses are placed under the appropriate Income Statement columns, while assets, liabilities, and stockholders' equity are extended to the Balance Sheet columns.

Step 4. Total Income Statement and Balance Sheet columns. The difference between the totals in the Income Statement *must* be the same as the difference between the totals in the Balance Sheet. This difference represents either the net income or net loss for the period. In this case, there is a net income of $6,000.

Step 5. Enter net income or net loss to balance the columns. Because net income increases retained earnings, the net income is transferred to the credit column of Balance Sheet. After this is done, the total debits and total credits of the Balance Sheet columns must prove. In Fig. 5-2, they prove to $29,700. If there had been a net loss, the total debit column (expenses) would have exceeded the total credit column (revenue) of Income Statement. The figure would then be entered in the credit column to balance Income Statement. Because a net loss decreases retained earnings, it would be entered in the debit column of Balance Sheet.

Once we see that the Income Statement columns and Balance Sheet columns agree, we can prepare the financial statements.

5.3 FINANCIAL STATEMENT PREPARATION

The financial statements for Quick Service Corporation may easily be prepared from the worksheet shown in Fig. 5-2 since all data needed for the income statement, the statement of retained earnings, and the balance sheet have been conveniently arranged.

Quick Service Corporation
Income Statement
For the Year Ending December 31, 20X4

Service Fee Income		$15,500
Less: Expenses		
Salaries Expense	$5,150	
Telephone Expense	2,500	
Supplies Expense	300	
Insurance Expense	500	
Depreciation Expense	1,000	
Interest Expense	50	
Total Expenses		$ 9,500
Net Income		$ 6,000

Quick Service Corporation
Statement of Retained Earnings
For the Year Ending December 31, 20X4

Retained Earnings—January 1, 20X4	$3,000
Net Income for year	6,000
Retained Earnings—December 31, 20X4	$9,000

Quick Service Corporation
Balance Sheet
December 31, 20X4

ASSETS

Current Assets		
Cash	$ 6,000	
Accounts Receivable	12,000	
Supplies	200	
Prepaid Insurance	1,500	
Total Current Assets		$19,700
Fixed Assets		
Machinery	$10,000	
Less: Accumulated Depreciation	4,000	6,000
Total Assets		$25,700

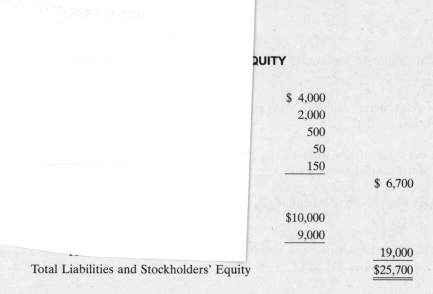

QUITY

$ 4,000
2,000
500
50
150
                                                                    $ 6,700

$10,000
9,000
                                                                    19,000
Total Liabilities and Stockholders' Equity $25,700

5.4 AFTER THE FINANCIAL STATEMENTS ARE PREPARED

After the financial statements are prepared from the worksheet, the adjusting entries are made in the journal from the amounts in the *Adjustments* column of the worksheet. When the adjusting entries have been journalized and posted, the ledger account balances will agree with the account balances indicated in the financial statements.

Closing entries for revenue and expenses and for transfer of net income to retained earnings are then prepared in the journal and posted. After the closing entries, the income statement accounts will have zero balances and hence income statement data for the next fiscal year can be entered. A post-closing trial balance is then prepared to ensure that the total debits and total credits for the balance sheet accounts agree.

5.5 THE ACCOUNTING CYCLE

The *accounting cycle* is the sequence of procedures from the beginning to the end for the reporting period in accumulating and summarizing accounting data. It consists of the following:

1. Journalize transactions.
2. Post from the journal to the ledger.
3. Prepare the worksheet.
4. Prepare the financial statements.
5. Journalize and post the adjusting entries.
6. Journalize and post the closing entries.
7. Prepare a post-closing trial balance.

Summary

(1) To simplify the accounting work at the end of the reporting period and to reduce errors in the formal accounting records, a(n) _____ should be prepared.

(2) The four major categories of the worksheet are: _____, _____, _____, and _____ .

(3) The Trial Balance columns of the worksheet contain account balances from the _____ .

(4) For cross-referencing, each adjusting entry shown in the Adjustments column is _____ in alphabetical order.

(5) In the worksheet, if the total of the credit column exceeds the total of the debit column of Income Statement, there is a(n) _____ for the period.

(6) A net loss should be horizontally transferred to the _____ column of Balance Sheet.

(7) A $10,000, 12 percent, one-year note is issued on April 1, 20X4. The interest expense for the year ended December 31, 20X4, is _____ .

(8) On the worksheet, the salaries expense is extended to the _____ column of Income Statement.

(9) Capital stock is extended to the _____ column of Balance Sheet.

(10) After the adjusting entries have been journalized and posted, the ledger account balances will _____ with the account balances listed in the financial statements.

Answers: (1) worksheet; (2) trial balance, adjustments, income statement, balance sheet; (3) ledger; (4) keyed; (5) net income; (6) debit; (7) $900; (8) debit; (9) credit; (10) agree

Solved Problems

5.1 Prepare the adjusting entry for each of the following:

(*a*) The supplies inventory at the beginning of the month was $600. At the end of the month, there was a remaining balance of $200.

(*b*) Prepaid insurance at the beginning of the month was $1,200. Insurance expired for the month was $100.

SOLUTION

(*a*)	Supplies Expense	400	
	Supplies		400
(*b*)	Insurance Expense	100	
	Prepaid Insurance		100

5.2 An auto having an estimated life of five years was purchased on January 2, 20X1, for $8,000. Straight-line depreciation was used.

(*a*) What is the depreciation for 20X1?

(*b*) Prepare the appropriate journal entry at December 31, 20X1.

(c) How would this information be presented in the income statement and balance sheet for 20X1?

SOLUTION

(a) Depreciation is $1,600 ($8,000/5 years).

(b) Dec. 31   Depreciation Expense   1,600
                            Accumulated Depreciation   1,600

(c) The income statement for the year ended December 31, 20X1, would show a depreciation expense of $1,600.
        The balance sheet as of December 31, 20X1, would show

Auto	$8,000
Less: Accumulated Depreciation	1,600
Book Value	$6,400

5.3 Assume the same information as in Problem 5.2 except that the auto was acquired on April 1, 20X1.

(a) What adjusting entry is needed to record the depreciation expense as of December 31, 20X1?

(b) What is the entry for depreciation expense for 20X2?

(c) What is the book value of the auto to be reported on the balance sheet as of December 31, 20X2?

SOLUTION

(a)   Depreciation Expense   1,200
                        Accumulated Depreciation   1,200

The calculations are

Depreciation per year = $8,000/5 years	$1,600
The auto was held for 9 months (April 1–December 31)	× 9/12
Depreciation expense for 20X1	$1,200

(b)   Depreciation Expense   1,600
                        Accumulated Depreciation   1,600

In 20X2, a full year's depreciation was realized.

(c)   Auto $8,000
                  Less: Accumulated Depreciation   2,800
                  Book Value $5,200

The calculation for accumulated depreciation is

20X1	$1,200
20X2	1,600
Accumulated	$2,800

5.4   On September 1, a six-month note payable for $10,000 bearing a 15 percent interest rate was issued. Prepare the appropriate adjusting entry as of December 31.

SOLUTION

Dec. 31	Interest Expense	500	
	Interest Payable		500

Accrued interest is for four months (September 1 to December 31). Therefore the interest expense is $500 ($10,000 × 15% × 4/12).

5.5   Based on the following information, prepare the adjusting journal entries at December 31.

(a)   Prepaid rent expired during the year, $500.
(b)   Salaries earned but unpaid are $1,000.
(c)   Unearned commission revenue of $2,000 was earned during the year.
(d)   Depreciation for the period was $200 (with no previous depreciation).
(e)   Accrued interest earned on a customer's note was $100.

SOLUTION

General Journal

(a)	Rent Expense	500	
	Prepaid Rent		500
(b)	Salaries Expense	1,000	
	Salaries Payable		1,000
(c)	Unearned Commission Revenue	2,000	
	Commission Income		2,000
(d)	Depreciation Expense	200	
	Accumulated Depreciation		200
(e)	Interest Receivable	100	
	Interest Income		100

5.6   For each of the accounts listed below, place an **X** in the column in which the account would appear in the worksheet.

Account	Income Statement Dr.	Income Statement Cr.	Balance Sheet Dr.	Balance Sheet Cr.
Accounts Receivable				
Retained Earnings				
Depreciation Expense				
Commission Income				
Accumulated Depreciation				
Prepaid Insurance				
Unearned Commission Income				
Interest Receivable				

SOLUTION

Account	Income Statement Dr.	Income Statement Cr.	Balance Sheet Dr.	Balance Sheet Cr.
Accounts Receivable			X	
Retained Earnings				X
Depreciation Expense	X			
Commission Income		X		
Accumulated Depreciation				X
Prepaid Insurance			X	
Unearned Commission Income				X
Interest Receivable			X	

5.7 A partial worksheet appears below. (*a*) Determine the net income or loss. (*b*) Explain what determines net income or loss and how it affects the Balance Sheet columns.

Account	Trial Balance Dr.	Trial Balance Cr.	Adjustments Dr.	Adjustments Cr.	Income Statement Dr.	Income Statement Cr.	Balance Sheet Dr.	Balance Sheet Cr.
					40,500	52,000	80,000	68,500

SOLUTION

(*a*)

Total credits in the Income Statement column	$52,000	
Total debits in the Income Statement column	40,500	
Net Income	$11,500	

	Trial Balance		Adjustments		Income Statement		Balance Sheet	
Account	Dr.	Cr.	Dr.	Cr.	Dr.	Cr.	Dr.	Cr.
Net Income					40,500	52,000	80,000	68,500
					11,500			11,500
					52,000	52,000	80,000	80,000

(*b*) The net income of $11,500 arose because total revenues ($52,000) exceeded total expenses ($40,500). Net income increases stockholders' equity and hence net income is extended to the credit column of Balance Sheet.

5.8   Complete the following partial worksheet:

	Trial Balance		Adjustments		Income Statement		Balance Sheet	
Account	Dr.	Cr.	Dr.	Cr.	Dr.	Cr.	Dr.	Cr.
					30,000	24,000	90,000	96,000

SOLUTION

	Trial Balance		Adjustments		Income Statement		Balance Sheet	
Account	Dr.	Cr.	Dr.	Cr.	Dr.	Cr.	Dr.	Cr.
Net Loss					30,000	24,000	90,000	96,000
						6,000	6,000	
					30,000	30,000	96,000	96,000

Note that the net loss is extended to the debit column of Balance Sheet because it decreases stockholders' equity.

5.9	Below is the Income Statement portion of a worksheet. Determine the net income.

	Income Statement	
Account	Dr.	Cr.
Commission Income		10,000
Interest Income		4,000
Telephone Expense	1,000	
Salaries Expense	4,000	
Advertising Expense	1,800	

SOLUTION

Total Credits	$14,000
Total Debits	6,800
Net Income	$ 7,200

5.10	The worksheet for Summit Service Corporation is shown below.

Summit Service Corporation
Worksheet
For the Year Ended December 31, 20XX

Account	Trial Balance Dr.	Trial Balance Cr.	Adjustments Dr.	Adjustments Cr.	Income Statement Dr.	Income Statement Cr.	Balance Sheet Dr.	Balance Sheet Cr.
Cash	28,000							
Accounts Receivable	21,000							
Prepaid Insurance	18,000							
Supplies	30,000							
Long-term Investments	9,000							
Land	90,000							
Trucks	45,000							
Accumulated Depreciation		20,000						
Accounts Payable		25,000						
Unearned Commission Income		15,000						
Common Stock		115,000						
Retained Earnings		30,000						
Commission Income		75,000						
Advertising Expense	12,000							
Salaries Expense	27,000							
	280,000	280,000						

Prepare adjusting entries on the worksheet based upon the following information:

(*a*)	Insurance expired, $9,000

(*b*)	Depreciation expense on trucks, $5,000

(*c*)	Portion earned of prepaid commissions, $10,000

(*d*)	Salaries due employees at the end of the period, $17,000

SOLUTION

Summit Service Corporation
Worksheet
For the Year Ended December 31, 20XX

Account	Trial Balance Dr.	Trial Balance Cr.	Adjustments Dr.	Adjustments Cr.	Income Statement Dr.	Income Statement Cr.	Balance Sheet Dr.	Balance Sheet Cr.
Cash	28,000							
Accounts Receivable	21,000							
Prepaid Insurance	18,000			(a) 9,000				
Supplies	30,000							
Long-term Investments	9,000							
Land	90,000							
Trucks	45,000							
Accumulated Depreciation		20,000		(b) 5,000				
Accounts Payable		25,000						
Unearned Commission Income		15,000	(c) 10,000					
Common Stock		115,000						
Retained Earnings		30,000						
Commission Income		75,000		(c) 10,000				
Advertising Expense	12,000							
Salaries Expense	27,000		(d) 17,000					
	280,000	280,000						
Insurance Expense			(a) 9,000					
Depreciation Expense			(b) 5,000					
Salaries Payable				(d) 17,000				
			41,000	41,000				

5.11 Based on the information in Problem 5.10, complete the worksheet above by filling in the Income Statement and Balance Sheet columns.

SOLUTION

Summit Service Corporation
Worksheet
For the Year Ended December 31, 20XX

Account	Trial Balance Dr.	Trial Balance Cr.	Adjustments Dr.	Adjustments Cr.	Income Statement Dr.	Income Statement Cr.	Balance Sheet Dr.	Balance Sheet Cr.
Cash	28,000						28,000	
Accounts Receivable	21,000						21,000	
Prepaid Insurance	18,000			(a) 9,000			9,000	
Supplies	30,000						30,000	
Long-term Investments	9,000						9,000	
Land	90,000						90,000	
Trucks	45,000						45,000	
Accumulated Depreciation		20,000		(b) 5,000				25,000
Accounts Payable		25,000						25,000
Unearned Commission Income		15,000	(c) 10,000					5,000
Common Stock		115,000						115,000
Retained Earnings		30,000						30,000
Commission Income		75,000		(c) 10,000		85,000		
Advertising Expense	12,000				12,000			
Salaries Expense	27,000		(d) 17,000		44,000			
	280,000	280,000						
Insurance Expense			(a) 9,000		9,000			
Depreciation Expense			(b) 5,000		5,000			
Salaries Payable				(d) 17,000				17,000
			41,000	41,000	70,000	85,000	232,000	217,000
Net Income					15,000			15,000
					85,000	85,000	232,000	232,000

5.12 Complete the following worksheet by supplying the missing amounts.

Garco Maintenance Company
Worksheet
For the Year Ended December 31, 20XX

Account	Trial Balance Dr.	Trial Balance Cr.	Adjustments Dr.	Adjustments Cr.	Income Statement Dr.	Income Statement Cr.	Balance Sheet Dr.	Balance Sheet Cr.
Cash	22,000							
Accounts Receivable	4,000							
Prepaid Rent				2,000			6,000	
Land							32,200	
Building	20,000							
Accumulated Depreciation		8,000						10,400
Accounts Payable		12,000						
Unearned Commission Income		25,000	5,500					
Common Stock		30,000						
Retained Earnings		2,000						
Dividends							700	
Commission Income		12,200						
Salaries Expense	2,000				4,500			
Advertising Expense	800							
	89,700	89,700						
Salaries Payable								
Depreciation Expense			2,400					
Rent Expense					2,000			
			12,400	12,400		17,700	84,900	76,900
Net Income					8,000			

SOLUTION

Garco Maintenance Company
Worksheet
For the Year Ended December 31, 20XX

Account	Trial Balance Dr.	Trial Balance Cr.	Adjustments Dr.	Adjustments Cr.	Income Statement Dr.	Income Statement Cr.	Balance Sheet Dr.	Balance Sheet Cr.
Cash	22,000						22,000*	
Accounts Receivable	4,000						4,000*	
Prepaid Rent	8,000*			2,000			6,000	
Land	32,200*						32,200	
Building	20,000						20,000*	
Accumulated Depreciation		8,000		2,400*				10,400
Accounts Payable		12,000						12,000*
Unearned Commission Income		25,500	5,500					20,000*
Common Stock		30,000						30,000*
Retained Earnings		2,000						2,000*
Dividends	700*						700	
Commission Income		12,200		5,500*		17,700*		
Salaries Expense	2,000		2,500*		4,500			
Advertising Expense	800				800*			
	89,700	89,700						
Salaries Payable				2,500*				2,500*
Depreciation Expense			2,400		2,400*			
Rent Expense			2,000*		2,000			
			12,400	12,400	9,700*	17,700	84,900	76,900
Net Income					8,000			8,000*
					17,700*	17,700*	84,900	84,900*

---
*Answer

5.13   Complete the worksheet below after making adjusting entries for the following data:

    (*a*)   Insurance expired, $50

    (*b*)   Depreciation, $2,000

    (*c*)   Earned $250 of unearned commission income

    (*d*)   Accrued salaries, $100

    (*e*)   Accrued interest expense on the note payable, $20

    (*f*)   Commission income earned but not received, $150

    (*g*)   Supplies on hand at year's end, $1,500

Lindac Servicing Corporation
Worksheet
For the Year Ended December 31, 20XX

Account	Trial Balance		Adjustments		Income Statement		Balance Sheet	
	Dr.	Cr.	Dr.	Cr.	Dr.	Cr.	Dr.	Cr.
Cash	12,900							
Accounts Receivable	8,000							
Prepaid Insurance	750							
Supplies	2,000							
Land	13,700							
Building	39,000							
Accumulated Depreciation		10,000						
Notes Payable		2,000						
Unearned Commission Income		1,750						
Common Stock		40,000						
Retained Earnings		20,000						
Dividends	200							
Commission Income		5,000						
Salaries Expense	1,000							
Telephone Expense	1,200							
	78,750	78,750						

SOLUTION

Lindac Servicing Corporation
Worksheet
For the Year Ended December 31, 20XX

Account	Trial Balance Dr.	Trial Balance Cr.	Adjustments Dr.	Adjustments Cr.	Income Statement Dr.	Income Statement Cr.	Balance Sheet Dr.	Balance Sheet Cr.
Cash	12,900						12,900	
Accounts Receivable	8,000						8,000	
Prepaid Insurance	750			(a) 50			700	
Supplies	2,000			(g) 500			1,500	
Land	13,700						13,700	
Building	39,000						39,000	
Accumulated Depreciation		10,000		(b) 2,000				12,000
Notes Payable		2,000						2,000
Unearned Commission Income		1,750	(c) 250					1,500
Common Stock		40,000						40,000
Retained Earnings		20,000						20,000
Dividends	200						200	
				(c) 250				
Commission Income		5,000		(f) 150		5,400		
Salaries Expense	1,000		(d) 100		1,100			
Telephone Expense	1,200				1,200			
	78,750	78,750						
Insurance Expense			(a) 50		50			
Depreciation Expense			(b) 2,000		2,000			
Salaries Payable				(d) 100				100
Interest Expense			(e) 20		20			
Interest Payable				(e) 20				20
Commission Receivable			(f) 150				150	
Supplies Expense			(g) 500		500			
			3,070	3,070	4,870	5,400	76,150	75,620
Net Income					530			530
					5,400	5,400	76,150	76,150

5.14 Based upon the information in Problem 5.13, prepare all adjusting and closing entries for the journal.

SOLUTION

Adjusting Entries

(a)	Insurance Expense	50	
	Prepaid Insurance		50
(b)	Depreciation Expense	2,000	
	Accumulated Depreciation		2,000

(c)	Unearned Commission Income	250	
	Commission Income		250
(d)	Salaries Expense	100	
	Salaries Payable		100
(e)	Interest Expense	20	
	Interest Payable		20
(f)	Commission Receivable	150	
	Commission Income		150
(g)	Supplies Expense	500	
	Supplies		500

Closing Entries

Commission Income	5,400	
Income Summary		5,400
Income Summary	4,870	
Salaries Expense		1,100
Telephone Expense		1,200
Insurance Expense		50
Depreciation Expense		2,000
Interest Expense		20
Supplies Expense		500
Income Summary	530	
Retained Earnings		530

5.15 Based upon the data in Problem 5.13, prepare the income statement, balance sheet, and statement of retained earnings.

SOLUTION

Lindac Servicing Corporation
Income Statement
For the Year Ended December 31, 20XX

Commission Income		$5,400
Less: Expenses		
Salaries Expense	$1,100	
Telephone Expense	1,200	
Insurance Expense	50	
Depreciation Expense	2,000	
Interest Expense	20	
Supplies Expense	500	
Total Expenses		4,870
Net Income		$ 530

Lindac Servicing Corporation
Balance Sheet
December 31, 20XX

ASSETS

Current Assets

Cash	$12,900	
Accounts Receivable	8,000	
Commission Receivable	150	
Prepaid Insurance	700	
Supplies	1,500	
Total Current Assets		$23,250

Fixed Assets

Land		$13,700	
Building	$39,000		
Less: Accumulated Depreciation	12,000	27,000	
Total Fixed Assets			40,700
Total Assets			$63,950

LIABILITIES AND STOCKHOLDERS' EQUITY

Liabilities

Notes Payable	$2,000	
Salaries Payable	100	
Interest Payable	20	
Unearned Commission Income	1,500	
Total Liabilities		$ 3,620

Stockholders' Equity

Common Stock	$40,000	
Retained Earnings	20,330	
Total Stockholders' Equity		60,330
Total Liabilities and Stockholders' Equity		$63,950

Lindac Servicing Corporation
Statement of Retained Earnings
For the Year Ended December 31, 20XX

Retained Earnings, January 1, 20XX	$20,000
Net Income	530
Subtotal	$20,530
Dividends	200
Retained Earnings, December 31, 20XX	$20,330

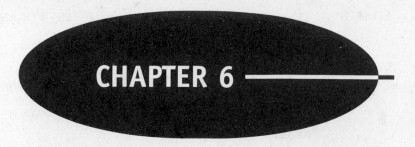

CHAPTER 6

Accounting for a Merchandising Business

6.1 INTRODUCTION

A merchandising business is one that buys goods for *resale* to customers. An example is a department store. The same accounting procedures apply as for a service-oriented business except that additional accounts are needed to reflect the purchase and sale of merchandise.

Every merchandising business has inventory. Inventory is the dollar value of merchandise on hand at either the beginning or end of the reporting period. Ending inventory consists of unsold merchandise as of the end of the period.

There are two alternative inventory systems—perpetual and periodic. Under the perpetual inventory system, *daily* records are maintained of each inventory item. The perpetual method is used for high-dollar-value items such as automobiles. Under the periodic inventory system, the inventory at the *end* of the reporting period is determined by taking a physical count of the merchandise on hand. The periodic approach is used for low-dollar-value items such as candy since it is impractical to keep daily records for such items.

6.2 ACCOUNTING FOR SALES OF MERCHANDISE

Sales may be made either for cash or on credit. An asset is debited and sales (revenue) is credited. The journal entry for a cash sale is

Cash
　　Sales

The entry for a credit sale is

Accounts Receivable
　　Sales

Revenue from merchandise sales is deemed earned in the reporting period that the merchandise is delivered to the customer, *not* when the cash is received.

Declining sales are a negative indicator about the financial health of the company because reduced earnings may be forthcoming.

Sales returns and allowances reduce the gross sales of the firm. Returns mean that the merchandise is given back to the seller because of defects. Allowances mean that the seller gives the buyer a certain amount off the selling price of the goods because of quality problems, but the buyer agrees to keep such goods. The appropriate journal entry in these situations is

Sales Returns and Allowances
    Cash (or Accounts Receivable)

Sales discounts represent cash discounts given by the seller to the purchaser for early payment of the account due. For example, assume that the credit terms of a sale are 1/10, net/30. This means that if the customer pays in 10 days, he or she gets 1 percent off the invoice price; however, the customer must pay for the goods no later than 30 days. Note that if the customer remits after 10 days (but before 30 days), he or she will not get any cash discount. The journal entry for a sales discount is

Cash
Sales Discount
    Accounts Receivable

EXAMPLE 1 Loft Company sold $10,000 of merchandise to a customer on terms of 1/10, n/30 (the n stands for net). Payment was made within 10 days. The amount of the discount is therefore $100 ($10,000 × 1%). Thus, the vendor will receive $9,900 ($10,000 − $100). Appropriate journal entries for the original credit sale and for the payment from the customer are

Accounts Receivable	10,000	
Sales		10,000
Cash	9,900	
Sales Discount	100	
Accounts Receivable		10,000

A trade discount is different from a cash discount. A trade discount represents a reduction from the listed retail price if substantial quantities are ordered or allowances are made to dealers. Such discount is *not* reflected in the seller's or purchaser's accounting records. For example, if the retail selling price of an item is $5,000 and the trade discount of 20 percent is given, the recorded sale would be $4,000 ($5,000 − $1,000). The journal entry is

Accounts Receivable	4,000	
Sales		4,000

A partial income statement highlighting the presentation of the sales revenue for a merchandising business is shown in the following example.

EXAMPLE 2

Income Statement (partial)

Gross Sales		$300,000
Less: Sales Returns and Allowances	$15,000	
Sales Discounts	8,000	23,000
Net Sales		$277,000

6.3   ACCOUNTING FOR PURCHASES

The inventory account represents the amount of goods in stock at a given point in time. In the periodic system, this is the amount on hand at the end of the reporting period. Purchases of *merchandise* from suppliers are entered in a separate account called Purchases at the *cost* of buying such goods. The Purchase account is for merchandise intended for resale. It is *not* for entering the acquisition of assets to be employed in the business (e.g., a machine); these are entered in their respective asset accounts (e.g., Machinery). The journal entry for a merchandise purchase is

Purchases
Cash (or Accounts Payable)

The Purchase account is shown in the Cost of Goods Sold section of the income statement. At the end of the reporting period it is closed out to the income summary account.

Purchase returns and allowances reduce the cost of gross purchases. They apply to unsatisfactory merchandise which is returned to the supplier or to goods for which price allowances are given. The journal entry is

Cash (or Accounts Payable)
Purchase Returns and Allowances

Purchase discounts are cash discounts given by the supplier to the purchaser for early payment of an account. The entry for a purchase discount is

Accounts Payable
Purchase Discounts
Cash

EXAMPLE 3   Merchandise is purchased by LSJ Company for $6,000 from a supplier on terms of 2/15, n/30. LSJ remits within 15 days. The amount of the discount is $120 ($6,000 × 2%). The payment to the supplier is $5,880 ($6,000 − $120). LSJ's journal entries for the purchase and for the payment are

Purchases	6,000	
Accounts Payable		6,000
Accounts Payable	6,000	
Purchase Discounts		120
Cash		5,880

Freight In (Transportation In) is an account set up to reflect the transportation charges paid by the *purchaser* for merchandise delivered. The journal entry is

Freight In

Cash (or Accounts Payable)

Freight In is added to the purchases account because it is an element of the delivered cost of the merchandise.

A partial income statement showing the presentation of purchases follows.

EXAMPLE 4

Income Statement (partial)

Purchases		$150,000
Freight In		3,000
Delivered Cost of Purchases		$153,000
Less: Purchase Returns and Allowances	$25,000	
Purchase Discounts	13,000	38,000
Net Purchases		$115,000

6.4 COST OF GOODS SOLD

Under the periodic method, merchandising businesses do not reflect purchases or sales of goods in inventory during the year. Hence, the closing inventory must be determined by a physical count, and any required adjustments must be provided. The ending inventory amount is an *asset* to be reflected in the balance sheet. In the income statement, the cost of goods sold is deducted from sales to arrive at gross profit.

The Cost of Goods Sold section of the income statement is shown in Example 5.

EXAMPLE 5 Cost of Goods Sold

Income Statement (partial)

Inventory, January 1, 20XX (beginning inventory)	$ 75,000
Net Purchases (Example 4)	115,000
Gost of Goods Available for Sale	$190,000
Less: Inventory, December 31, 20XX (ending inventory)	60,000
Cost of Goods Sold	$130,000

6.5 CONDENSED INCOME STATEMENT

An income statement for a merchanding firm comprises three major categories: Sales, Cost of Goods Sold, and Operating Expenses.

EXAMPLE 6

TV Retail Corporation
Income Statement
For the Year Ended December 31, 20XX

Net Sales (Example 2)	$277,000
Gost of Goods Sold (Example 5)	130,000
Gross Profit	$147,000
Operating Expenses	52,000
Income before Income Taxes (Operating Income)	$ 95,000
Income Tax Expense*	38,000
Net Income	$ 57,000

*Income Tax Expense is the tax the company incurs based
upon its operating income. We assumed a tax rate of 40
percent here, so the income tax expense for the year is $38,000
($95,000 × 40%).

6.6 THE WORKSHEET FOR A MERCHANDISING BUSINESS

The worksheet for a service-oriented business was discussed in Chapter 5. In addition to the accounts mentioned there, the worksheet for a merchandising business will have some new accounts, namely Sales, Inventory, Purchases, and Income Summary, which serves to show the cost of goods sold.

Under the periodic inventory method, entries in the Inventory account are made only at the *end* of the accounting period to show the replacement of the old by the new inventory. During the period, the Inventory account shows only the cost of merchandise which was on hand at the beginning of the period.

The beginning inventory in the normal course of business would be sold by the *end* of the reporting period. Thus, inventory would be reduced, requiring a credit to the account. The appropriate journal entry for January 1, 20X4 (beginning) inventory of $15,000 is

Dec. 31, 20X4	Income Summary	15,000	
	Merchandise Inventory		15,000

Any ending inventory represents an asset and consequently must be debited. If the December 31, 20X4, inventory was $17,000, the appropriate journal entry is

Dec. 31, 20X4	Merchandise Inventory	17,000	
	Income Summary		17,000

The impact of the preceding entries on the Merchandise Inventory and Income Summary accounts in the ledger is as follows:

Merchandise Inventory				Income Summary			
Jan. 1	15,000	Dec. 31	15,000	Dec. 31	15,000	Dec. 31	17,000
Dec. 31	17,000						

A typical trial balance and worksheet for a merchandising business are shown in the next example and figure. To simplify matters, Quick Merchandising Corporation's trial balance and worksheet are identical to those provided for Quick Service Corporation in Chapter 5 (Example 1 of Chapter 5 and Fig. 5-2), except that new accounts have been added in order to convert from a service company to a merchandising business. Also, all adjustments are identical to the worksheet (Fig. 5-2) in Chapter 5, except for the addition of adjusting entries for merchandise inventory and the omission of adjusting entry (d) in Fig. 5-2 for earned service fee income.

EXAMPLE 7   Additional information for the merchandising company follows:

(a)	Merchandise inventory (beginning)	$15,000
(b)	Merchandise inventory (ending)	17,000
(c)	Supplies on hand	200
(d)	Insurance expired	500
(e)	Depreciation for year	1,000
(f)	Accrued interest expense	50
(g)	Accrued salaries	150

Quick Merchandising Corporation
Trial Balance
December 31, 20X4

	Debit	Credit
Cash	$ 6,000	
Accounts Receivable	12,000	
Merchandise Inventory*	15,000	
Supplies	500	
Prepaid Insurance	2,000	
Machinery	10,000	
Accumulated Depreciation		$ 3,000
Accounts Payable		4,000
Notes Payable		2,000
Capital Stock		10,000
Retained Earnings**		16,000
Sales*		38,000
Purchases*	20,000	
Salaries Expense	5,000	
Telephone Expense	2,500	
	$73,000	$73,000

---

*New account
**Same account as in Example 1 of Chap. 5 but with new amount

Quick Merchandising Corporation
Worksheet
For the Year Ending December 31, 20X4

Account	Trial Balance Debit	Trial Balance Credit	Adjustments Debit	Adjustments Credit	Income Statement Debit	Income Statement Credit	Balance Sheet Debit	Balance Sheet Credit
Cash	6,000						6,000	
Accounts Receivable	12,000						12,000	
Merchandise Inventory*	15,000		(b) 17,000	(a) 15,000			17,000	
Supplies	500			(c) 300			200	
Prepaid Insurance	2,000			(d) 500			1,500	
Machinery	10,000						10,000	
Accumulated Depreciation		3,000		(e) 1,000				4,000
Accounts Payable		4,000						4,000
Notes Payable		2,000						2,000
Capital Stock		10,000						10,000
Retained Earnings**		16,000						16,000
Sales*		38,000				38,000		
Purchases*	20,000				20,000			
Salaries Expense	5,000		(g) 150		5,150			
Telephone Expense	2,500				2,500			
	73,000	73,000						
Income Summary*			(a) 15,000	(b) 17,000	15,000	17,000		
Supplies Expense			(c) 300		300			
Insurance Expense			(d) 500		500			
Depreciation Expense			(e) 1,000		1,000			
Interest Expense			(f) 50		50			
Interest Payable				(f) 50				50
Salaries Payable				(g) 150				150
			34,000	34,000	44,500	55,000	46,700	36,200
Net Income					10,500			10,500
					55,000	55,000	46,700	46,700

*New account

**Same account as in Fig. 5-2, but with new amount

Fig. 6-1

In the Trial Balance column, the merchandise inventory of $15,000 is the beginning balance (January 1, 20X4). Entry (a) in the Adjustments columns reflects the appropriate adjustment for the disposition of the beginning inventory by year's end. Entry (b) in the Adjustments columns is to establish the ending inventory (December 31, 20X4).

Note that the debit and credit amounts for the Income Summary account listed in the Adjustments columns are extended to the appropriate Income Statement columns. This procedure is unique to the income summary account and is unlike any other account. This is done since beginning and ending inventories must be shown in the Cost of Goods Sold section of the income statement. The debit amount of $15,000 represents the beginning inventory. The credit adjustment of $17,000 constitutes the ending inventory. We *cannot* net the two inventory amounts because needed details regarding inventory (beginning and ending) would be lost. Also note that the merchandise inventory account has a balance of $17,000, which is the ending inventory, and is thus extended to the debit side of Balance Sheet columns since remaining inventory is an asset.

6.7 AN INCOME STATEMENT FOR A MERCHANDISING BUSINESS

Upon completion of the worksheet, the income statement for the merchandiser may be prepared.

EXAMPLE 8

Quick Merchandising Corporation
Income Statement
For the Year Ended December 31, 20X4

Sales		$38,000
Cost of Goods Sold		
Merchandise Inventory, Jan. 1, 20X4	$15,000	
Purchases	20,000	
Cost of Goods Available for Sale	$35,000	
Merchandise Inventory, Dec. 31, 20X4	17,000	
Cost of Goods Sold		18,000
Gross Profit		$20,000
Operating Expenses		
Salaries Expense	$ 5,150	
Telephone Expense	2,500	
Supplies Expense	300	
Insurance Expense	500	
Depreciation Expense	1,000	
Interest Expense	50	
Total Operating Expenses		9,500
Net Income		$10,500

Summary

(1) A(n) _____ business is one in which income is generated by resale of bought goods.

(2) The entry for a credit sale is to debit the _____ account and credit the _____ account.

(3) Gross sales less _____ less _____ equal net sales.

(4) If a $1,000 sale is made on credit terms of 3/10, n/60, the amount of cash discount allowed if payment is made to the seller within 10 days is _____ .

(5) The entry on the seller's books for a sales discount is to debit the _____ account and the _____ account and credit the _____ account.

(6) A(n) _____ discount is not recorded in the seller's or purchaser's accounting records.

(7) Merchandise on hand at either the beginning or end of the reporting period is called _____ .

(8) Two alternative inventory systems are _____ and _____ .

(9) Under the _____ inventory system, we are generally dealing with low-dollar-value merchandise.

(10) Ending inventory appears in the balance sheet as a(n) _____ .

(11) Both beginning inventory and ending inventory appear in the _____ section of the income statement.

(12) The beginning inventory for 20X6 is the same as the _____ inventory for 20X5.

(13) When goods are acquired from a supplier, the gross cost of such goods is recorded in the _____ account.

(14) Cost of goods available for sale is equal to _____ inventory plus net purchases.

(15) Freight In is _____ to the Purchases account to obtain the delivered cost of merchandise.

(16) Purchase discounts are _____ from purchases to get net purchases.

(17) The adjusting entry for both beginning inventory and ending inventory at the end of the accounting period involves the _____ account.

Answers: (1) merchandising; (2) accounts receivable, sales; (3) sales returns and allowances, sales discounts; (4) $30; (5) Cash, Sales Discounts, Accounts Receivable; (6) trade; (7) inventory; (8) periodic, perpetual; (9) periodic; (10) asset; (11) Cost of Goods Sold; (12) ending; (13) Purchases; (14) beginning; (15) added; (16) subtracted; (17) Income Summary

Solved Problems

6.1 On February 3, a store made a cash sale of $5,000. On February 12, the customer returned $600 of the goods shipped. Prepare the appropriate journal entries.

SOLUTION

Feb. 3	Cash		5,000	
	Sales			5,000
12	Sales Returns and Allowances		600	
	Cash			600

6.2   Assuming Problem 6.1 involves a cash purchase rather than a cash sale, what would be the appropriate journal entries?

SOLUTION

Feb. 3	Purchases	5,000	
	Cash		5,000
12	Cash	600	
	Purchase Returns and Allowances		600

6.3   On April 8, $1,000 of merchandise was sold to a customer on terms of 2/10, n/30. How much cash will be received if the customer pays on (*a*) April 15? (*b*) April 27? Prepare appropriate journal entries to record the collection on each of these dates.

SOLUTION

(*a*)

Accounts Receivable	$1,000
Less: Discount (2% × $1,000)	20
Proceeds	$ 980

April 15	Cash	980	
	Sales Discount	20	
	Accounts Receivable		1,000

(*b*)   Since the discount period ended on April 18, no discount is allowed. Thus, the full $1,000 will be received and entered in the journal as follows:

April 27	Cash	1,000	
	Accounts Receivable		1,000

6.4   Assuming Problem 6.3 involved cash payments instead of cash receipts, what journal entries would be required to record parts (*a*) and (*b*)?

SOLUTION

(*a*)

April 15	Accounts Payable	1,000	
	Purchase Discount		20
	Cash		980

(*b*)

27	Accounts Payable	1,000	
	Cash		1,000

6.5   Prepare journal entries for the following transactions:

October   3—Sold merchandise to a customer for $800, terms 3/20, n/60

October   6—The customer returned $100 of the goods because of damages

October 11—Received payment from the customer for the balance due

SOLUTION

Oct.	3	Accounts Receivable	800	
		Sales		800
	6	Sales Returns and Allowances	100	
		Accounts Receivable		100
	11	Cash	679	
		Sales Discount*	21	
		Accounts Receivable		700

*$800 − $100 = $700 × 3% = $21

6.6   Assuming Problem 6.5 dealt with purchases rather than sales, prepare the appropriate journal entries.

SOLUTION

Oct.	3	Purchases	800	
		Accounts Payable		800
	6	Accounts Payable	100	
		Purchase Returns and Allowances		100
	11	Accounts Payable	700	
		Purchase Discount		21
		Cash		679

6.7   Information relating to sales is shown below. Determine the net sales.

Sales Discount	$ 20,000
Gross Sales	400,000
Sales Returns and Allowances	50,000

SOLUTION

Gross Sales		$400,000
Less: Sales Returns and Allowances	$50,000	
Sales Discount	20,000	70,000
Net Sales		$330,000

6.8   Information regarding purchases is presented below. Compute the net purchases.

Freight In	$ 15,000
Purchase Discount	12,000
Purchases	210,000
Purchase Returns and Allowances	30,000

SOLUTION

Purchases	$210,000
Freight In	15,000
Delivered Cost of Purchases	$225,000
Less: Purchase Returns and Allowances	$30,000
Purchase Discount	12,000 42,000
Net Purchases	$183,000

6.9 Arjay Corporation purchased merchandise at a cost of $210,000. Determine the cost of goods sold in each case below.

	Beginning Inventory	Ending Inventory
(a)	$ 80,000	$50,000
(b)	40,000	60,000
(c)	120,000	90,000

SOLUTION

	Beginning Inventory	+	Purchases	−	Ending Inventory	=	Cost of Goods Sold
(a)	$ 80,000		$210,000		$50,000		$240,000
(b)	40,000		210,000		60,000		190,000
(c)	120,000		210,000		90,000		240,000

6.10 Determine the cost of goods sold based upon the following data: beginning inventory, $30,000; purchases, $60,000; ending inventory, $35,000.

SOLUTION

Beginning Inventory	$30,000
Purchases	60,000
Cost of Goods Available for Sale	$90,000
Ending Inventory	35,000
Cost of Goods Sold	$55,000

6.11 Fill in the missing numbers for the following situations:

	Beginning Inventory	Purchases	Ending Inventory	Cost of Goods Sold
(a)	$_____	$20,000	$13,000	$28,000
(b)	30,000	_____	20,000	45,000
(c)	12,000	14,000	10,000	_____
(d)	19,000	30,000	_____	29,000

SOLUTION

(a) $21,000; (b) $35,000; (c) $16,000; (d) $20,000

6.12 Based upon the following data, prepare adjusting journal entries at December 31, 20X1.

(a) Merchandise inventory at January 1 is $52,000; at December 31, $57,000.

(b) The prepaid advertising at January 1, 20X1, of $3,000 is applicable for a three-year period.

(c) Of the unearned commission income of $10,000, 40 percent has been earned at year's end.

SOLUTION

(a)

| Income Summary | 52,000 | |
| Merchandise Inventory | | 52,000 |

| Merchandise Inventory | 57,000 | |
| Income Summary | | 57,000 |

(b)

| Advertising Expense | 1,000 | |
| Prepaid Advertising | | 1,000 |

(c)

| Unearned Commission Income | 4,000 | |
| Commission Income | | 4,000 |

6.13 For each item listed below, prepare the appropriate adjusting entry.

(a) Merchandise inventory at January 1 was $40,000; at December 31, $33,000.

(b) As of January 1, there was $6,000 in office supplies. At year's end, the amount of supplies on hand was $1,500.

(c) The last payroll day was December 27, a Tuesday. The weekly payroll (five-day work week) is $20,000.

SOLUTION

(a)

| Income Summary | 40,000 | |
| Merchandise Inventory | | 40,000 |

| Merchandise Inventory | 33,000 | |
| Income Summary | | 33,000 |

(b)

| Office Supplies Expense | 4,500 | |
| Office Supplies | | 4,500 |

(c)

| Salaries Expense* | 12,000 | |
| Salaries Payable | | 12,000 |

---

*Three payroll days (December 28–December 30) must be accrued. December 31 is not counted because it falls on a Saturday. The computation is

$$\$20,000 \times 3/5 = \$12,000$$

6.14 A company's trial balance includes merchandise inventory balance of $30,600. At year's end, merchandise inventory was $36,500. Fill in the Trial Balance and Adjustment columns of the worksheet.

Account	Trial Balance		Adjustments		Income Statement		Balance Sheet	
	Dr.	Cr.	Dr.	Cr.	Dr.	Cr.	Dr.	Cr.

SOLUTION

Account	Trial Balance		Adjustments		Income Statement		Balance Sheet	
	Dr.	Cr.	Dr.	Cr.	Dr.	Cr.	Dr.	Cr.
Merchandise Inventory	30,600		(b) 36,500	(a) 30,600				
Income Summary			(a) 30,600	(b) 36,500				

6.15 Based on the solution to Problem 6.14, fill in the Income Statement and Balance Sheet columns of the worksheet.

SOLUTION

Account	Trial Balance		Adjustments		Income Statement		Balance Sheet	
	Dr.	Cr.	Dr.	Cr.	Dr.	Cr.	Dr.	Cr.
Merchandise Inventory	30,600		(b) 36,500	(a) 30,600			36,500	
Income Summary			(a) 30,600	(b) 36,500	30,600	36,500		

6.16 A company's worksheet is shown below. The merchandise inventory at year's end is $47,000. Fill in the Adjustments columns.

Account	Trial Balance		Adjustments		Income Statement		Balance Sheet	
	Dr.	Cr.	Dr.	Cr.	Dr.	Cr.	Dr.	Cr.
Merchandise Inventory	39,000							
Income Summary								

SOLUTION

Account	Trial Balance		Adjustments		Income Statement		Balance Sheet	
	Dr.	Cr.	Dr.	Cr.	Dr.	Cr.	Dr.	Cr.
Merchandise Inventory	39,000		(b) 47,000	(a) 39,000				
Income Summary			(a) 39,000	(b) 47,000				

6.17 Based upon the solution to Problem 6.16, fill in the Income Statement and Balance Sheet columns of the worksheet. What is the significance of the debit balance in the Balance Sheet column? What do the debit and credit balances in the Income Statement columns represent?

SOLUTION

Account	Trial Balance		Adjustments		Income Statement		Balance Sheet	
	Dr.	Cr.	Dr.	Cr.	Dr.	Cr.	Dr.	Cr.
Merchandise Inventory	39,000		(b) 47,000	(a) 39,000			47,000	
Income Summary			(a) 39,000	(b) 47,000	39,000	47,000		

The debit balance of $47,000 in the Balance Sheet column represents the inventory left at year's end.

In the Income Statement columns, the debit balance of $39,000 represents the beginning inventory, while the credit balance of $47,000 constitutes the ending inventory.

6.18 The following information is from the Income Statement columns of a worksheet. Prepare the income statement.

Income Summary	21,000	28,000
Sales		105,000
Purchases	40,000	
Salaries Expense	12,000	
Telephone Expense	9,000	
Advertising Expense	6,000	
Rent Expense	14,000	

SOLUTION

Income Statement

Sales		$105,000
Cost of Goods Sold		
Merchandise Inventory, beginning	$21,000	
Purchases	40,000	
Cost of Goods Available for Sale	$61,000	
Merchandise Inventory, ending	28,000	
Cost of Goods Sold		33,000
Gross Profit		$ 72,000

Operating Expenses

Salaries Expense	$12,000	
Telephone Expense	9,000	
Advertising Expense	6,000	
Rent Expense	14,000	
Total Operating Expenses		41,000
Net Income		$ 31,000

6.19 The Trial Balance for Gitland Manufacturing Company is presented below. Using the following information for adjusting entries, complete the worksheet.

(*a*) Merchandise inventory, December 31, 20XX, $21,000

(*b*) Depreciation expense, $10,000

(*c*) Insurance expired, $2,000

(*d*) Accrued interest on notes payable, $5,000

Gitland Manufacturing Company
Worksheet
For the Year Ended December 31, 20XX

Account	Trial Balance		Adjustments		Income Statement		Balance Sheet	
	Dr.	Cr.	Dr.	Cr.	Dr.	Cr.	Dr.	Cr.
Cash	50,000							
Accounts Receivable	75,000							
Marketable Securities	16,000							
Prepaid Insurance	9,215							
Merchandise Inventory	18,800							
Machinery	300,000							
Accumulated Depreciation		75,000						
Patents	17,000							
Accounts Payable		37,600						
Notes Payable		57,180						
Common Stock		190,000						
Retained Earnings		54,915						
Dividends	26,000							
Sales		961,470						
Purchases	280,000							
Freight In	4,150							
Salaries Expense	275,000							
Rent Expense	170,000							
Advertising Expense	75,000							
Travel Expense	60,000							
	1,376,165	1,376,165						

SOLUTION

Gitland Manufacturing Company
Worksheet
For the Year Ended December 31, 20XX

Account	Trial Balance Dr.	Trial Balance Cr.	Adjustments Dr.	Adjustments Cr.	Income Statement Dr.	Income Statement Cr.	Balance Sheet Dr.	Balance Sheet Cr.
Cash	50,000						50,000	
Accounts Receivable	75,000						75,000	
Marketable Securities	16,000						16,000	
Prepaid Insurance	9,215			(c) 2,000			7,215	
Merchandise Inventory	18,800		(a) 21,000	(a) 18,800			21,000	
Machinery	300,000						300,000	
Accumulated Depreciation		75,000		(b) 10,000				85,000
Patents	17,000						17,000	
Accounts Payable		37,600						37,600
Notes Payable		57,180						57,180
Common Stock		190,000						190,000
Retained Earnings		54,915						54,915
Dividends	26,000						26,000	
Sales		961,470				961,470		
Purchases	280,000				280,000			
Freight In	4,150				4,150			
Salaries Expense	275,000				275,000			
Rent Expense	170,000				170,000			
Advertising Expense	75,000				75,000			
Travel Expense	60,000				60,000			
	1,376,165	1,376,165						
Income Summary			(a) 18,800	(a) 21,000	18,800	21,000		
Depreciation Expense			(b) 10,000		10,000			
Insurance Expense			(c) 2,000		2,000			
Interest Expense			(d) 5,000		5,000			
Interest Payable				(d) 5,000				5,000
			56,800	56,800	899,950	982,470	512,215	429,695
Net Income					82,520			82,520
					982,470	982,470	512,215	512,215

6.20 Based upon the solution to Problem 6.19, prepare an income statement.

SOLUTION

Gitland Manufacturing Company
Income Statement
For the Year Ended December 31, 20XX

Sales			$961,470
Cost of Goods Sold			
Merchandise Inventory, January 1		$ 18,800	
Purchases	$280,000		
Freight In	4,150		
Delivered Cost of Purchases		284,150	
Cost of Goods Available for Sale		$302,950	
Less: Merchandise Inventory, December 31		21,000	
Cost of Goods Sold			281,950
Gross Profit			$679,520
Operating Expenses			
Salaries Expense		$275,000	
Rent Expense		170,000	
Advertising Expense		75,000	
Travel Expense		60,000	
Depreciation Expense		10,000	
Insurance Expense		2,000	
Interest Expense		5,000	
Total Operating Expenses			597,000
Net Income			$ 82,520

6.21 The Trial Balance columns of a worksheet for James Corporation are shown below. Using the data provided for adjusting entries at December 31, 20XX, complete the worksheet.

(*a*) Merchandise inventory, December 31, 20XX, $42,000

(*b*) Supplies on hand, $300

(*c*) Accrued interest on notes payable, $800

(*d*) Depreciation for the period, $12,000

(*e*) Accrued salaries, $1,500

James Corporation
Worksheet
For the Year Ended December 31, 20XX

Account	Trial Balance Dr.	Trial Balance Cr.	Adjustments Dr.	Adjustments Cr.	Income Statement Dr.	Income Statement Cr.	Balance Sheet Dr.	Balance Sheet Cr.
Cash	10,000							
Accounts Receivable	23,000							
Merchandise Inventory	37,000							
Supplies	1,200							
Equipment	50,000							
Accumulated Depreciation		22,000						
Accounts Payable		13,000						
Notes Payable		10,000						
Common Stock		30,000						
Retained Earnings		11,200						
Dividends	3,000							
Sales		150,000						
Purchases	80,000							
Salaries Expense	16,000							
Rent Expense	10,000							
Advertising Expense	6,000							
	236,200	236,200						

SOLUTION

James Corporation
Worksheet
For the Year Ended December 31, 20XX

Account	Trial Balance Dr.	Trial Balance Cr.	Adjustments Dr.	Adjustments Cr.	Income Statement Dr.	Income Statement Cr.	Balance Sheet Dr.	Balance Sheet Cr.
Cash	10,000						10,000	
Accounts Receivable	23,000						23,000	
Merchandise Inventory	37,000		(a) 42,000	(a) 37,000			42,000	
Supplies	1,200			(b) 900			300	
Equipment	50,000						50,000	
Accumulated Depreciation		22,000		(d) 12,000				34,000
Accounts Payable		13,000						13,000
Notes Payable		10,000						10,000
Common Stock		30,000						30,000
Retained Earnings		11,200						11,200
Dividends	3,000						3,000	
Sales		150,000				150,000		
Purchases	80,000				80,000			
Salaries Expense	16,000		(e) 1,500		17,500			
Rent Expense	10,000				10,000			
Advertising Expense	6,000				6,000			
	236,200	236,200						
Income Summary			(a) 37,000	(a) 42,000	37,000	42,000		
Supplies Expense			(b) 900		900			
Interest Expense			(c) 800		800			
Interest Payable				(c) 800				800
Depreciation Expense			(d) 12,000		12,000			
Salaries Payable				(e) 1,500				1,500
			94,200	94,200	164,200	192,000	128,300	100,500
Net Income					27,800			27,800
					192,000	192,000	128,300	128,300

6.22   Based upon the completed worksheet of Problem 6.21, prepare adjusting and closing entries.

SOLUTION

Adjusting Entries

(a)	Merchandise Inventory	42,000	
	Income Summary		42,000
	Income Summary	37,000	
	Merchandise Inventory		37,000
(b)	Supplies Expense	900	
	Supplies		900
(c)	Interest Expense	800	
	Interest Payable		800
(d)	Depreciation Expense	12,000	
	Accumulated Depreciation		12,000
(e)	Salaries Expense	1,500	
	Salaries Payable		1,500

Closing Entries

(a)	Sales	150,000	
	Income Summary		150,000
(b)	Income Summary	127,200	
	Purchases		80,000
	Salaries Expense		17,500
	Rent Expense		10,000
	Advertising Expense		6,000
	Supplies Expense		900
	Interest Expense		800
	Depreciation Expense		12,000
(c)	Income Summary	27,800	
	Retained Earnings		27,800

6.23 Based upon the completed worksheet in Problem 6.21, prepare

(*a*) an income statement, (*b*) a statement of retained earnings, and (*c*) a balance sheet.

SOLUTION

(*a*)

James Corporation
Income Statement
For the Year Ended December 31, 20XX

Sales		$150,000
Cost of Goods Sold		
Merchandise Inventory, January 1	$ 37,000	
Purchases	80,000	
Cost of Goods Available for Sale	$117,000	
Less: Merchandise Inventory, December 31	42,000	
Cost of Goods Sold		75,000
Gross Profit		$ 75,000
Operating Expenses		
Salaries Expense	$ 17,500	
Rent Expense	10,000	
Advertising Expense	6,000	
Supplies Expense	900	
Interest Expense	800	
Depreciation Expense	12,000	
Total Operating Expenses		47,200
Net Income		$ 27,800

(*b*)

James Corporation
Statement of Retained Earnings
For the Year Ended December 31, 20XX

Retained Earnings, January 1	$11,200
Net Income	27,800
Subtotal	39,000
Dividends	3,000
Retained Earnings, December 31	$36,000

(*c*)

James Corporation
Balance Sheet
December 31, 20XX

ASSETS

Current Assets		
Cash	$10,000	
Accounts Receivable	23,000	
Merchandise Inventory	42,000	
Supplies	300	
Total Current Assets		$75,300
Fixed Assets		
Equipment	$50,000	
Less: Accumulated Depreciation	34,000	16,000
Total Assets		$91,300

LIABILITIES AND STOCKHOLDERS' EQUITY

Current Liabilities

Accounts Payable	$13,000	
Notes Payable	10,000	
Salaries Payable	1,500	
Interest Payable	800	
Total Current Liabilities		$25,300

Stockholders' Equity

Common Stock	$30,000	
Retained Earnings	36,000	
Total Stockholders' Equity		66,000
Total Liabilities and Stockholders' Equity		$91,300

Chapters 4-6

1. Why are adjusting entries required?

2. What are the four types of adjusting entries? For each type of adjusting entry, define and give an example.

3. Prepare adjusting entries at December 31 for the following transactions:

   (a) Weekly salaries of $10,000 for a five-day week are payable on Friday. The last payroll date was Friday, December 25.

   (b) The supplies on hand at the beginning of the year were $2,000. On December 31, $500 of supplies were left.

   (c) Unearned rental income at the beginning of the year was $5,000. At December 31, 40 percent of that income has been earned.

   (d) Interest earned on a customer's note receivable was $100.

4. What is the purpose of making closing entries?

5. At the end of the reporting period, a company had the following balances in its expense accounts:

Salaries Expense	$4,000
Rent Expense	3,000
Advertising Expense	1,000

   Prepare the closing entry.

6. After all revenue and expense accounts had been closed at year's end, the Income Summary account had a debit balance of $83,000 and a credit balance of $95,000. Retained Earnings had a credit balance of $38,000.

   (a) Prepare the closing entry to transfer the net income.

   (b) What is the ending balance in Retained Earnings?

7. On July 1, 20X1, the company purchased an auto for $12,000. The auto's life is eight years. The company uses the straight-line depreciation method.

    (*a*)   What is the depreciation expense for 20X1?

    (*b*)   What is the depreciation expense for 20X2?

    (*c*)   What is the book value of the auto at December 31, 20X2?

8. The trial balance for Host Servicing Corporation as of December 31, 20X4, is presented below. From the data provided for adjusting entries, complete the worksheet.

    (*a*)   Supplies used, $300

    (*b*)   Depreciation on machinery, $500

    (*c*)   Of the unearned fee income, $400 has been earned during the period

    (*d*)   Interest earned on a customer's note receivable, $80

Host Servicing Corporation
Worksheet
For the Year Ended December 31, 20X4

Account	Trial Balance Dr.	Trial Balance Cr.	Adjustments Dr.	Adjustments Cr.	Income Statement Dr.	Income Statement Cr.	Balance Sheet Dr.	Balance Sheet Cr.
Cash	2,500							
Notes Receivable	1,000							
Supplies	800							
Land	22,600							
Machinery	22,000							
Accumulated Depreciation		2,400						
Accounts Payable		5,000						
Unearned Fee Income		1,200						
Common Stock		20,000						
Retained Earnings		3,000						
Dividends	200							
Fee Income		31,000						
Salaries Expense	8,000							
Rent Expense	4,000							
Repair Expense	1,500							
	62,600	62,600						

9. Prepare journal entries for the following transactions:

    (*a*)   On October 3, merchandise was sold on credit for $20,000. The terms of sale were 1/10, n/30.

    (*b*)   On October 6, the customer returned defective merchandise amounting to $3,000.

    (*c*)   On October 11, the customer remitted the balance due.

10. Listed below is a partial trial balance of the A&G Retail Store at December 31, 20X9.

Trial Balance (partial)

Merchandise Inventory	$80,000	
Sales		$190,000
Sales Returns and Allowances	20,000	
Purchases	60,000	
Purchase Discount		3,000
Freight In	1,000	

The merchandise inventory on December 31 is $74,000.

(*a*) Prepare the adjusting entries needed for merchandise inventory.

(*b*) Prepare the income statement down to gross profit.

11. Presented below is the trial balance for Walter Corporation at December 31, 20X3. From the data provided for adjusting entries, complete the worksheet.

(*a*) Merchandise inventory, December 31, $43,000

(*b*) Insurance expired, $1,200

(*c*) Depreciation on equipment, $2,000

(*d*) Accrued salaries, $1,300

(*e*) Accrued interest on notes payable, $100

Walter Corporation
Worksheet
For the Year Ended December 31, 20X3

Account	Trial Balance Dr.	Trial Balance Cr.	Adjustments Dr.	Adjustments Cr.	Income Statement Dr.	Income Statement Cr.	Balance Sheet Dr.	Balance Sheet Cr.
Cash	10,000							
Accounts Receivable	15,000							
Merchandise Inventory	37,000							
Prepaid Insurance	2,500							
Equipment	46,000							
Accumulated Depreciation		6,000						
Notes Payable		3,000						
Common Stock		10,000						
Retained Earnings		14,000						
Dividends	2,000							
Sales		200,500						
Sales Discount	4,000							
Purchases	60,000							
Purchase Returns & Allowances		3,000						
Salaries Expense	25,000							
Rent Expense	22,000							
Advertising Expense	13,000							
	236,500	236,500						

Answers to Examination II

1. Adjusting entries are prepared so that accounts will reflect both the results of operations for the reporting period and the financial position at the end of the period.

2. The four types of adjusting entries are

   (1) Prepaid (Unexpired) Expenses. An expense is prepaid when the expenditure for an item is made prior to the consumption of that item. An example is prepaid insurance.

   (2) Unearned (Deferred) Revenue. Unearned revenue refers to revenue that has been received in advance. An example is unearned professional fee income.

   (3) Accrued Expenses. An expense is accrued when an item's consumption occurs before its payment. An example is accrued salaries.

   (4) Accrued Revenue. Accrued revenue is revenue that has been earned but not received. An example is the interest earned on a customer's note receivable.

3.
(a)	Salaries Expense	8,000*	
	Salaries Payable		8,000
(b)	Supplies Expense	1,500	
	Supplies		1,500
(c)	Unearned Rental Income	2,000	
	Rental Income		2,000
(d)	Interest Receivable	100	
	Interest Income		100

*Monday, December 28 to Thursday, December 31 = 4 days, so the calculation is

$$\$10,000 \times 4/5 = \$8,000$$

4. Closing entries are used for summarizing the activities of the period by matching expenses against revenue in order to arrive at the net income (or net loss) and therefore the increase (or decrease) in stockholders' equity. Closing entries have the effect of keeping the operations of each period separate. Closing entries relate to the nominal or temporary accounts that are in essence only extensions of the stockholders' equity accounts.

5.
Income Summary	8,000	
Salaries Expense		4,000
Rent Expense		3,000
Advertising Expense		1,000

6. (a)
Income Summary	12,000	
Retained Earnings		12,000

   (b) $50,000 ($38,000 + $12,000)

7.

(a) Depreciation per year = $12,000/8 $ 1,500
Period held in 20X1 (July 1–Dec. 31)   × 6/12
Depreciation expense for 20X1 $ 750

(b) Depreciation expense for 20X2 $1,500

(c) Cost $12,000
Less: Accumulated depreciation   2,250
Book value $ 9,750

8.

Host Servicing Corporation
Worksheet
For the Year Ended December 31, 20X4

Account	Trial Balance Dr.	Trial Balance Cr.	Adjustments Dr.	Adjustments Cr.	Income Statement Dr.	Income Statement Cr.	Balance Sheet Dr.	Balance Sheet Cr.
Cash	2,500						2,500	
Notes Receivable	1,000						1,000	
Supplies	800			(a) 300			500	
Land	22,600						22,600	
Machinery	22,000						22,000	
Accumulated Depreciation		2,400		(b) 500				2,900
Accounts Payable		5,000						5,000
Unearned Fee Income		1,200	(c) 400					800
Common Stock		20,000						20,000
Retained Earnings		3,000						3,000
Dividends	200						200	
Fee Income		31,000		(c) 400		31,400		
Salaries Expense	8,000				8,000			
Rent Expense	4,000				4,000			
Repair Expense	1,500				1,500			
	62,600	62,600						
Supplies Expense			(a) 300		300			
Depreciation Expense			(b) 500		500			
Interest Receivable			(d) 80				80	
Interest Income				(d) 80		80		
			1,280	1,280	14,300	31,480	48,880	31,700
Net Income					17,180			17,180
					31,480	31,480	48,880	48,880

9.

    (*a*) Accounts Receivable   20,000

              Sales   20,000

    (*b*) Sales Returns and Allowances   3,000

              Accounts Receivable   3,000

    (*c*) Cash   16,830

           Sales Discount*   170

              Accounts Receivable   17,000

*The Sales Discount is calculated as follows:

$$\$20,000 - \$3,000 = \$17,000 \times 1\% = \$170$$

10. (*a*)

                Income Summary   80,000

                   Merchandise Inventory   80,000

                Merchandise Inventory   74,000

                   Income Summary   74,000

  (*b*)

A&G Retail Store
Income Statement
For the Year Ended December 31, 20X9

Sales			$190,000
Less: Sales Returns and Allowances			20,000	$170,000
Cost of Goods Sold				
Merchandise Inventory, January 1			$ 80,000	
Purchases	$60,000			
Freight In	1,000			
Delivered Cost of Purchases	$61,000			
Less: Purchase Discount	3,000			
Net Purchases			58,000	
Cost of Goods Available for Sale			$138,000	
Less: Merchandise Inventory, December 31			74,000	
Cost of Goods Sold				64,000
Gross Profit				$106,000

11.

Walter Corporation
Worksheet
For the Year Ended December 31, 20X3

Account	Trial Balance Dr.	Trial Balance Cr.	Adjustments Dr.	Adjustments Cr.	Income Statement Dr.	Income Statement Cr.	Balance Sheet Dr.	Balance Sheet Cr.
Cash	10,000						10,000	
Accounts Receivable	15,000						15,000	
Merchandise Inventory	37,000		(a) 43,000	(a) 37,000			43,000	
Prepaid Insurance	2,500			(b) 1,200			1,300	
Equipment	46,000						46,000	
Accumulated Depreciation		6,000		(c) 2,000				8,000
Notes Payable		3,000						3,000
Common Stock		10,000						10,000
Retained Earnings		14,000						14,000
Dividends	2,000						2,000	
Sales		200,500				200,500		
Sales Discount	4,000				4,000			
Purchases	60,000				60,000			
Purchase Returns & Allowances		3,000				3,000		
Salaries Expense	25,000		(d) 1,300		26,300			
Rent Expense	22,000				22,000			
Advertising Expense	13,000				13,000			
	236,500	236,500						
Income Summary			(a) 37,000	(a) 43,000	37,000	43,000		
Insurance Expense			(b) 1,200		1,200			
Depreciation Expense			(c) 2,000		2,000			
Salaries Payable				(d) 1,300				1,300
Interest Expense			(e) 100		100			
Interest Payable				(e) 100				100
			84,600	84,600	165,600	246,500	117,300	36,400
Net Income					80,900			80,900
					246,500	246,500	117,300	117,300

CHAPTER 7

Cash and Short-term Investments

7.1 INTRODUCTION

Transactions involving cash occur frequently. Cash is the most liquid asset of a business and is immediately available for paying current obligations. Creditors are particularly interested in ratios involving cash—for example, the ratio of cash to total current liabilities—because such ratios represent the funds available to repay them. Since cash is the easiest asset to steal, stringent accounting procedures and recordkeeping must be followed for cash transactions.

Short-term investments (marketable securities) are those that management intends to hold for one year or less. Hence, they are highly liquid assets. When idle cash exists, it is financially advantageous to invest excess funds in securities so that a return is earned.

7.2 WHAT IS CASH?

Cash is what the bank accepts for deposit, crediting the company's account. The cash account includes currency, coin, demand deposits (checking account), savings deposits, petty cash, and money orders. Although other items, such as postage stamps and postdated checks, are controlled by the cashier, they are *not* cash. Postage represents a prepaid expense, while postdated checks are receivables. Creditors are interested in restrictions upon corporate bank accounts since the applicable cash subject to the restriction is not currently available to meet debts. An example is a compensating balance. This represents the amount of cash that must be kept as collateral with the bank in support of a loan.

Sinking funds set up to meet the principal on bonds are not available cash and hence represent noncurrent assets.

7.3 THE CONTROL OF CASH

Internal control over cash through the separation of duties is essential because of this asset's susceptibility to theft. The individual having the physical custody over cash should not have responsibility for handling the accounting records regarding it. For cash on hand, there should be frequent surprise counts.

Some controls applicable to cash receipts are:

1. Cash sales should have supporting documentation such as sales tickets.
2. A receipt should be received when cash is given to another party.
3. Cash receipts should be deposited at the end of each day.

Some controls dealing with cash disbursements are:

1. Cash payments should be made only by an authorized individual.
2. Approved supporting documentation should exist prior to payment.
3. The person who approves the expenditure should not be the one who signs the check.
4. Prenumbered checks should be used.
5. Spoiled checks should be voided.
6. The individual making out the checks should perform no other function having to do with cash.

Two controls are important regarding the preparation of the bank reconciliation:

1. The person preparing the bank reconciliation should not be involved in cash receipt or cash payment functions.
2. The envelope containing the bank statement and cleared checks should not be opened by any party other than the preparer of the bank reconciliation.

7.4 THE BANK STATEMENT

A bank statement shows for a monthly period the deposits made, checks cleared, various charges and credits (to be mentioned in the next section), and the account balances at the beginning and end of the period.

The three parties involved in a check are the drawer, drawee, and payee. The drawer is the party issuing the check; the drawee is the bank upon which the check is drawn; and the payee is the party receiving payment. The cancelled check is proof that the amount due to the payee has been credited to his or her account. When the payee deposits the check, he or she must sign (endorse) the back of it. Three types of endorsements will be defined here.

Blank Endorsement. The endorser only signs his or her name. If lost or stolen, the blank endorsement check may be cashed. Hence, such endorsement is recommended only when the depositor is already at his or her bank (Fig. 7-1).

Full Endorsement. This endorsement restricts payment to the order of a specific person (Fig. 7-2).

Restrictive Endorsement. Here, the receiver of the check is limited as to how the amount is to be collected. This type of endorsement is customarily made when the check is prepared for deposit (Fig. 7-3).

L Jones	*Pay to the order of* *L Jones*	*For deposit only* *L Jones*
Fig. 7-1	**Fig. 7-2**	**Fig. 7-3**

7.5 BANK RECONCILIATION

A bank reconciliation is prepared based upon the information contained in the bank statement. Indicated thereon are deposits made, checks cleared, and charges or credits (deductions or additions) to the account. An example of a deduction to the company's account is a bank charge, while an example of an addition to the account is the amount collected on a customer's note. Enclosed with the bank statement are the cancelled checks, debit memoranda for charges, and credit memoranda for credits.

Rarely does the ending balance in the bank statement agree with the ending balance in the cash account per books. To reflect the reconciling items, a bank reconciliation is required. Once completed, the adjusted bank balance must prove to the adjusted book balance. When it does, it indicates that both records are correct. Journal entries are then prepared to update the records per books and to arrive at an ending balance in the cash account that agrees with the ending balance in the bank statement. In other words, the cash balance per books must be the same as the balance in the bank account at the end of the period. Reconciling differences relate to (1) items shown on the company's books but not on the bank statement and (2) items shown on the bank statement but not on the depositor's books.

RECONCILING ITEMS FOR THE BANK STATEMENT

The bank balance is adjusted for items reflected on the company's books that are not on the bank statement. They include several types of items.

Outstanding checks. These are checks that have been issued by the company but have not as yet cleared the bank. The total of the outstanding checks is deducted from the bank balance. The exception is an uncleared certified check, which is not considered outstanding since both parties, the company and the bank, know about it. A certified check is one for which the bank immediately sets aside funds for payment when the check is presented for certification.

Deposits in transit. This refers to cash received by the company at the end of the period that has not been deposited yet or was deposited after the bank prepared its statement. Such deposits are added to the bank balance.

Errors in recording checks. Mistakes, such as transposition errors, can be made in the recording of checks. For example, an item should be added to the bank balance when it was previously overstated on the books.

Bank errors in charging or crediting the company's account. If a company's account is charged in error for another firm's cleared check, the company's bank balance is understated. Hence, the company should add the amount of the check to its bank balance. On the other hand, if a deposit made by a firm is incorrectly credited to the account of another company, the latter should reduce its bank balance.

RECONCILING ITEMS FOR THE BOOKS

The book balance (cash account) is adjusted for items shown on the bank statement that are not reflected on the books. They include the following:

Bank charges. Fees for bank services are a reduction of the book balance. These amounts are not known until the bank statement is received. Examples include the monthly service charge, cost per check, check printing costs, and stop payment fees.

NSF checks. These are checks that have bounced because of insufficient funds in the customer's checking account. (NSF stands for Not Sufficient Funds.) In this case, the company's bank issues a debit memorandum for the dishonored amount and hence the book balance is reduced.

Collections. Notes and other items are collected by the bank for a nominal fee. The proceeds received less the charge (in the form of a credit memorandum) is credited to the corporate account. The net amount acts as an addition to the book balance.

Interest earned. Interest income credited by the bank on the checking account increases the book balance.

Errors on the books. Various types of mistakes can be made on the books. Two examples of them and explanations of how they would be corrected follow (assume that the amount of the check is correct):

1. A check is written ($50) for more than the amount entered as a cash disbursement ($45). In this case, cash disbursements are understated by $5 and hence the balance per books should be reduced by that amount.

2. A check is written ($100) for less than the amount shown as a cash disbursement ($120). Here, cash disbursements are overstated. Thus, the book balance should be increased by $20 to correct for the error.

After the bank reconciliation has been prepared, journal entries are made for the reconciling items affecting the *book* balance. This is because the amounts on the books will have to be updated for any items reflected on the bank statement that the firm did not know about during the period. However, reconciling items entered as an adjustment to the bank balance are not journalized since they are already on the books. Such reconciling items undoubtedly would be shown on the next bank statement.

EXAMPLE 1   Windor Corporation provides the following data in connection with the preparation of its bank reconciliation at June 30, 20XX: balance per bank, $4,889; balance per books, $4,400; outstanding checks—#410, $500 and #423, $200; deposit in transit, $300; collection on note—principal, $200 and interest, $16; collection fee on note, $12; NSF check, $100; and monthly service charge, $15.

Windor Corporation
Bank Reconciliation
June 30, 20XX

Balance per bank		$4,889	Balance per books	$4,400
Add: Deposit in transit		300	Add: Proceeds on note	216
		$5,189		$4,616
Less: Outstanding checks			Less:	
#410	$500			
#423	200		NSF check	$100
		700	Collection fee	12
			Service charge	15
				127
Adjusted bank balance		$4,489	Adjusted book balance	$4,489

The following journal entries are required at June 30, 20XX:

General Journal

June 30	Cash	216	
	Notes receivable		200
	Interest income		16
	Accounts receivable	100	
	Cash		100
	Bank service charge	27	
	Cash		27

After the journal entries have been posted, the books are up to date. For example, the cash balance per books will now agree with the bank balance, namely $4,489. The cash "T" account is shown below for clarification.

Cash

6/30 Balance before adjustment	4,400	100
	216	27
	4,616	127
6/30 Balance after adjustment	4,489	

7.6 CASH SHORTAGE AND OVERAGE

In a business involving over-the-counter cash receipts, occasional errors may occur in making change. The cash shortage or overage is revealed when the cash count at the end of the day does not agree with the cash register tape. Assuming that the count is $600 and the cash register reading shows $620, the appropriate journal entry is

Cash	600	
Cash Short and Over	20	
Sales		620

Cash Short and Over is an income statement account that is grouped with miscellaneous expenses or miscellaneous revenue, respectively.

7.7 PETTY CASH

Companies write out checks for cash payments. However, in the case of small expenditures such as postage, taxi fare, and delivery charges it is not feasible to issue a check. Such expenditures are made through a petty cash fund (imprest fund). One individual (custodian) should be responsible for the fund. The fund is available currency and is periodically reimbursed over short intervals of time, usually monthly. At any given point, the fixed amount of the fund consists of the total currency left and the receipts for the expenditures made.

The following procedure is involved in the maintenance of a petty cash fund:

1. *Estimate the amount needed in the fund.* A check is cashed for the anticipated funds to be disbursed for a given period of time. An entry is made in the Petty Cash account when the fund is established, as well as when it is subsequently reimbursed for expenditures made. For a fund set up for $100, the appropriate journal entry is

Petty Cash	100	
Cash		100

2. *Issue petty cash vouchers.* Currency and signed petty cash vouchers are kept in a safe place. When an employee receives currency, the voucher number, date, amount, payee, nature of expenditure, and recipient's signature is written on the voucher. After the expenditure has been made, an entry is prepared in the petty cash book and the voucher is kept along with the money in the petty cash box.

3. *Make entries in the petty cash book.* An illustrative petty cash book follows.

EXAMPLE 2

Petty Cash Book

Date	Explanation	Voucher #	Receipts	Payments	Postage	Taxi	Sundry
Jan. 1	Initiate fund		$100				
3	Taxi fare	1		$ 15		$15	
16	Stamps	2		20	$20		
29	Coffee	3		5			$5
			$100	$ 40	$20	$15	$5
	Balance			60			
			$100	$100			
Feb. 1	Balance		$ 60				
	Replenishment		40				
....							

4. *Replenish the fund when necessary.* The appropriate journal entry for the replenishment of petty cash shown in Example 2 is:

Postage expense	20	
Taxi expense	15	
Miscellaneous expense	5	
Cash		40

The vouchers in support of the amount replenished should be perforated so they will not be used again.

7.8 SHORT-TERM INVESTMENTS

Short-term investments (marketable securities) are investments that a company plans to hold for one year or less. They are classified as current assets. Examples of securities in which idle funds can be invested are corporate stocks (common and preferred), bonds, Treasury bills, and notes.

Marketable securities are highly liquid because they can quickly be converted to cash. The group of marketable securities represents an investment portfolio.

Short-term investments fall into three categories:

1. *Held-to-maturity securities*, which the company intends to hold until the securities' maturity date and on which it earns interest revenue.

2. *Trading securities*, which the company holds primarily for sale in the near term to generate profits on short-term price movements.

3. *Available-for-sale securities*, which are not classified as held-to-maturity securities or trading securities.

All trading securities are short-term in nature, because companies intend to hold them for only a few months or less. Available-for-sale securities may be either short- or long-term investments, depending on the length of time that the company expects to hold them.

7.9 HELD-TO-MATURITY SECURITIES

Only debt securities can be classified as held-to-maturity because, by definition, equity securities have no maturity date. Companies buy held-to-maturity securities to earn interest revenue, and they plan to hold these investments until their maturity date. Many held-to-maturity securities are virtually risk-free. Examples include U.S. Treasury bills, the commercial paper of companies with excellent credit ratings, and bonds.

EXAMPLE 3   On June 1, 20X1, ABC pays $1,500 million for XYZ commercial paper that will mature at $1,500 million in 90 days. All investments are recorded initially at cost.

20X1		(In Millions)	
June 1	Short-term Investments	1,500	
	Cash		1,500

EXAMPLE 4   ABC's fiscal year ends on June 30, so at year-end the company would accrue 30 days' interest revenue that it has earned on the investment. With investments such as commercial paper and U.S. Treasury bills, the accrual of interest revenue increases the carrying (book) value of the investment, as follows:

20X1		(In Millions)	
June 30	Short-term Investments	40	
	Interest revenue ($120 million × 30/90)		40

REPORTING HELD-TO-MATURITY SECURITIES AT AMORTIZED COST ON THE BALANCE SHEET

Held-to-maturity securities are reported on the balance sheet at *amortized cost*, which means cost adjusted for discount or premium amortization.

EXAMPLE 5   At June 30, 20X1, ABC's amortized cost of its investment in XYZ commercial paper is $1,540 million ($1,500 million cost + $40 million accrued interest to date). Assuming that this is ABC's only short-term investment at June 30, 20X1, ABC would report short-term investments at $1,540 million on its balance sheet. Suppose that ABC collects the maturity amount of the XYZ commercial paper on September 1, 20X2. On that day, ABC would record the transaction as follows:

20X2		(In Millions)	
Sept. 1	Cash	1,620	
	Short-term Investments		1,540
	Interest revenue ($120 million × 60/90)		80

7.10 TRADING SECURITIES

Trading securities can be either the stock of another company (equity securities) or debt instruments purchased as a short-term investment. Companies intend to hold trading investments for a very short period of time—a few months at most. Trading securities are classified as current assets on the balance sheet and valued at fair value, which is usually the same as market value—for example, when securities are sold on a stock exchange or in the over-the-counter market. Cost is used only as the initial amount for recording trading investments.

EXAMPLE 6   ABC buys DEF Company stock for $100 million on November 23, 20X2. Assume further that ABC's top management hopes to sell this stock within three months at a gain, so the investment is a trading security. The entry to record the investment in a trading security is as follows:

20X2		(In Millions)	
Nov. 23	Trading Securities	100	
	Cash		100

EXAMPLE 7   DEF stock pays a cash dividend of $2.00 per share, so ABC would receive a dividend on the investment. ABC's entry to record receipt of a $1.5 million dividend on December 14, 20X1, is

20X1		(In Millions)	
Dec. 14	Cash	1.5	
	Dividend Revenue		1.5

REPORTING TRADING SECURITIES AT MARKET VALUE ON THE BALANCE SHEET

Trading investments are reported on the balance sheet at current market value, not at their cost. This rule requires a year-end adjustment of the trading investments from their last carrying amount to current market value.

EXAMPLE 8   Assume that the DEF stock has increased in value, and at June 30, 20X2, ABC's investment in DEF stock is worth $110 million (which is $10 million more than the purchase price). At year-end, ABC would make the following adjustment:

20X2		(In Millions)	
Dec. 31	Allowance to Adjust Trading Securities to Market Value	10	
	Unrealized Gain on Trading Securities		10

An unrealized gain (or loss) is one that is not the result of a sale transaction.

EXAMPLE 9   If the market value of the stock had been less than $100 million, the entry would have been:

Unrealized Loss on Trading Securities	XX	
Allowance to Adjust Trading Securities to Market Value		XX

The next example shows how ABC would report its investment activity in 20X2.

EXAMPLE 10   Suppose that ABC holds both the DEF Company stock, a trading security, and U.S. Treasury bills as held-to-maturity securities with an amortized cost of $810 million. In our example, ABC's short-term investment portfolio consists of the following securities at June 30, 20X2:

	(In Millions)
Held-to-maturity securities:	
U.S. Treasury bills, at amortized cost	$810
Trading Securities:	
DEF Company stock, at current market value	110
Short-term investments, as reported on the balance sheet at June 30, 20X2	$920

The ABC balance sheet reports short-term investments of $920 million at June 30, 20X2.

A company that holds debt instruments (such as corporate bonds) as trading securities accounts for interest revenue in the same way as we showed above for held-to-maturity securities. It reports the trading investments at market value on the balance sheet. The company measures gains and losses as the difference between the securities' current market value and the previous carrying value. Unrealized gains and losses appear on the income statement.

EXAMPLE 11 Suppose that a company began investing in trading securities this year. At the end of 20X0, the following trading portfolio existed:

Stock	Cost	Market Value
Pfizer (2,000 shares)	$250,000	$200,000
Lucent (1,000 shares)	100,000	90,000
Total	$350,000	$290,000

Since the current fair value of the portfolio is $60,000 less than the original cost of $350,000, an adjusting entry is needed to record the unrealized loss as follows:

Date	Description	Debit	Credit
20X0			
Dec. 31	Unrealized Loss on Trading Securities	60,000	
	Allowance to Adjust Trading Securities to Market Value		60,000
	Year-end adjustment for market rise		

REPORTING INTEREST REVENUE, DIVIDEND REVENUE, AND INVESTMENT GAINS AND LOSSES ON THE INCOME STATEMENT

ABC could report its investment revenues, gains, and losses as Other Revenue and Expense on its income statement as shown in Table 7-1.

Table 7-1

ABC Corporation Income Statements Years Ended June 30, 20X2, and June 30, 20X1		
	20X2	20X1
1. Net revenues	$XXX	$XXX
2. Cost of sales	XX	XX
3. Research and development and other expenses	XX	XX
4. Operating income	XX	XX
5. Other revenue and (expense):		
6. Interest expense	(X)	(X)
7. Interest revenue (20X2 amount assumed)	125	30
8. Dividend revenue	1.5	
9. Unrealized gain on investments	10	
10. Income before taxes	XX	XX
11. Income tax expense	X	X
12. Net income	$X	$X

Operating income (line 4) reports on ABC's success in its main operations. Other revenue (line 5) arises from activities other than the company's main operations. When the individual amounts are small, companies like ABC combine the Other Revenues and Expenses and report the net amount as a single figure. For example, ABC could combine the dividend revenue and the unrealized gain (from lines 8 and 9) and report the total of $11.5 million as investment revenue.

GAIN AND LOSSES ON THE SALE OF TRADING SECURITIES

When a company sells a trading investment, the gain or loss on the sale is the difference between the sale proceeds and the last carrying amount of the investment.

EXAMPLE 12 Suppose that ABC sells the DEF stock for $95 million on January 19, 20X2. On that day ABC would record the sale as follows:

20X2		(In Millions)	
Jan. 19	Cash	95	
	Realized Loss on Trading Securities	5	
	Trading Securities		100

This loss results from the sale of the investment. Because the loss was based on a transaction, the loss has been *realized*. We labeled the gain in 20X2 as *unrealized* because ABC had not yet sold the DEF stock. For reporting on the income statement, ABC could combine all gains and losses on short-term investments—realized and unrealized—and report a single net amount under Other Revenue and Expense.

7.11 AVAILABLE-FOR-SALE SECURITIES

Available-for-sale securities are debt and equity securities that are not classified as held-to-maturity or trading. The purpose of this portfolio is to earn a return on funds that may be required for operating purposes in the future. Available-for-sale securities are accounted for in exactly the same way as trading securities, except that the unrealized gain or loss is *not* reported on the income statement, but is reported as a special item in the stockholders' equity section of the balance sheet.

Table 7-2 summarizes the accounting for investments.

Table 7-2
Accounting and Reporting Treatments of Investments

	Category of Investment		
	Held-to-Maturity	Trading	Available-for-Sale
Type	Debt	Debt and equity	Debt and equity
Objective	To earn interest at maturity	To generate profits on price movements	To earn a return for future operating purposes
Accounting method (valuation)	Amortized cost (cost plus accrued interest to date)	Fair value (current market value)	Fair value (current market value)
Classified in the balance sheet	Noncurrent asset	Current asset	Current or noncurrent asset
Unrealized gains and losses	Not recognized	Report on the income statement	Report on the balance sheet

Summary

(1) Creditors would like to see a high amount listed in their customer's _____ account because it shows an entity's ability to pay its obligations.

(2) A company's _____ balance held by a bank is an example of cash that is *not* free for the company's use.

(3) The three parties involved in a check are the _____, _____, and _____ .

(4) A major aspect of internal control is the _____ of duties between the physical custody of cash and its record keeping.

(5) One of the means of controlling cash payments is to _____ the checks.

(6) The signature on the back of a check when it is cashed is referred to as a(n) _____ .

(7) An endorsement that says "pay to the order of" is an example of a(n) _____ endorsement.

(8) The interest income earned by an entity on its bank account is indicated on a(n) _____ memorandum.

(9) A customer's check that "bounces" is termed a(n) _____ check.

(10) In preparing a bank reconciliation, a deposit in transit is _____ to the _____ balance.

(11) When doing a bank reconciliation, if a cash disbursement is overstated relative to the issued check, there should be a(n) _____ to the _____ balance.

(12) After journal entries have been made to adjust the books, the updated _____ account should agree with the bank balance.

(13) If at the end of the day the physical count of cash exceeds that which is indicated by the cash receipts for the day we have a cash _____ .

(14) Cash available for minor expenditures is placed in a(n) _____ fund.

(15) Marketable securities are classified under _____ assets.

(16) Investment portfolio risk can be reduced through _____ .

(17) The cost of a marketable equity security is equal to the _____ plus _____ plus _____ .

(18) Cash dividends earned on a marketable equity security are credited to the _____ account.

(19) A stock dividend or stock split requires only a(n) _____ entry.

(20) After a stock dividend is given, the cost per share _____ .

(21) Short-term investments, also called _____ , are investments that a company plans to hold for one year or less.

(22) _____ can only be debt (not equity), because only debt has a maturity date.

(23) The _____ method is used to account for all _____ investments because they will be sold in the near term at their current market value on the date of sale.

(24) A(n) _____ is one that is the result of a sale transaction.

(25) _____ on available-for-sale securities are reported on the balance sheet as a separate element of _____ .

(26) _____ securities are reported on the balance sheet at amortized cost.

Answers: (1) cash; (2) compensating; (3) drawer, drawee, payee; (4) segregation; (5) prenumber; (6) endorsement; (7) full; (8) credit; (9) NSF; (10) added, bank; (11) addition, book; (12) Cash; (13) overage; (14) petty cash; (15) current; (16) diversification; (17) list price, brokerage commission, transfer taxes; (18) Dividend Income; (19) memorandum; (20) decreases; (21) marketable securities; (22) Held-to-maturity securities; (23) market-value, trading; (24) realized gain (or loss); (25) Unrealized gains and losses, stockholders' equity; (26) Held-to-maturity

Solved Problems

7.1 What are five sources of cash receipts?

SOLUTION

The sources of cash receipts include

1. Sales of merchandise or the rendering of services
2. Collecting on accounts receivable
3. Sale of marketable securities
4. Sale of fixed assets
5. Taking out a bank loan
6. Issuance of a bond payable
7. Issuance of common stock

7.2 What are five types of cash payments?

SOLUTION

Cash payments include

1. Purchase of goods
2. Paying expenses

3. Buying a fixed asset
4. Acquiring marketable securities
5. Paying off a loan
6. Retiring bonds payable or common stock
7. Paying dividends

7.3 A check is shown below. Answer the questions that follow.

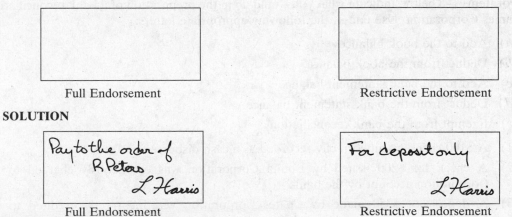

(*a*) Who is the drawer?
(*b*) Who is the drawee?
(*c*) Who is the payee?

SOLUTION

(*a*) Charles Bird is the drawer.
(*b*) Cook County Bank is the drawee.
(*c*) Larry Wink is the payee.

7.4 L. Harris banks at Chemical Bank. She wishes to make an endorsement for R. Peters. (*a*) Prepare a full endorsement. (*b*) Prepare a restrictive endorsement for a deposit.

Full Endorsement	Restrictive Endorsement

SOLUTION

Pay to the order of R. Peters L. Harris	For deposit only L. Harris
Full Endorsement	Restrictive Endorsement

7.5 In preparing a bank reconciliation for Adler Corporation, you note a number of reconciling items. For each item listed below, place an **X** in the appropriate column to indicate how you would treat it in order to produce equal adjusted balances for the books and bank.

	Increase Book Balance	Decrease Book Balance	Increase Bank Balance	Decrease Bank Balance	No Effect
1. Outstanding check					
2. Outstanding certified check					
3. Deposit in transit					
4. Proceeds of a customer note collected by the bank					
5. Proceeds of a loan made to the company by the bank					
6. A customer's bounced check					
7. Bank service charge					

SOLUTION

	Increase Book Balance	Decrease Book Balance	Increase Bank Balance	Decrease Bank Balance	No Effect
1. Outstanding check				X	
2. Outstanding certified check					X
3. Deposit in transit			X		
4. Proceeds of a customer note collected by the bank	X				
5. Proceeds of a loan made to the company by the bank	X				
6. A customer's bounced check		X			
7. Bank service charge		X			

7.6 For items 1–6 below, indicate what you would do in the preparation of a bank reconciliation for James Corporation. Use one of the following appropriate letters:

(a) Add to the book balance

(b) Deduct from the book balance

(c) Add to the bank statement balance

(d) Deduct from the bank statement balance

(e) Exempt from the bank reconciliation

(1) A $100 check was incorrectly recorded as a cash disbursement of $90.

(2) A check for $200 issued by Bonita Corporation was erroneously charged to James Corporation account by the bank.

(3) A deposit of $350 made by Coates Corporation was incorrectly credited to James Corporation.

(4) The company received a customer check of $600 that was incorrectly entered as a cash receipt of $560.

(5) A mistake was made in making out a check and the check was immediately voided.

(6)   A deposit made by the company was erroneously not included in the bank statement.

SOLUTION

1. (*b*); 2. (*c*); 3. (*d*); 4. (*a*); 5. (*e*); 6. (*c*)

7.7   Listed below are transactions involving the bank reconciliation statement. Some transactions require adjusting entries on the depositor's books. Identify those that do and prepare the appropriate adjusting entries.

(1)   Deposit in transit, $650

(2)   Bank charge for printing checks, $30

(3)   Incorrect entry of $440 on depositor's records for a check for rent expense of $400

(4)   Erroneous bank charge of $70 against depositor's account for check issued by another company

(5)   Return of a customer's check marked NSF for $80

SOLUTION

(2)	Bank Service Charge	30	
	Cash		30
(3)	Cash	40	
	Rent Expense		40
(5)	Accounts Receivable	80	
	Cash		80

Transaction (1)—deposit in transit—would be added to the bank balance but requires no adjusting entry. Transaction (4)—bank error—requires the addition of $70 to the bank balance but no adjusting entry.

7.8   The records of XYZ Printing Company showed the following for the month of April:

(1)   Cash balance per books—April 30, $15,000

(2)   Cash balance per bank statement—April 30, $12,850

(3)   On April 30, the following checks were outstanding:

#510	$ 46
#541	$493
#547	$ 89
#601	$ 14

(4)   The following two customer checks deposited by XYZ were returned to the company and were marked NSF:

ABC Shirts	$300
Sign Inc.	$840

(5)   A deposit of $3,100 was made on April 30 but was not included on the bank statement.

(6)   The bank collected a $2,000 note for XYZ from the Uniform Company.

(7)   The bank service charge was $25.

(8)   The bank charged XYZ $527 in error.

Prepare a bank reconciliation as of April 30.

SOLUTION

Balance per books	$15,000	Balance per bank		$12,850
Add: Note receivable collected	2,000	Add:		
	$17,000	Deposit in transit	$3,100	
Less:		Bank error	527	
				3,627
				$16,477
NSF checks	$1,140			
		Less: Outstanding checks		
Service charge	25	#510	$ 46	
	1,165	#541	493	
		#547	89	
		#601	14	
				642
Adjusted balance	$15,835	Adjusted balance		$15,835

7.9 Prepare the bank reconciliation of Stone Insurance Agency as of November 30 using the following information:

(1) Balance per depositor's records, $11,550

(2) Balance per bank statement, $16,840

(3) Outstanding checks, $2,442

(4) Erroneous recording of check #1,558 for telephone expense, $171; actual amount issued by check, $117

(5) Bank service charge, $6

(6) Deposit in transit, $2,760

(7) Note collected by bank acting as Stone's agent, $6,400

(8) NSF check of L. Green, $840

SOLUTION

Balance per depositor's records		$11,550
Add: Noted collected	$6,400	
Error in check #1,558	54	6,454
		$18,004
Deduct: Bank service charge	$ 6	
NSF check of L. Green	840	846
Adjusted balance		$17,158
Balance per bank statement		$16,840
Add: Deposit in transit		2,760
		$19,600
Deduct: Outstanding checks		2,442
Adjusted balance		$17,158

7.10 With regard to Problem 7.9, prepare appropriate adjusting entries.

SOLUTION

Cash	6,454	
Notes Receivable		6,400
Telephone Expense		54

Bank Service Charge	6	
Accounts Receivable	840	
Cash		846

7.11 The accountant for Vida Corporation was unable to prepare correctly the bank reconciliation shown below. He has asked you to correct any mistakes that he has made and to complete the bank reconciliation.

Vida Corporation
Bank Reconciliation
August 31, 20X1

Balance per depositor's books		$7,540
Add: Deposit in transit	$500	
Bank error in crediting another company's deposit to our account	100	600
		$8,140
Deduct: NSF check	$ 70	
Outstanding checks	300	370
Adjusted balance		$7,770
Balance per bank statement		$7,600
Add: Note collected by bank	$200	
Check #107 for $300 applicable to advertising expense was incorrectly written in the checkbook as $330	30	230
		$7,830
Deduct: Transportation costs to and from the bank		50
Adjusted balance		$7,780

SOLUTION

Vida Corporation
Bank Reconciliation
August 31, 20X1

Balance per depositor's books		$7,540
Add: Note collected by bank	$200	
Check $107 for $300 for advertising expense was incorrectly written in the checkbook as $330	30	230
		$7,770
Deduct: NSF check		70
Adjusted balance		$7,700

Balance per bank statement		$7,600
Add: Deposit in transit		500
		$8,100
Deduct: Outstanding checks	$300	
Bank error in crediting another company's deposit to our account	100	
Adjusted balance		400
		$7,700

7.12 Prepare the appropriate adjusting entries for Problem 7.11.

SOLUTION

Cash	230	
Notes Receivable		200
Advertising Expense		30
Accounts Receivable	70	
Cash		70

7.13 Based on the information presented below, prepare a bank reconciliation for Smith Corporation at December 31, 20X1.

  (1) Balance per bank statement—December 31, 20X1, $101,240

  (2) Balance per books—November 30, 20X1, $87,000

  (3) Cash receipts for December 20X1, $40,000

  (4) Cash payments for December 20X1, $38,000

  (5) Outstanding checks—December 31, 20X1:

> #108 for $12,000
> #112 Certified Check for $7,000
> #114 for $5,000

  (6) Received cash—December 31, 20X1, $4,000; deposited on January 2, 20X2

  (7) Return of $300 check, made out to Lakeside Corporation, by the bank on December 26, 20X1, due to absence of countersignature

  (8) Incorrect entry on bank statement for December 16, 20X1, deposit, $2,010; actual deposit, $2,100

  (9) Erroneous charge for $200 against Smith Corporation account for check issued by Stone Corporation

 (10) December 20, 20X1: collection on a note receivable by bank for Smith Corporation, $1,100, including $100 in interest; collection charge, $20

 (11) Bank service charge for December 20X1 per debit memorandum, $50

 (12) Erroneous debit memorandum of December 21, 20X1, to charge the firm's account for settlement of a bank loan in which check #82 was issued on December 20, 20X1, $2,000

 (13) Incorrect credit to Smith Corporation account for December 14, 20X1, Smart Corporation deposit, $800

SOLUTION

Balance per books— December 31, 20X1		$89,000*
Add: Collection of note receivable		
Principal	$ 1,000	
Interest	100	1,100
		$90,100
Deduct: Charge back of Lakeside Corp. check	$ 300	
Service charge	50	
Collection charge	20	370
Adjusted balance		$89,730

Balance per bank statement— December 31, 20X1			$101,240
Add: Deposit in transit		$ 4,000	
Error in deposit		90	
Check of Stone Corp. incorrectly charged to our account		200	
Debit memorandum of December 21, 20X1		2,000	6,290
			$107,530
Deduct: Outstanding checks			
#108	$12,000		
#114	5,000	$17,000	
Deposit of Smart Corp. credited to our account in error		800	17,800
Adjusted balance			$ 89,730

*To determine the *December* book balance, the calculations are

Balance per books—November 30, 20X1	$ 87,000
Add: Cash receipts for December 20X1	40,000
Total	$127,000
Deduct: Cash payments for December 20X1	38,000
Balance per books—December 31, 20X1	$ 89,000

7.14 With regard to Problem 7.13, prepare the appropriate adjusting entries.

SOLUTION

Cash	1,100	
Notes Receivable		1,000
Interest Income		100
Accounts Receivable	300	
Bank Charges	70	
Cash		370

7.15 For the month of January, Smith Corporation had the following transactions relating to the establishment of its petty cash fund:

January 1—An imprest petty cash fund of $300 was set up.

January 31—The petty cash box contained $90 cash plus the following paid vouchers: postage, $80; taxi fares, $60; office supplies, $50; miscellaneous expense, $20.

Prepare appropriate journal entries for the above information.

SOLUTION

Jan. 1	Petty Cash	300	
	Cash		300
31	Postage Expense	80	
	Taxi Fare Expense	60	
	Office Supplies Expense	50	
	Miscellaneous Expense	20	
	Cash		210

7.16 If in Problem 7.15 the cash on hand was $86, prepare the entry for the reimbursement at January 31.

SOLUTION

Postage Expense	80	
Taxi Fare Expense	60	
Office Supplies Expense	50	
Miscellaneous Expense	20	
Cash Short & Over	4	
Cash		214

Note that Cash Short & Over is an income statement account that is closed out at the end of the reporting period to Income Summary.

7.17 If in Problem 7.15 the cash on hand happened to be $97, would there be a cash shortage or overage? Would the account Cash Short & Over be debited or credited?

SOLUTION

There would be a cash overage of $7 ($97 − $90). Cash Short & Over would be credited.

7.18 At the end of the day, the cashier for Marthe's retail store noticed an error. The total cash sales as determined by the sales register tape were $5,600, while the total cash receipts were $5,590. Prepare the appropriate entry to record the cash sales and to reflect the error.

SOLUTION

Cash	5,590	
Cash Short & Over	10	
Sales		5.600

7.19 Park, Inc., paid $1.5 million when it purchased marketable securities in June 20X1. At June 30, 20X1, their amortized cost is $1.52 million, and their market value is $1.6 million.

(*a*) The company plans to hold the marketable securities until maturity. At what amount will the company report the investment on the balance sheet at June 30, 20X1? What will the company report on its 20X1 income statement?

(*b*) The company holds the marketable securities in the hope of selling them at a profit within a few days or weeks. At what amount will the company report the investment on the balance sheet at June 30, 20X1? What will the company report on its income statement for 20X1?

SOLUTION

(*a*) Held-to-maturity, reported as follows on the balance sheet:

	(In millions)
Current Assets:	
Cash	$XX
Short-term Investments at Amortized Cost	1.52

The company's income statement reports:

	(In millions)
Other Revenue and Expenses:	
Interest Revenue ($1.52 − $1.5)	$0.02

(*b*) Trading securities are reported as follows on the balance sheet:

	(In millions)
Current Assets:	
Cash	$XX
Short-term Investments at Market Value	1.6

The company's income statement reports:

	(In millions)
Other Revenue and Expense:	
Unrealized Gain on Investments ($1.6 − $1.5)	0.1

7.20 Prepare the entries for the transactions described below.

March 17—Purchased 90-day Treasury bills for $5,925. This investment will be held to maturity.

June   15—Treasury bills matured; $6,000 received.

SOLUTION

Date	Description	Debit	Credit
March 17	Short-term Investments	5,925	
	Cash		5,925
June 15	Cash	6,000	
	Short-term Investments		5,925
	Interest Income		75

7.21 Howell Equipment Company sells and services a major line of farm equipment. Both sales and service have been profitable. The following transactions affected the company during 20X1:

Jan.   1—Purchased 2,000 shares of Dolphic stock at $40 per share. The purchase was made for trading purposes.

Dec. 28—Received $4,000 cash dividend on the Dolphic stock.

Dec. 31—The current market price is $39.

Give the journal entry for each of the above transactions. Provide all explanations.

SOLUTION

Date	Description	Debit	Credit
Jan. 1	Trading Securities	80,000	
	Cash		80,000
	Purchases Dolphic stock for trading		
Dec. 28	Cash	4,000	
	Revenue from Investments		4,000
	Receipt of dividend on Dolphic stock		
Dec. 31	Unrealized Loss on Trading Securities	2,000	
	Allowance to Adjust Trading		
	Securities to Market Value		2,000
	To record unrealized loss on the stock:		
	2,000 shares × $1 ($40 − $39) = $2,000		

7.22 On June 15, 20X0, Johnson Corporation purchased 3,000 shares of Yum Corporation stock for $30 per share. The purchase was made for trading purposes. At December 31, 20X0, the stock has a market value of $28 per share. On August 12, 20X1, Johnson sold all 3,000 shares for $110,000. Prepare the journal entries for June 15, December 31, and March 12. Provide all explanations.

SOLUTION

Date	Description	Debit	Credit
June 15	Trading Securities	90,000	
	Cash		90,000
	Purchase of Yum stock for trading		
Dec. 31	Unrealized Loss on Trading Securities	6,000	
	Allowance to Adjust Trading		
	Securities to Market Value		6,000
	Year-end adjustment for market decline		
March 12	Cash	110,000	
	Trading Securities		90,000
	Realized Gain on Trading Securities		20,000
	To record sale of Yum stock		

7.23 Make journal entries to record the following transactions for Davidson Corporation for 20X1 and 20X2. Provide all explanations.

20X1

Aug. 13—Purchased 1,000 shares of Constas Corporation stock for $30,000. This purchase was made for trading purposes.

Oct.   5—Purchased 4,000 shares of Perlman Corporation stock for $68,000. This purchase was made for trading purposes.

Nov. 1—Invested $98,000 in 120-day U.S. Treasury bills that have a maturity value of $100,000.

Dec. 31—The market value of Constas shares is $31,000, and the market value of the Perlman shares is $63,000. A year-end adjustment is made.

A year-end adjustment is made to accrue interest on the Treasury bills.

20X2

Mar.   1—Received maturity value of U.S. Treasury bills in cash.

Apr. 14—Sold all 1,000 shares of Constas stock for $30,800.

Sept. 22—Received dividends of $1 per share from Perlman.

Dec. 31—The market value of the Perlman Corporation shares is $70,000. A year-end adjustment is made.

SOLUTION

Date	Description	Debit	Credit
20X1			
Aug. 13	Trading Securities	30,000	
	Cash		30,000
	Purchase of Constas stock for trading		
Oct. 3	Trading Securities	68,000	
	Cash		68,000
	Purchase of Perlman stock for trading		
Nov. 1	Short-term Investments	98,000	
	Cash		98,000
	Purchase of 120-day U.S. Treasury bills		
Dec. 31	Unrealized Loss on Trading Securities	4,000	
	Allowance to Adjust Trading		
	Securities to Market Value		4,000
	Year-end adjustment for market decline		
	Short-term Investments	1,000	
	Interest Income		1,000
	To record accrued interest on T-bills		

Date	Description	Debit	Credit
20X2			
Mar. 1	Cash	100,000	
	Short-term Investments		99,000
	Interest Income		1,000
	Received cash upon maturity of T-bills		
Apr. 14	Cash	30,800	
	Trading Securities		30,000
	Realized Gains on Trading Securities		800
	Sale of Constas stock		
Sept. 22	Cash	4,000	
	Dividend Income		4,000
	Received dividend on Perlman stock		
Dec. 31	Allowance to Adjust Trading Securities		
	to Market Value	6,000	
	Unrealized Gain on Trading Securities		6,000
	Year-end adjustment for market rise		

7.24 On May 31, Haas Corporation invested $59,000 in U.S. Treasury bills. The bills mature in 120 days at $60,000. Prepare entries to record the purchase on May 31; the adjustment to accrue interest on June 30, which is the end of the fiscal year; and the receipt of cash at the maturity date of September 28.

SOLUTION

Date	Description	Debit	Credit
May 31	Short-term Investments	59,000	
	Cash		59,000
	Purchase of 120-day U.S. Treasury bills		
June 30	Short-term Investments	250	
	Interest Income		250
	Accrued interest ($1,000 $\times$ 30/120)		
Sept. 28	Cash	60,000	
	Interest Income		750
	Short-term Investments		59,250
	Receipt of cash and recognition of related interest income		

7.25 Seri Company began investing in trading securities this year. At the end of 20X0, the following trading portfolio existed:

Stock	Cost	Market Value
GM (2,500 shares)	$200,000	$300,000
IBM (1,000 shares)	100,000	75,000
Total	$300,000	$375,000

Prepare the necessary year-end adjusting entry on December 31 and the entry for the sale of all the IBM shares on the following March 23 for $85,000.

SOLUTION

Date	Description	Debit	Credit
20X0			
Dec. 31	Allowance to Adjust Trading Securities		
	to Market Value	75,000	
	Unrealized Gain on Trading Securities		75,000
	Year-end adjustment for market rise		
20X1			
March 23	Cash	85,000	
	Realized Loss on Trading Securities	15,000	
	Trading Securities		100,000
	Sale of 1,000 shares of IBM at less than cost		

7.26 Delta Publishing Company, Inc., purchased 10,000 shares of KMart stock at a price of $25 per share on February 1, 20X1. Management intends to hold these securities for a long period of time as a cushion against a future business downturn. Journalize this investment.

SOLUTION

Feb. 1	Available-for-Sale Securities	250,000	
	Cash		250.000

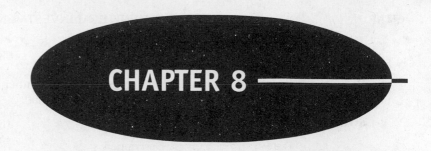

Inventories

8.1 INTRODUCTION

A merchandising business or retail store is mainly involved in selling goods. The merchandise it has on hand for resale is called inventory. Inventory is classified as a *current asset* since it will be converted into cash within one year. For a manufacturing business, three types of inventories exist: raw materials, goods in process, and finished goods.

8.2 PERPETUAL AND PERIODIC INVENTORY METHODS

In the *perpetual method* of inventory valuation an account of the inventory is made upon each purchase and sale. This method is usually used in the type of business where units sold are of relatively *high value*, since the expense of maintaining individual inventory records otherwise would be considered prohibitive.

	Perpetual	Periodic

Purchases	Inventory
	    Cash
		Purchases
		    Cash

Sales	Cash
	    Sales
	
	Cost of Goods Sold
	    Inventory
		Cash
		    Sales

Periodic close-outs	Sales
	    Income Summary
	
	Income Summary
	    Cost of Goods Sold
	
	Income Summary
	    Retained Earnings
		Sales
		    Income Summary
		
		Cost of Goods Sold
		    Inventory (Beginning)
		    Purchases
		
		Inventory (Ending)
		    Cost of Goods Sold
		
		Income Summary
		    Retained Earnings

In the *periodic method* the inventory is counted manually at regular intervals, either monthly, quarterly, semi-annually, or annually. Businesses engaged in the sale of *low-priced* items use the periodic system.

The period system is common in the retail trade, where profits on individual units are meager and the business depends on the sale of large quantities, as is the case with hardware and stationery stores. In this chapter, we are concerned only with the periodic method.

A summary of the accounting for inventory under the perpetual and periodic methods is shown in the following table.

8.3   INVENTORY VALUATION METHODS

There are various methods of determining the value of inventory when identical goods are acquired at different times and prices. The method used does *not* have to conform to the actual, physical flow of the goods. The following data will be used to illustrate the first three methods:

Date/Type	Units	Cost per Unit	Total Cost
Jan. 1 Inventory	150	$ 8	$1,200
Feb. 20 Purchases	200	9	1,800
April 12 Purchases	250	10	2,500
Sept. 20 Purchases	200	11	2,200
Goods available for sale	800		$7,700

Assume that the physical inventory on December 31 is 430 units.

FIRST-IN, FIRST-OUT (FIFO) METHOD

This method assumes that merchandise is sold in the order of its receipt.

EXAMPLE 1   Under the FIFO method, merchandise on hand is considered to be that which was most recently received. Hence, year-end inventory of 430 units is valued as follows:

Last purchase (Sept. 20)	200 units @ $11 =	$2,200
Next most recent purchase (April 12)	230 units @ $10 =	2,300
Total	430	$4,500

The FIFO method really turns out to be first-price-in, first-price-out. Hence, cost of goods sold is based on the older costs. Ending inventory is reflected at the latest costs.

LAST-IN, FIRST-OUT (LIFO) METHOD

In this method we assume that goods are sold in the reverse order of their acquisition.

EXAMPLE 2   Under the LIFO method, ending inventory is reflected at the beginning costs of the purchases made. Therefore, cost of goods sold is based upon the most recent costs. The year-end inventory is computed as follows:

Initial purchase (Jan. 1)	150 units @ $8 =	$1,200
Next purchase (Feb. 20)	200 units @ $9 =	1,800
Next later purchase (April 12)	80 units @ $10 =	800
Total	430	$3,800

LIFO has two advantages over FIFO. First, LIFO matches most recent costs with current sales. Therefore, in a rising spiral net income and thus tax would be reduced. Second, LIFO results in a more accurate measurement of net income in an inflationary period because current costs are matched against current revenue. It therefore results in less "paper" profit.

WEIGHTED-AVERAGE METHOD

To obtain a weighted-average unit cost, the total cost of goods available for sale is divided by the total units available for sale. This average unit cost is then used to determine inventory and cost of goods sold. The advantage of the method is that costs are assigned equally to both inventory and goods sold.

EXAMPLE 3   The average unit cost is computed as follows:

$$\text{Cost per unit} = \frac{\text{Cost of goods available}}{\text{Units available}} = \frac{\$7,700}{800} = \$9.63$$

The value of the ending inventory is therefore

$$430 \text{ units @ } \$9.63 = \$4,141$$

Example 4 compares the results of the three methods discussed above in terms of ending inventory and cost of goods sold. It should be remembered that

$$\text{Cost of goods available for sale} - \text{Ending inventory} = \text{Cost of goods sold}$$

EXAMPLE 4   The tabulated results of these three methods reveal the following comparisons:

	First-In, First-Out	Last-In, First-Out	Weighted Average
Cost of Goods Available for Sale	$7,700	$7,700	$7,700
Less: Ending Inventory, Dec. 31	4,500	3,800	4,141
Cost of Goods Sold	$3,200	$3,900	$3,559

It is to be noted that if the ending inventory is overstated, then the cost of goods sold will be understated and net income overstated. On the other hand, if the ending inventory is understated, then the cost of goods sold will be overstated and net income understated. It is thus evident that the method selected can have a material effect upon the entity's net income and related tax. It also has an effect upon the balance sheet in terms of the inventory valuation.

SPECIFIC IDENTIFICATION METHOD

A fourth method identifies the actual costs by reference to the specific invoices. It is often used when the cost per unit is very high.

EXAMPLE 5

Purchase invoice #1,416 (Feb. 20)	180 units @ $ 9 =	$1,620
Purchase invoice #1,453 (April 12)	130 units @ $10 =	1,300
Purchase invoice #1,498 (Sept. 20)	120 units @ $11 =	1,320
Total	430	$4,240

LOWER OF COST OR MARKET METHOD

A *conservative* means of valuing inventory is derived from the use of the lower of cost or market method. The decline in inventory value is reflected as a loss for the period, regardless of the fact that the inventory has not been sold. Under this method, the *lower* of the unit cost (as determined under FIFO or weighted average) or market price (current replacement cost) of the item is used. The tax law prohibits the use of this approach in conjunction with the LIFO method. Increases in value of inventory are *not* shown since this would violate the conservatism principle.

The lower of cost or market rule is also applicable when the inventory consists of separate lots. Assume the following data:

Lot	Quantity in Units	Unit Cost	Unit Replacement Cost	Total Cost	Total Replacement Cost	Lower of Cost or Market Value
W	200	$ 7.00	$ 7.50	$ 1,400	$ 1,500	$ 1,400
X	250	9.00	10.00	2,250	2,500	2,250
Y	300	10.00	9.00	3,000	2,700	2,700
Z	400	11.00	12.00	4,400	4,800	4,400
Total				$11,050	$11,500	$10,750

If the lower of cost or market rule is applied on an item-by-item basis, inventory would be valued at $10,750. However, an alternative means of applying the rule is to take the lower of the total cost or total market value of the inventory. In this case, inventory would be reflected at $11,050. A third alternative approach is to apply the lower of cost or market value concept to the categories of inventory rather than individual items.

GROSS PROFIT METHOD

The gross profit method can be used to estimate the inventory at the end of an interim period (e.g., quarterly, monthly). This method can also be used to estimate the inventory at the date of a fire for insurance reimbursement.

Under the method, the expected gross profit rate (gross profit to net sales) for the period is used. The ending inventory can be computed by preparing a partial income statement starting with sales and ending with gross profit. The amounts for the beginning inventory, net purchases, and net sales are entered in the partial income statement.

EXAMPLE 6   Assume that the beginning inventory is $15,000, net purchases are $90,000, and net sales are $200,000. The gross profit rate has been running 60 percent of net sales.

Income Statement (partial)

Net Sales		$200,000
Less: Cost of Goods Sold		
Beginning Inventory	$ 15,000	
Net Purchases	90,000	
Cost of Goods Available	$105,000	
Less: Ending Inventory	?	
Cost of Goods Sold		80,000
Gross Profit on Sales (60% × $200,000)		$120,000

Since cost of goods available less ending inventory is equal to cost of goods sold, the ending inventory must be $25,000. The proof is

$$\text{Cost of Goods Available} - \text{Ending Inventory} = \text{Cost of Goods Sold}$$
$$\$105,000 \quad - \quad \$25,000 \quad = \quad \$80,000$$

RETAIL METHOD

Mainly used by department stores and other types of retail establishments, the retail method is based on the relationship between the cost of the goods available for sale and the retail price of such goods. The ending inventory at retail is the difference between the retail price of the goods available for sale less the sales for the period. The inventory is converted from retail to cost based upon the ratio of cost to selling price.

EXAMPLE 7

	Cost	Retail
Merchandise Inventory, December 1	$45,000	$ 60,000
Purchases	50,000	68,000
Merchandise Available for Sale	$95,000	$128,000
Sales for December		100,000
Merchandise Inventory, December 31, at retail		$ 28,000
Merchandise Inventory, December 31, at cost	$20,776*	

$$*\text{Ratio} = \frac{\text{Cost}}{\text{Retail}} = \frac{\$95,000}{\$128,000} = 74.2\%$$

$$\$28,000 \times 74.2\% = \$20,776$$

This method is beneficial in that it provides inventory figures for interim reporting and assists in detecting inventory shortages. However, a complication may arise in practice, if frequent markups and markdowns modify the initially established sales prices.

The topics of purchase discounts, purchase returns and allowances, and transportation in have already been discussed in Chapter 6.

Summary

(1) Inventory is reported in the balance sheet as a(n) _____ asset.

(2) When a daily record is kept of the inventory balance after purchases and sales are made the _____ inventory method is being used.

(3) Retail businesses generally use the _____ method to determine inventory value.

(4) The inventory valuation method which assumes that goods are sold in the order in which they are received is called the _____ method.

(5) The inventory valuation method which assumes that goods are sold in the reverse order of their acquisition is known as the _____ method.

(6) The inventory valuation method which is based upon the determination of unit price by dividing the total cost of goods available for sale by the total number of available units is known as the _____ method.

(7) A company should select the _____ inventory method if it wishes to keep its taxes to a minimum.

(8) Cost of goods available for sale less ending inventory is equal to _____ .

(9) If ending inventory is understated, net income will be _____ .

(10) A valuation system that is used with FIFO or the weighted-average method whose purpose is to obtain the lowest inventory valuation is the _____ method.

(11) The _____ inventory method can be used to estimate the ending inventory for insurance reimbursement in case of a fire.

(12) The _____ method is used by many department stores.

(13) Under the retail method, ending inventory is changed from retail to _____ by application of the ratio of cost to selling price.

Answer: (1) current; (2) perpetual; (3) periodic; (4) first-in, first-out; (5) last-in, first-out; (6) weighted-average; (7) LIFO; (8) cost of goods sold; (9) understated; (10) lower of cost or market; (11) gross profit; (12) retail; (13) cost

Solved Problems

8.1 The following information pertains to a given product:

Jan 1	Inventory	15 units	$20
Feb. 20	Purchase	12 units	24
April 10	Purchase	20 units	25
Nov. 15	Purchase	8 units	16

The physical count of ending inventory reveals that 16 units are on hand. Using the first-in, first-out method, what is the inventory cost?

SOLUTION

Last purchase (Nov. 15)	8	units @ $16 =	$128
Next most recent purchase (April 10)	8	unit @ $25 =	200
Total	16		$328

8.2 Referring to the information in Problem 8.1, what is the ending inventory cost using the last-in, first-out method?

SOLUTION

Initial cost (Inventory)	15	units @ $20 =	$300
Next to earliest purchase (Feb. 20)	1	unit @ $24 =	24
Total	16		$324

8.3 Referring to the data in Problem 8.1, what is the inventory cost using the weighted-average method?

SOLUTION

Jan 1	15	units @ $20 =	$ 300
Feb. 20	12	units @ $24 =	288
April 10	20	units @ $25 =	500
Nov. 15	8	units @ $16 =	128
Total	55		$1,216

$$\text{Average unit cost} = \frac{\$1,216}{55} = \$22.11$$

$$\text{Ending inventory} = \$22.11 \times 16 \text{ units} = \underline{\$353.76}$$

8.4 Using the data in Problem 8.1, determine the inventory value by using the specific identification method. Assume that 5 of the units in ending inventory were purchased on February 20 and 11 of them were purchased on April 10.

SOLUTION

Feb. 20	5	units @ $24 =	$120
April 10	11	units @ $25 =	275
Total	16	units	$395

8.5 Using the information given in the table below, calculate the value of the inventory using the lower of cost or market method applied on an item-by-item basis.

Item	Units	Cost per Unit	Replacement Cost per Unit
M	200	$4.00	$4.50
N	250	5.00	5.50
P	300	6.00	5.00
R	350	7.00	6.00

SOLUTION

Item	Units	Unit Valuation	Lower of Cost or Market
M	200	$4.00 (C)	$ 800
N	250	5.00 (C)	1,250
P	300	5.00 (M)	1,500
R	350	6.00 (M)	2,100
Total			$5,650

The (C) refers to the cost per unit, while the (M) is the replacement cost or market value.

8.6 Based on the information provided in Problem 8.5, determine the inventory value by using the lower of cost or market method applied on a total inventory basis.

SOLUTION

Item	Units	Unit Cost	Total Cost	Unit Replacement Cost	Total Replacement Cost
M	200	$4.00	$ 800	$4.50	$ 900
N	250	5.00	1,250	5.50	1,375
P	300	6.00	1,800	5.00	1,500
R	350	7.00	2,450	6.00	2,100
			$6,300		$5,875

The ending inventory would be valued at $5,875, since total market value is less than total cost.

8.7 The beginning inventory and subsequent purchases of product N follow:

Jan. 1	Balance	10 units @ $11
Mar. 10	Purchase	14 units @ $12
June 12	Purchase	18 units @ $13
Sept. 16	Purchase	16 units @ $14
Dec. 8	Purchase	20 units @ $15

A count of ending inventory revealed that 32 units were on hand. Compute the ending inventory using the following methods: (*a*) first-in, first-out; (*b*) last-in, first-out; and (*c*) weighted average.

SOLUTION

(a)

	Last purchase (Dec. 8)	20 @ $15 = $300
	Next most recent purchase (Sept. 16)	12 @ $14 = 168
	Total	32 $468

(b)

	Inventory (Jan. 1)	10 @ $11 = $110
	Next earliest purchase (March 10)	14 @ $12 = 168
	Next earliest purchase (June 12)	8 @ $13 = 104
	Total	32 $382

(c)

10 @ $11 = $ 110
14 @ $12 = 168
18 @ $13 = 234
16 @ $14 = 224
20 @ $15 = 300
78        $1,036

$$\text{Average unit cost} = \frac{\$1,036}{78} = \$ 13.28$$

$$\text{Ending inventory} = 32 \text{ units} \times \$13.28 = \$424.96$$

8.8 A condensed income statement for Lakeside Corporation is presented below.

Sales		$100,000
Less: Cost of Goods Sold		
Beginning Inventory	$20,000	
Purchases	30,000	
Cost of Goods Available	$50,000	
Less: Ending Inventory	14,000	
Cost of Goods Sold		36,000
Gross Profit		$ 64,000
Operating Expenses		29,000
Net Income		$ 35,000

It has been determined that the ending inventory is overstated by $2,000. What is the effect on (a) cost of goods sold and (b) net income?

SOLUTION

(a) Cost of goods sold is understated by $2,000.

(b) Net income is overstated by $2,000.

8.9 Winston Corporation has hired you to estimate its inventory on March 31 by the gross profit method for interim reporting purposes. The gross profit rate has been 35 percent. The following data are provided:

Inventory—March 1	$ 40,000
Sales	250,000
Purchases	150,000

SOLUTION

Sales		$250,000
Less: Cost of Goods Sold		
Inventory—March 1	$ 40,000	
Purchases	150,000	
Cost of Goods Available	$190,000	
Less: Inventory—March 31	27,500*	
Cost of Goods Sold (Sales − Gross Profit)		
Gross Profit (35% × $250,000)		162,500
		$ 87,500

*The ending inventory is equal to goods available minus goods sold in that period:

$$\$190,000 - \$162,500 = \$27,500$$

8.10　On January 1, 20X6, the merchandise inventory of Manuel Company was $300,000. During 20X6 Manuel Co. purchased $1,900,000 of merchandise and recorded sales of $2,000,000. The gross profit on these sales was 20 percent. What is the merchandise inventory of Manuel Co. at December 31, 20X6? (AICPA Adapted)

SOLUTION

Sales		$2,000,000
Less: Cost of Goods Sold		
Inventory—January 1	$ 300,000	
Purchases	1,900,000	
Cost of Goods Available	$2,200,000	
Less: Inventory—December 31	600,000*	
Cost of Goods Sold		1,600,000
Gross Profit (20% × $2,000,000)		$ 400,000

*Ending Inventory equals: $2,200,000 − $1,600,000 = $600,000

8.11　The following information is available for The Gant Company for 20X6:

Freight in	$ 20,000
Purchase returns	80,000
Selling expenses	200,000
Ending inventory	90,000

The cost of goods sold is equal to seven times the selling expenses. What is the cost of goods available for sale? (AICPA Adapted)

SOLUTION

    The cost of goods available for sale is equal to the cost of goods sold plus the ending inventory. Since the cost of goods sold is equal to seven times the selling expenses, it is 7 × $200,000, or $1,400,000. Since the ending inventory is $90,000, the cost of goods available for sale is $1,400,000 plus $90,000, or $1,490,000.

8.12   Using the retail method, what is the estimated cost of the December 31 inventory?

	Cost	Retail
Inventory—December 1	$340,000	$480,000
Purchases	120,000	200,000
Goods available for sale	$460,000	$680,000
Sales		400,000

SOLUTION

	Cost	Retail
Inventory—December 1	$340,000	$480,000
Purchases	120,000	200,000
Goods available for sale	$460,000	$680,000
Sales		400,000
Inventory at retail—December 31		$280,000
Inventory at cost—December 31	$189,280*	

*Cost ratio: $\dfrac{\$460,000}{\$680,000} = 67.6\%$

Ending inventory: $280,000 \times 67.6\% = \$189,280$

8.13   Using the retail method, compute the cost of the following June 30 inventory.

	Cost	Retail
Inventory—June 1	$24,000	$30,000
Purchases	40,000	60,000
Sales		40,000

SOLUTION

	Cost	Retail
Inventory—June 1	$24,000	$30,000
Purchases	40,000	60,000
Goods available for sale	$64,000	$90,000
Sales		40,000
Inventory at retail—June 30		$50,000
Inventory at cost—June 30	$35,550*	

*Cost ratio: $\dfrac{\$64,000}{\$90,000} = 71.1\%$

Ending inventory: $50,000 \times 71.1\% = \$35,550$

CHAPTER 9

Receivables and Payables

9.1 ACCOUNTS RECEIVABLE

It is expected that some customers will not pay their balances. Therefore, provision must be made in the accounting records to reflect this fact. Under operating expenses in the income statement is shown an account called Uncollectible Accounts Expense, representing the *anticipated* uncollectible accounts on sales made for the current year. In the balance sheet is shown the *net* amount of accounts receivable, representing the amount expected to be collected rather than the gross amount of the receivables. The difference between the gross and net amounts represents the expected uncollectible accounts.

The direct-write-off method and the allowance method are two ways of accounting for uncollectible accounts.

DIRECT-WRITE-OFF METHOD

Under this method, the uncollectible accounts expense is recognized in the period that receivables *actually* become worthless. The journal entry is

Uncollectible Accounts Expense
Accounts Receivable

EXAMPLE 1 Merchandise of $1,000 was sold to Franklin Jones on July 6, 20X7. His account was considered uncollectible on February 7, 20X8. The journal entry on February 7 is

Feb. 7	Uncollectible Accounts Expense	1,000	
	Accounts Receivable		1,000

Note that the expense is recorded in the year *after* revenue is recognized. Therefore, a deficiency of the direct-write-off method is that it fails to match the uncollectible accounts expense against revenue in the year of sale.

Since there is no valuation allowance account, accounts receivable are shown in the balance sheet at their gross amount.

ALLOWANCE METHOD

The allowance method *corrects* for the drawback of the direct-write-off method in terms of *matching* expenses against revenue. The uncollectible accounts expense is deducted in the year of sale. Unless uncollectible accounts are *estimated* and reflected in the balance sheet and income statement, the financial statements will be misstated.

The following journal entry is made at *year's end* to record the anticipated uncollectibles of accounts receivable:

Uncollectible Accounts Expense
Allowance for Uncollectible Accounts

The allowance account is shown as an offset (contra) to gross accounts receivable in order to arrive at net accounts receivable. The net figure represents the *realizable value* of the receivables.

EXAMPLE 2 EIZ Corporation was formed this year. At year's end, the accounts receivable balance is $50,000. It is estimated that $2,000 of the customer balances will be uncollectible. The journal entry is

Uncollectible Accounts Expense	2,000	
Allowance for Uncollectible Accounts		2,000

The year-end balance sheet shows the estimated realizable value of the accounts receivable:

Accounts Receivable	$50,000	
Less: Allowance for Uncollectible Accounts	2,000	$48,000

9.2 COMPUTING THE PROVISION FOR UNCOLLECTIBLE ACCOUNTS

The uncollectible accounts expense may be computed based upon a given percentage of current year *net credit* sales, a stated percentage of gross accounts receivable, or an *aging* of the year-end gross accounts receivable balance.

PERCENT-OF-SALES METHOD

This method is an income statement approach to estimating bad debts. The expense provision is computed by multiplying the current year's net credit sales by a flat rate for uncollectibles. The rate is based upon past experience and modified in light of the current environment.

EXAMPLE 3 Charge sales for 20X3 are $220,000. The anticipated uncollectibility rate is 1 percent of sales. The allowance account currently has a balance of $1,200. The journal entry is

Uncollectible Accounts Expense	2,200	
Allowance for Uncollectible Accounts		2,220

Under this method, the balance in the allowance account of $1,200 is *irrelevant* in making the year-end journal entry. We must add to the allowance account for the anticipated uncollectibility of *current* year credit sales. The relationship stressed here is between the current year's uncollectible accounts expense and the current year's net credit sales. However, if the balance in the allowance account is significant, a change in the percentage for uncollectibles may be required. For example, an excessively high credit balance would warrant a reduction in the bad-debt percentage.

AGING METHOD

This method is balance-sheet oriented in that each customer's account balance is *aged* based upon the date of sale. The longer an account is past due, the greater is the probability of it being uncollectible.

EXAMPLE 4

Age of Account	Year-End Gross Accounts Receivable Balance	Uncollectible Percentage	Amount Needed in Allowance Account at Year's End
1–30 days	$12,000	1	$ 120
31–60 days	28,000	3	840
61–90 days	8,000	5	400
Over 90 days	2,000	12	240
	$50,000		$1,600

Since the amount needed in the allowance account is $1,600 based upon an analysis of year-end receivables, an adjusting entry is needed to bring the current allowance account balance up to that amount. The amount of the adjusting entry is therefore equal to the difference between the current amount and the amount needed according to the aging schedule. If the allowance account has a credit balance of $1,200, the year-end journal entry is

Uncollectible Accounts Expense	400	
Allowance for Uncollectible Accounts		400

EXAMPLE 5 Assume the same information as in Example 4 except that the allowance account has a debit balance of $1,200. The journal entry is

Uncollectible Accounts Expense	2,800	
Allowance for Uncollectible Accounts		2,800

After this entry, the allowance account will have the desired $1,600 balance in it ($2,800 − $1,200).

9.3 WRITING OFF A CUSTOMER'S ACCOUNT

When it is obvious that a customer is no longer able to pay the amount due (for example, the customer has declared bankruptcy), the account should be written off. The journal entry is

Allowance for Uncollectible Accounts	
Accounts Receivable	

The allowance account is debited because part of the allowance provision established for future uncollectibles has now been used up.

EXAMPLE 6   Joy Butler owes us $1,000. Her account is deemed worthless. The entry is

Allowance for Uncollectible Accounts	1,000	
Accounts Receivable		1,000

The *net* amount of the accounts receivable is *not* affected by the write-off since the gross receivables and the allowance account are reduced by the same amount.

9.4 SUBSEQUENT RECOVERY OF WRITTEN-OFF RECEIVABLE

A full or partial recovery of a previously written-off customer account balance may occur. For example, the customer may unexpectedly receive funds from another source and wish to reinstate his or her business activities. The journal entry to restore the account is

Accounts Receivable
Allowance for Uncollectible Accounts

The receipt of funds to settle the account in full or in part would be recorded in the usual fashion by debiting cash and crediting accounts receivable.

EXAMPLE 7   Referring to Example 6, assume that Butler agrees to pay back only $600. The journal entries are

Accounts Receivable	600	
Allowance for Uncollectible Accounts		600
Cash	600	
Accounts Receivable		600

9.5 PROMISSORY NOTES

The maker of a promissory note agrees to pay a given amount to a payee at a future date. Therefore, a promissory note is a payable to the maker and a receivable to the payee.

There are several advantages to a promissory note. The holder may obtain money for the note prior to its maturity from a bank. This is referred to as *discounting* the note. The note also serves as written evidence of a debt due and as such represents a priority lien compared to an open account receivable.

9.6 INTEREST COMPUTATION

Interest is usually computed on the basis of a 360-day year (12 months × 30 days per month). The following formula is used:

$$\text{Interest} = \text{Principal} \times \text{Interest Rate} \times \text{Time}$$

The *principal* is the face amount of the note. The *interest rate* is what is being earned on an annual basis on the note. The *time* is the fraction of the year that the note is held.

EXAMPLE 8   An $800, 16 percent, 90-day note is issued. The interest is

$$\$800 \times 16\% \times 90/360 = \$32$$

EXAMPLE 9   A $1,200, 15 percent, 45-day note is issued. The interest is

$$\$1,200 \times 15\% \times 45/360 = \$22.50$$

9.7 DETERMINING THE MATURITY DATE

The date upon which the note is due may be determined through the following steps:

1. In the month that the note is issued, determine the number of days in that month subsequent to the issuance date. The day upon which the note was issued is *not* counted.
2. Add the days in each *full* month after the note's issuance date.
3. Deduct the total days arrived at in steps 1 and 2 from the time period of the note. This will give the due date in the appropriate month (the month after the last full month in step 2).

EXAMPLE 10   The maturity date of a 90-day note dated May 6 is

Time Period of Note		90
	May 31	
Issuance Date	−6	25
	June	30
	July	31
	Total	86
Maturity Date	August	4

If the due date is given in months, the maturity date is found by counting the months from the date upon which the note was written.

EXAMPLE 11   A four-month note dated February 10 is due on June 10. A one-month note dated October 31 is due November 30.

9.8 NOTES RECEIVABLE

A note receivable is an asset because a claim exists for future collection. Interest earned on the note is credited to the interest income account.

EXAMPLE 12   John Cahill owes Roberta Hawkins $600. Mrs. Hawkins receives a 90-day, 16 percent note as settlement. Her journal entry is

Notes Receivable	600	
Accounts Receivable		600

The interest is not recorded until it is *due*, 90 days later. At that time, the interest income will become part of the journal entry as follows:

Cash	624	
Notes Receivable		600
Interest Income		24*

---

*$600 × 16% × 90/360 = $24

9.9 DISCOUNTING A NOTE RECEIVABLE

The holder of a note may receive money for it from a bank or finance company prior to its maturity date. This is referred to as "discounting a note receivable." The proceeds received by the holder at the time the note is discounted is equal to the *maturity value* less the bank discount (interest charge). The bank discount is based upon the period of time the bank will be holding the note and the note's interest rate. The interest rate charged by the bank need *not* be the same as the interest rate on the maker's note. This may be due to changes in the going interest rate over time due to current money market conditions. The maturity value of the note is

$$\text{Maturity Value} = \text{Face of Note} + \text{Interest Income}$$

The bank discount is

$$\text{Bank Discount} = \text{Maturity Value} \times \text{Discount Rate} \times \text{Period Note is Held by Bank}$$

The net proceeds received by the payee at the time of discounting equal

$$\text{Net Proceeds} = \text{Maturity Value} - \text{Bank Discount}$$

On the date that a note is discounted, cash is debited for the net proceeds received, notes receivable is credited for the face amount of the note, and interest income is credited for the *net* interest earned by the holder.

If the maker pays to the bank his or her note at maturity, no further entry is required by the payee. In this case, the bank has received the maturity value of the note.

A default on a note receivable is discussed in a subsequent section.

EXAMPLE 13 Mr. Small holds a $1,000, 120-day, 18 percent note dated September 6. It is discounted at 18 percent on October 6. The interest on the note is

$$\$1,000 \times 18\% \times 120/360 = \$60$$

The maturity value is

$$\$1,000 + \$60 = \$1,060$$

At the time Mr. Small discounted the note, he had already held it for 30 days. The bank will therefore be holding it for 90 days. The bank discount charge is

$$\$1,060 \times 18\% \times 90/360 = \$47.70$$

Therefore, the net proceeds received by Mr. Small are

$$\$1,060.00 - \$47.70 = \$1,012.30$$

The journal entry to record the discounting of the note is

Cash	1,012.30	
Notes Receivable		1,000.00
Interest Income		12.30

If the note is paid by the maker at maturity, no further entry is required by Mr. Small.

The same computational procedure is followed even when the bank discount rate is different from the interest rate on the face of the note. The only numbers that change are the bank discount charge and the net proceeds.

EXAMPLE 14   Assume the same information as in Example 13 except that the bank discount rate is 19 percent rather than 18 percent.

The interest on the note and the maturity value are the same as before. The bank discount charge is now

$$\$1,060 \times 19\% \times 90/360 = \$50.35$$

The net proceeds become

$$\$1,060.00 - \$50.35 = \$1,009.65$$

The entry to record the discounting of the note is now

Cash	1,009.65	
Notes Receivable		1,000.00
Interest Income		9.65

The interest income is less than before since the higher bank discount charge reduces the interest earned by Mr. Small for the 30 days he held the note.

If the bank discount rate significantly exceeds the interest rate on the note, it is possible that the proceeds received may be less than the face value of the note. In this case, interest expense would be debited for the difference.

EXAMPLE 15   Assume that in Example 13 the bank discount rate was 24 percent. The bank discount charge is now

$$\$1,060 \times 24\% \times 90/360 = \$63.60$$

The net proceeds become

$$\$1,060.00 - \$63.60 = \$996.40$$

The journal entry is

Cash	996.40	
Interest Expense	3.60	
Notes Receivable		1,000.00

9.10   DEFAULT ON A NOTE RECEIVABLE

A note is *dishonored* if the issuer does not pay it at maturity. In this case, the principal and interest earned are charged to the maker's account. The journal entry is

Accounts Receivable		
Notes Receivable		
Interest Income		

Note that interest income is recorded even though not collected, since the payee is entitled to it.

EXAMPLE 16 A $600, 60-day, 16 percent note issued by a customer is dishonored at the maturity date. The journal entry is

Accounts Receivable	616	
Notes Receivable		600
Interest Income		16*

———————————

*$600 × 16% × 60/360 = $16

The discounting of a note receivable results in a *contingent* (potential) liability upon the part of the payee that requires disclosure as a footnote in financial statements. If the maker defaults on the note, the payee—who already has received payment upon the note from the bank—must make good on the note's maturity value. In addition, the payee is charged a protest fee by the bank, but payment of the protest fee is ultimately the responsibility of the maker of the note; that is, the amount paid by the payee is charged back to the maker. The journal entry is

Accounts Receivable
   Cash

EXAMPLE 17 A $5,000, 60-day, 15 percent note was discounted at the bank. On the due date, the note is dishonored by the maker. A protest fee of $10 is charged. The journal entry is

Accounts Receivable	5,135*	
Cash		5,135

———————————

*Face of the note	$5,000
Interest ($5,000 × 15% × 60/360)	125
Maturity value	$5,125
Protest fee	10
Chargeback to the maker of the note	$5,135

9.11 NOTES PAYABLE

A note payable may be issued either to make a purchase, settle an open account payable, or borrow from the bank.

EXAMPLE 18 A machine was purchased for $5,000 by issuing a note payable. The journal entry is

Machinery	5,000	
Notes Payable		5,000

EXAMPLE 19 A company owes $4,000 to a creditor on open account. The creditor is aware of current financial problems with the company and desires a written, signed promise. Hence, at the creditor's request, a 90-day, 15 percent note is issued in substitution of the open account. The journal entry for the company is

Accounts Payable	4,000	
Notes Payable		4,000

At the maturity date, the entry is

Notes Payable	4,000	
Interest Expense	150*	
Cash		4,150

———————————

*$4,000 × 15% × 90/360 = $150

A note payable is typically issued to the bank when money is borrowed. Often, the bank immediately deducts the interest on the loan from the face of the note. The borrower receives the net proceeds. The term "discounting a note payable" refers to the case where interest is paid in advance.

EXAMPLE 20   A company borrows $10,000 for 60 days at 18 percent from a bank. The loan is made on a *discount* basis, where interest of $300 ($10,000 × 18% × 60/360) is deducted in advance. The journal entry is

Cash	9,700	
Interest Expense	300	
Notes Payable		10,000

At the maturity date, the entry is

Notes Payable	10,000	
Cash		10,000

Summary

(1)   The method of recording the uncollectible accounts expense at the time of actual customer uncollectibility is known as the _____ method.

(2)   The _____ method accounts for the expected uncollectibility of customer accounts and involves the matching of expenses to sales.

(3)   Determining the amount and time outstanding in each customer's account is referred to as _____ the accounts receivable.

(4)   The entry for the uncollectible accounts expense should be made at _____.

(5)   Uncollectible accounts expense is shown in the _____.

(6)   The Allowance for Uncollectible Accounts is a(n) _____ account to accounts receivable in the _____.

(7)   The write-off of a customer's account under the allowance method will have _____ upon net accounts receivable.

(8)   Interest on a note is equal to _____ × rate × time.
(9)   The interest on a $1,600, 90-day, 20 percent note is _____.

(10)   The maturity date of a 90-day note issued May 14 is _____.

(11)   The _____ of a note is equal to the principal plus interest.

(12)   If Ralph Winslow issues a $500 note to Althea Baker, Winslow is called the _____ and Baker is the _____.

(13)   A note is considered a _____ to the payee.

(14) When a promissory note is received from an open account, _____ receivable is debited and _____ receivable is credited.

(15) The term _____ is used when the payee of a note obtains funds for it from the bank prior to the maturity date.

(16) When a note receivable is discounted, the bank's discount charge is equal to the _____ × discount rate × unexpired time.

(17) When a note is discounted at the bank, the net proceeds received by the payee is equal to the _____ less the _____ .

(18) Notes receivable discounted represents a(n) _____ liability.

(19) If a note is dishonored by the maker at maturity, _____ is debited, _____ is credited, and _____ is credited.

Answers: (1) direct-write-off; (2) allowance; (3) aging; (4) year's end; (5) income statement; (6) contra (offset), balance sheet; (7) no effect; (8) principal; (9) $80; (10) August 12; (11) maturity value; (12) maker, payee; (13) receivable; (14) notes, accounts; (15) discounting; (16) maturity value; (17) maturity value, bank discount; (18) contingent; (19) accounts receivable, notes receivable, interest income

Solved Problems

9.1 Atlas Company uses the direct-write-off method to account for its uncollectible accounts. In 20X1, credit sales were $130,000. On March 7, 20X2, a customer owing $1,600 was declared bankrupt. Prepare journal entries relating to uncollectible accounts for (*a*) 20X1 and (*b*) March 7, 20X2.

SOLUTION

(*a*) No entry is made since the uncollectible is recognized when the receivable actually becomes worthless.

(*b*)   March 7   Uncollectible Accounts Expense   1,600
                                   Accounts Receivable   1,600

9.2 The December 31, 20XX, trial balance of the Mark Company before adjustments included the following accounts:

	Debit	Credit
Allowance for doubtful accounts	$2,000	
Sales		$830,000
Sales returns and allowances	10,000	

Mark estimates its bad debts based upon 2 percent of net sales. What amount should Mark record as bad debt expense for 20XX? (AICPA Adapted)

SOLUTION

Net Sales	$820,000
Percent of Net Sales	×2%
Bad-Debt Expense	$16,400

9.3   The following account balances are for Cobb Incorporated:

Accounts Receivable	Sales	Allowance for Uncollectible Accounts
110,000	320,000	300

Prepare the adjusting entry to provide for bad debts if the uncollectible expense is estimated (*a*) at 1 percent of net sales and (*b*) by aging the accounts receivable and assuming the needed allowance balance is estimated at $3,300.

SOLUTION

(*a*)   Uncollectible Accounts Expense   3,200*

               Allowance for Uncollectible Accounts   3,200

*1% × $320,000 = $3,200

(*b*)   Uncollectible Accounts Expense   3,000*

               Allowance for Uncollectible Accounts   3,000

*Desired Allowance Balance	$3,300
Current Allowance Balance	300
Additional Allowance Needed	$3,000

9.4   Use the aging schedule below to make the adjusting entry needed to provide for the uncollectible accounts expense. Assume the allowance account has a credit balance of $2,400.

Age of Account	Amount	Percentage Uncollectible	Amount Needed in Allowance Account at Year's End
1–30 days	$28,000	1	$ 280
31–60 days	19,000	4	760
61–180 days	9,000	20	1,800
181 days and over	5,000	50	2,500
Total	$61,000		$5,340

SOLUTION

Uncollectible Accounts Expense   2,940*

          Allowance for Uncollectible Accounts   2,940

*Desired Allowance Balance	$5,340
Current Credit Allowance Balance	2,400
Additional Allowance Needed	$2,940

9.5   With regard to Problem 9.4, what will be reported in the balance sheet?

SOLUTION

Account Receivable	$61,000
Less: Allowance for Uncollectible Accounts	5,340
Net Realizable Value	$55,660

9.6   Assume the same facts as in Problem 9.4 except that the allowance account has a debit balance of $2,400. Prepare the appropriate journal entry.

SOLUTION

Uncollectible Accounts Expense	7,740*	
Allowance for Uncollectible Accounts		7,740

*Desired Allowance Balance	$5,340
Current Debit Allowance Balance	2,400
Additional Allowance Needed	$7,740

9.7   At December 31, 20X7, the Avec Company's account balances for accounts receivable and the related allowance for uncollectible accounts were $800,000 and $40,000, respectively. An aging of accounts receivable indicated that $71,100 of the December 31 receivable may be uncollectible. What is the realizable value of accounts receivable? (AICPA Adapted)

SOLUTION

Accounts Receivable	$800,000
Less: Allowance for Uncollectible Accounts	71,100
Net Realizable Value	$728,900

9.8   Prepare journal entries for the following transactions:

May 10—W. Hook's account of $1,100 was deemed uncollectible.

June 20—S. Brooks, who owes us $900, has been declared bankrupt.

July   7—W. Hook paid us back $800.

SOLUTION

May 10	Allowance for Uncollectible Accounts	1,100	
	Accounts Receivable		1,100
June 20	Allowance for Uncollectible Accounts	900	
	Accounts Receivable		900
July 7	Accounts Receivable	800	
	Allowance for Uncollectible Accounts		800
	Cash	800	
	Accounts Receivable		800

9.9   During 20X8 Boyd Corporation, which uses the allowance method of accounting for uncollectible accounts, recorded charges of $50,000 to bad-debt expense and in addition wrote off, as uncollectible, accounts receivable of $42,000. As a result of these transactions by how much was working capital decreased? (AICPA Adapted)

SOLUTION

Working capital = Current assets − Current liabilities

Of the two transactions mentioned, only the charge (see Example 2) to bad-debt expense had any effect on working capital. Working capital was reduced because *net* accounts receivable, a current asset, was decreased as the allowance increased.

The write-off (see Example 6) of bad debts has no working capital effect. In a write-off both the allowance account and accounts receivable are reduced, so there is no effect on *net* accounts receivable. Therefore, the answer is $50,000.

9.10   An example of a note receivable follows:

Date: May 15, 20X2

I, Juanita Sentry, promise to pay Anchor Hardware $400 at
15% interest 60 days from now.

Juanita Sentry

(*a*) Who is the payee?

(*b*) Who is the maker?

(*c*) What is the maturity date?

(*d*) What is the maturity value?

SOLUTION

(*a*) Anchor Hardware

(*b*) Juanita Sentry

(*c*) July 14, 20X2

The maturity date is determined as follows:

Time Period of Note			60
Issuance Date	May 31		
	−15	16	
	June	30	
	Total		46
Maturity Date	July		14

(d) $410

The maturity value is determined as follows:

Principal	$400
Interest ($400 × 15% × 60/360)	10
Maturity Value	$410

9.11 Determine the interest on a $10,000, 150-day, 20 percent note.

SOLUTION

$$\$10,000 \times 20\% \times 150/360 = \$833.33$$

9.12 A note dated March 1 is due June 25. It was discounted at the bank on May 15. (a) How many days is the note for? (b) How many days did the bank hold the note?

SOLUTION

(a)

March	31	
Issued	−1	30
April		30
May		31
June		25
Time Period of Note		116 days

(b)

May	31	
Discounted	−15	16
June		25
Held by Bank		41 days

9.13 An $8,000, 90-day, 16 percent note is discounted at the bank after it has been held for 30 days. The bank discount rate is 16 percent. Determine the proceeds of the note.

SOLUTION

Interest: $8,000 × 16% × 90/360 = $320
Maturity value: $8,000 + $320 = $8,320
Bank discount charge: $8,320 × 16% × 60/360 = $221.87
Proceeds: $8,320.000 − $221.87 = $8,098.13

9.14 Prepare the journal entries needed for the information given in Problem 9.13 (a) at the time of discounting and (b) when the note is paid at maturity.

SOLUTION

(a)

Cash	8,098.13	
Notes Receivable		8,000.00
Interest Income		98.13

(b) No further entry is needed since the note was paid at maturity (see Section 9.9).

9.15 Journalize the following transactions:

March 1—Received a $3,000, 90-day, 18 percent note to settle Kenny Smith's account.

March 31—Discounted the note at the bank (discount rate = 19 percent).

May 30—Kenny Smith dishonored the note at maturity. A protest fee of $4 was charged.

June 4—Smith paid the note and the protest fee.

SOLUTION

March 1	Notes Receivable	3,000	
	Accounts Receivable		3,000
31	Cash	3,035.72*	
	Notes Receivable		3,000.00
	Interest Income		35.72
May 30	Accounts Receivable	3,139**	
	Cash		3,139
June 4	Cash	3,139	
	Accounts Receivable		3,139

*Interest on the note is: $3,000 × 18% × 90/360 = $135
The maturity value is: $3,000 + $135 = $3,135
The bank discount charge is: $3,135 × 19% × 60/360 = $99.28
The net proceeds are: $3,135.00 − $99.28 = $3,035.72

**$3,135 + $4 = $3,139

9.16 A $10,000, 120-day, 15 percent note is discounted at the bank after 30 days have elapsed. The bank discount rate is 20 percent. Prepare the journal entry at the time of discounting.

SOLUTION

Cash	9,975*	
Interest Expense	25	
Notes Receivable		10,000

*The interest on the note is: $10,000 × 15% × 120/360 = $500.
The maturity value is: $10,000 + $500 = $10,500.
The bank discount charge is: $10,500 × 20% × 90/360 = $525.
The proceeds are: $10,500 − $525 = $9,975.

9.17 James Corporation borrowed $6,000 for 60 days at 20 percent interest from the Sunset Bank. Interest is to be paid in advance. Prepare the journal entries to record (*a*) the loan and (*b*) the payment.

SOLUTION

(*a*)	Cash	5,800	
	Interest Expense	200*	
	Notes Payable		6,000

*$6,000 × 20% × 60/360 = $200

(b)	Notes Payable	6,000	6,000
	Cash		

9.18   With regard to Problem 9.17, what entry would be made at the end of 60 days if James Corporation were unable to repay the loan and an additional 60-day renewal were given? Assume interest is to be paid in advance.

SOLUTION

Interest Expense	200	
Cash		200

Because the note has been renewed, only interest is to be paid at renewal date.

9.19   If in Problem 9.17 the interest was to be paid upon maturity of the note, what entries would be made to record (a) the loan and (b) the payment?

SOLUTION

(a)	Cash	6,000	
	Notes Payable		6,000

(b)	Notes Payable	6,000	
	Interest Expense	200	
	Cash		6.200

EXAMINATION III

Chapters 7-9

1. The following transactions relate to a petty cash fund for the month of January:

   January 1—Established a petty cash fund for $100.

   January 31—The petty cash box showed the following receipts for the month: office supplies, $15; cleaning, $12; and postage, $30.

   Prepare the necessary journal entries.

2. Based upon the following data, prepare (*a*) a bank reconciliation and (*b*) appropriate journal entries.

Balance per bank statement, October 31		$5,940
Balance per company's books, October 31		4,475
Bank service charge		10
Deposit in transit		390
Outstanding checks:		
#110	$1,000	
#114	1,200	
#116 Certified	500	2,700
Note receivable collected by the bank:		
Principal	$ 345	
Interest	5	350
NSF check		550
Our account was charged in error by the bank for another company's check		150
Check #106 made out for $100 to a creditor was incorrectly entered as a cash disbursement of $115		15

3. What are trading securities? How are they reported?

4. On June 15, 20X0, Sophia Corporation purchased 2,000 shares of Donna Corporation stock for $30 per share. The purchase was made for trading purposes. At December 31, 20X0, the stock had

a market value of $28 per share. On August 12, 20X1, Sophia sold all 2,000 shares for $66,000. Prepare the journal entries for June 15, December 31, and March 12.

5. The inventory of product Y at January 1 consisted of 15,000 units valued at a cost of $112,500. Purchases during the year were:

March 5	20,500 units @ $7.75
May 12	33,000 units @ $8.00
Sept. 15	23,000 units @ $8.30
Nov. 28	8,500 units @ $8.44

   On December 31, there were 30,000 units on hand. Compute the December 31 inventory using (a) the last-in, first-out method, (b) the first-in, first-out method, and (c) the weighted-average method.

6. If ending inventory is overstated, what effect will there be on cost of goods sold and net income?

7. Determine the value of the ending inventory using the lower of cost or market method applied on (a) an item-by-item basis and (b) a total inventory basis.

Lot	Quantity in Units	Unit Cost	Unit Market Price
A	120	$75	$80
B	90	60	55
C	200	40	37
D	175	35	40

8. A fire destroyed the inventory of Schwartz Corporation on April 27, 20X1. The records show that gross profit in recent years was approximately 35 percent of net sales. Determine the value of the ending inventory using the following information:

Beginning Inventory	$ 50,000
Net Purchases	43,500
Sales	101,230
Sales Returns	3,401

9. Determine the inventory cost under the retail method based upon the following data:

	Cost	Retail
Inventory, April 1	$ 40,000	$ 48,000
Sales for April		204,000
Purchases for April	123,000	177,000

10. Is the direct-write-off method of accounting for uncollectible accounts theoretically sound?

11. The following account balances are given for Harris Corporation for 20X2:

Accounts Receivable	Allowance for Uncollectible Accounts	Sales
300,000	4,300	800,000

Prepare the journal entries to record the provision for uncollectible accounts when uncollectibility is based on (*a*) 2 percent of sales and (*b*) an aging of accounts receivable that indicates a needed balance in the allowance account of $15,700.

12. Prepare journal entries for the following transactions:

(*a*) Four customer accounts totalling $2,700 were written off as uncollectible.

(*b*) One of the accounts written off amounting to $500 was paid in full.

13. A $7,000, 18 percent, 90-day note is received upon the sale of merchandise to a customer. The note is discounted at the bank 30 days later; the bank discount rate is 20 percent. At maturity, the note is dishonored. A protest fee of $15 is charged. Prepare the required journal entries when (*a*) the note is received, (*b*) the note is discounted, and (*c*) the note is dishonored.

14. Jones Corporation borrows $4,000 for 120 days at 18 percent from a bank. The loan is made on a discount basis.

(*a*) Prepare the journal entry at the time of the loan.

(*b*) Record the payment on the loan.

Answers to Examination III

1.

Jan.	1	Petty Cash	100	
		Cash		100
	31	Office Supplies Expense	15	
		Cleaning Expense	12	
		Postage	30	
		Cash		57

2. (*a*)

Bank Reconciliation

Balance per bank		$5,940	Balance per books		$4,475
Add: Deposit in transit	$390		Add: Notes Receivable	$345	
Account charged in error	150	540	Interest income	5	
		$6,480	Proceeds	$350	
Less: Outstanding checks			Check #106	15	365
#110	$1,000				$4,840
#114	1,200	2,200	Less: NSF check	$550	
			Service charge	10	560
Adjusted bank balance		$4,280	Adjusted book balance		$4,280

(b)   ***General Journal***

Cash		365	
Notes Receivable			345
Interest Income			5
Accounts Payable			15
Accounts Receivable		550	
Bank Service Charge		10	
Cash			560

3. Trading securities are primarily equity securities purchased with the intent of selling in the near term, and are carried at fair value with unrealized gains and losses included in income.

4.

Date	Description	Debit	Credit
June 15	Short-term Investments	60,000	
	Cash		60,000
	Purchase of Donna stock for trading		
Dec. 31	Unrealized Loss on Investments	4,000	
	Allowance to Adjust Short-term		
	Investments to Market		4,000
	Year-end adjustment for market decline		
March 12	Cash	66,000	
	Short-term Investments		60,000
	Realized Gain on Investments		6,000
	To record sale of Donna stock		

5. (a) LIFO

Beginning inventory	15,000 units @ $7.50 =	$112,500
March 5 purchase	15,000 units @ $7.75 =	116,250
Total	30,000	$228,750

(b) FIFO

Nov. 28 purchase	8,500 units @ $8.44 =	$ 71,740
Sept. 15 purchase	21,500 units @ $8.30 =	178,450
	30,000	$250,190

(c) Weighted average:

Date	Units	Cost per Unit	Total Cost
Beg. Inv.	15,000	$7.50	$112,500
March 5	20,500	7.75	158,875
May 12	33,000	8.00	264,000
Sept. 15	23,000	8.30	190,900
Nov. 28	8,500	8.44	71,740
Goods avail.	100,000		$798,015

The average unit cost is

$$\text{Cost per unit} = \frac{\text{Cost of goods available}}{\text{Units available}} = \frac{\$798,015}{100,000} = \$7.98$$

The value of the ending inventory is

30,000 units @ $7.98 = $239,400

6. Cost of goods sold will be understated and net income will be overstated.

7.

Lot	Total Cost	Total Market Value	Lower of Cost or Market
A	$ 9,000	$ 9,600	$ 9,000
B	5,400	4,950	4,950
C	8,000	7,400	7,400
D	6,125	7,000	6,125
	$28,525	$28,950	$27,475

(a) $27,475
(b) $28,525

8.

Sales	$101,230	
Less: Sales Returns	3,401	
Net Sales		$97,829
Less: Cost of Goods Sold		
Beginning Inventory	$50,000	
Net Purchases	43,500	
Cost of Goods Available	$93,500	
Less: Ending Inventory	29,911*	
Cost of Goods Sold		63,589
Gross Profit on Net Sales (35% × $97,829)		$34,240

*Since cost of goods available less ending inventory is equal to cost of goods sold, the ending inventory must be $29,911.

9.

	Cost	Retail
Inventory, April 1	$ 40,000	$ 48,000
Purchases	123,000	177,000
Merchandise Available for Sale	$163,000	$225,000
Sales for April		204,000
Inventory, April 30, at retail		$ 21,000
Inventory, April 30, at cost	$ 15,212*	

Ratio: $\frac{\text{Cost}}{\text{Retail}} = \frac{\$163,000}{\$225,000} = 72.44\%$

*$21,000 × 72.44% = $15,212

10. The direct-write-off method is not theoretically sound because it does not match expenses against revenue. The uncollectible accounts expense is recognized in a period subsequent to the time of sale.

11. (a)

Uncollectible Accounts Expense	16,000*	
Allowance for Uncollectible Accounts		16,000

*2% × $800,000 = $16,000

    (b)

Uncollectible Accounts Expense	11,400*	
Allowance for Uncollectible Accounts		11,400

*$15,700 − $4,300 = $11,400

12. (a)

Allowance for Uncollectible Accounts	2,700	
Accounts Receivable		2,700

    (b)

Accounts Receivable	500	
Allowance for Uncollectible Accounts	500	
Cash	500	
Accounts Receivable		500

13. (a)

Notes Receivable	7,000	
Sales		7,000

    (b)

Cash	7,071.17*	
Notes Receivable		7,000.00
Interest Income		71.17

    (c)

Accounts Receivable	7,330	
Cash		7,330

*Interest on the note is: $7,000 × 18% × 90/360 = $315
The maturity value is: $7,000 + $315 = $7,315
The bank discount charge is: $7,315 × 20% × 60/360 = $243.83
The proceeds are: $7,315.00 − $243.83 = $7,071.17

14. (a)

Cash	3,760	
Interest Expense	240*	
Notes Payable		4,000

    (b)

Notes Payable	4,000	
Cash		4,000

*$4,000 × 18% × 120/360 = $240

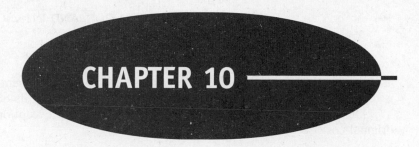

CHAPTER 10

Fixed Assets, Depreciation, and Intangible Assets

10.1 PROPERTY, PLANT, AND EQUIPMENT

Property, plant, and equipment are tangible, long-term assets used in the production or sale of goods or services. They are not held for the purpose of resale to customers. Items included in the fixed-asset category include land, building, machinery, equipment, and auto.

A fixed asset is recorded at historical cost, which is equal to the list price paid plus all normal incidental costs necessary to bring the asset into existing use and location. The asset's cost does *not* include unreasonable expenditures, such as the cost of a traffic ticket received in transporting the new machine.

EXAMPLE 1 The Atkins Corporation purchased a machine that was billed as follows: invoice price, $20,000; cash discount, $300; delivery, $535; insurance, $40; and installation, $800. The journal entry is

Machinery	21,075*	
Cash		21,075

*$20,000 − $300 + $535 + $40 + $800 = $21,075

10.2 DEPRECIATION

A fixed asset has a limited life because of physical deterioration and obsolescence. The asset will eventually be worth only its salvage value (scrap value). The yearly expiration of the original cost of a fixed asset is termed *depreciation*. Under the accrual concept, depreciation expense is matched against the revenue derived from the asset. Depreciation expense is listed as an operating expense in the income statement. The accumulated depreciation of an asset serves to reduce its original cost to arrive at the *book value* (carrying value). Accumulated depreciation constitutes the portion of the

195

asset's cost which has been recognized as expense up to the present time. The book value of the asset is reported on the balance sheet. As the asset becomes older, its book value declines.

All fixed assets are subject to depreciation with the exception of land. Land is retained at its original cost.

EXAMPLE 2 A machine was originally acquired for $25,000. The accumulated depreciation at year's end is $7,500. The machine's book value is reported on the balance sheet as follows:

Machinery	$25,000
Less: Accumulated Depreciation	7,500
Book Value	$17,500

10.3 DEPRECIATION METHODS

The depreciable cost of a fixed asset (original cost less salvage value) may be charged to expense over the asset's life under different methods. The straight-line method results in equal depreciation charges for every period. Accelerated methods result in higher depreciation charges in the earlier years and lower depreciation charges in the later years. Two accelerated methods are the double-declining-balance method and the sum-of-the-years'-digits method. Accelerated methods are generally more realistic in measuring the decline in value of fixed assets (e.g., autos) because fixed assets usually are most efficient when new. Variable charge methods also exist and depend upon the usage of the asset. An example is the units-of-production method where the depreciation expense is directly traceable to the volume produced.

STRAIGHT-LINE METHOD

This is the easiest and most popular method. It results in equal periodic depreciation charges. The method is most appropriate when the asset's usage is uniform from period to period, as is the case with furniture. Depreciation expense is equal to

$$\text{Depreciation expense} = \frac{\text{Cost} - \text{Salvage value}}{\text{Number of years of useful life}}$$

EXAMPLE 3 An auto is purchased for $20,000 with an expected salvage value of $2,000. The auto's estimated life is eight years. Depreciation per year equals

$$\frac{\$20,000 - \$2,000}{8 \text{ years}} = \$2,250 \text{ per year}$$

An alternative means of computation is to multiply the depreciable cost of $18,000 by the annual depreciation rate of 12.5 percent (1/8). The result is the same: $2,250 per year.

The journal entry is

Depreciation Expense	2,250	
Accumulated Depreciation		2,250

SUM-OF-THE-YEARS'-DIGITS METHOD

In this method the number of years of life expectancy is enumerated in reverse order in the numerator. For example, let us assume the life expectancy of a machine is eight years. If we write the numbers in reverse order we have 8, 7, 6, 5, 4, 3, 2, and 1. The denominator for each fraction is the sum of the years' digits $(8 + 7 + 6 + 5 + 4 + 3 + 2 + 1)$, which equals 36. Thus, the fraction for the first year is 8/36, while the fraction for the last year is 1/36. The sum of the eight fractions equals 36/36, or 1. Therefore, at the end of eight years, the machine is completely written down to its salvage value.

EXAMPLE 4   The cost of an auto having an estimated life of eight years is $20,000 and its salvage value is $2,000. The amount subject to depreciation is $18,000 ($20,000 − $2,000). The computation for each year's depreciation expense is shown below.

Year	Fraction	× Depreciable Amount	= Depreciation Expense
1	8/36	$18,000	$ 4,000
2	7/36	18,000	3,500
3	6/36	18,000	3,000
4	5/36	18,000	2,500
5	4/36	18,000	2,000
6	3/36	18,000	1,500
7	2/36	18,000	1,000
8	1/36	18,000	500
Total			$18,000

If the auto is expected to have a very long life, the following formula may be used to find the sum of the years' digits:

$$S = \frac{(N)(N+1)}{2}$$

where N represents the number of years of life expectancy.

In the case of eight years, the sum of the years' digits is

$$\frac{(8)(8+1)}{2} = \frac{(8)(9)}{2} = 36$$

EXAMPLE 5   If the life of a machine is expected to be 40 years, the sum of the years' digits would be

$$S = \frac{(40)(40+1)}{2} = 820$$

When an asset is acquired during the year, a pro rata (i.e., proportionate) amount for depreciation must be computed.

EXAMPLE 6   An auto is purchased on 7/1/X1 for $20,000. Its expected life is eight years and it has a salvage value of $2,000.

Depreciation expense for 20X1 is

7/1/X1–12/31/X1   8/36 × $18,000 = $4,000 × 6/12 = $2,000

Depreciation expense for 20X2 is

12/31/X1– 6/30/X2   8/36 × $18,000 = $4,000 × 6/12 = $2,000
7/1/X2–12/31/X2   7/36 ×   18,000 =   3,500 × 6/12 =   1,750
$3,750

DOUBLE-DECLINING-BALANCE METHOD

Under this method, depreciation expense is highest in the earlier years. First, a depreciation rate is determined by doubling the straight-line rate. For example, if an asset has a life of 10 years, the straight-line rate is 10 percent, and the double-declining rate is 20 percent. Second, depreciation expense is computed by multiplying the rate by the book value of the asset at the beginning of each year. Since book value declines over time, depreciation expense will become less each year. The method *ignores* salvage value in the computation. However, the book value of the fixed asset at the end of its useful life cannot be below its salvage value.

This method is advantageous for tax purposes since higher depreciation charges in the earlier years result in less income and thus less tax to be paid. The tax savings may then be invested for a return. Of course, over the life of the fixed asset, the total depreciation charges will be the same no matter what depreciation method is used. However, the timing of the tax savings will differ.

It should be noted that a company can use one depreciation method in its income tax report and another in its stockholders' report.

EXAMPLE 7   A $20,000 asset has a life expectancy of eight years. Since the straight-line rate is 12.5 percent (1/8), the double-declining-balance rate is 25 percent ($2 \times 12.5\%$). Depreciation expense per year is computed below.

Year	Book Value at Beginning of Year	× Rate	= Depreciation Expense	Year-end Book Value
1	$20,000	25%	$5,000	$15,000
2	15,000	25%	3,750	11,250
3	11,250	25%	2,813	8,437
4	8,437	25%	2,109	6,328
5	6,328	25%	1,582	4,746
6	4,746	25%	1,187	3,559
7	3,559	25%	890	2,669
8	2,669	25%	667	2,002

If there were an original estimated salvage value of $2,100, then the computations would be the same as above except for the eighth year. Since the asset cannot be depreciated below its salvage value, the depreciation expense for that year would have been $569 ($2,669 − $2,100) rather than $667.

EXAMPLE 8   Assume that in Example 7 the asset was purchased at the end of the fourth month. The pro rata portion of the first year's depreciation is

$$\$20,000 \times 25\% \times 8/12 = \$3,333$$

The book value at the end of year 1 is therefore $16,667 ($20,000 − $3,333).
Depreciation expense for year 2 is

$$\$16,667 \times 25\% = \$4,167$$

The book value at the end of year 2 is therefore $12,500 ($16,667 − $4,167). The rest of the calculations are as shown in Example 7, although the amounts will, of course, be different now.

UNITS-OF-PRODUCTION METHOD

This method is appropriate when the use of the asset materially varies from period to period. It has the benefit of optimally matching depreciation expense to revenue obtained. Under the method, the depreciation per unit or other output measure (e.g., machine hours, miles) is first determined by using the following formula:

$$\text{Depreciation per unit} = \frac{\text{Cost} - \text{Salvage value}}{\text{Estimated total units}}$$

The depreciation expense for a given year is determined as follows:

$$\text{Depreciation expense} = \text{Depreciation per unit} \times \text{Units produced}$$

EXAMPLE 9   The cost of a machine is $20,000, its salvage value is $2,000, and the estimated total usage is 8,000 hours. The depreciation per hour is

$$\frac{\$20,000 - \$2,000}{8,000 \text{ hours}} = \$2.25$$

In the first year the machine is used for 1,600 hours. Depreciation expense is

$$1,600 \text{ hours} \times \$2.25 \text{ per hour} = \$3,600$$

10.4   DISPOSAL OF PLANT AND EQUIPMENT

DISCARDING OF PLANT AND EQUIPMENT

When a fixed asset is no longer of value to the entity, the asset is often sold for its scrap value. If the asset is fully depreciated, then no depreciation is recorded at the time of its disposal.

EXAMPLE 10   Equipment purchased for $25,000 is fully depreciated in the accounts. The company decided to dispose of the asset. The journal entry is

Accumulated Depreciation	25,000	
Equipment		25,000

If the asset is not fully depreciated at the time of disposal, an entry is needed to update the depreciation.

EXAMPLE 11   Equipment of $20,000 with accumulated depreciation of $18,000 as of the end of the previous year (December 31) is being discarded on March 31. The annual depreciation rate is 10 percent. The depreciation expense for three months (January 1–March 31) is $500 ($20,000 $\times$ 10% $\times$ 3/12). The journal entry on March 31 to bring the accumulated depreciation account up to date is

Depreciation Expense	500	
Accumulated Depreciation		500

The entry to dispose of the asset is

Accumulated Depreciation	18,500	
Loss on Disposal of Fixed Assets	1,500	
Equipment		20,000

The loss account is shown under other expenses in the income statement.

SALE OF PLANT AND EQUIPMENT

Before the sale of plant or equipment may be recorded, depreciation is recognized for the fraction of the year ending with the disposal date. The difference between the asset's selling price and updated book value will result in a gain (selling price is greater than book value) or a loss (selling price is less than book value). Of course, in the unlikely case that an asset is sold for an amount identical to its book value, no gain or loss will arise.

EXAMPLE 12 On March 31, 20X2, equipment costing $20,000 with accumulated depreciation of $18,000 as of December 31, 20X1, is sold for $2,600. The annual straight-line depreciation rate is 10 percent. Two journal entries are required. The first is to update the accumulated depreciation account and the second is to record the sale.

20X2			
March 31	Depreciation Expense	500*	
	Accumulated Depreciation		500
	Cash	2,600	
	Accumulated Depreciation	18,500	
	Equipment		20,000
	Gain on Disposal of Fixed Assets		1,100

*$2,000 × 3/12 = $500

The gain may be proved by comparing the selling price to the book value as follows:

Selling Price		$2,600
Book Value		
Cost	$20,000	
Less: Accumulated Depreciation	18,500	1,500
Gain		$1,100

The gain account is shown under other income in the income statement.

EXAMPLE 13 If we assume the same information as in Example 12 except that the equipment is sold for $1,400, the journal entries are

20X2			
March 31	Depreciation Expense	500	
	Accumulated Depreciation		500
	Cash	1,400	
	Accumulated Depreciation	18,500	
	Less: Disposal of Fixed Assets	100	
	Equipment		20,000

The loss may be proved by comparing the selling price to the book value.

Selling Price		$1,400
Book Value		
Cost	$20,000	
Less: Accumulated Depreciation	18,500	1,500
Loss		$ 100

TRADING IN OF PLANT AND EQUIPMENT

An old asset is often traded in for a new one. In an exchange of similar assets, the price of the new asset less the credit given on the old asset represents the cash to be paid (called boot). If the trade-in value exceeds the book value of the old asset, a gain arises. According to *APB Opinion 29*, however, the gain is not recorded but rather serves as a reduction of the cost basis of the new asset. The new asset's recorded cost will be equal to the book value of the old asset plus the cash paid.

GAIN IS NOT RECOGNIZED

EXAMPLE 14   Assume the following information relating to a trade-in:

Old Equipment	
Cost	$20,000
Accumulated depreciation as of December 31 of the previous year	17,500
Depreciation expense for the current year up to the time of trade-in	500
New Equipment	
Cost	$22,000
Trade-in allowance	2,600
Cash paid	$19,400

The entry to bring the depreciation up to date is

Depreciation Expense	500	
Accumulated Depreciation		500

Before the trade-in can be recorded, any gain from the transaction must be determined.

Trade-in value	$2,600
Less: Book value of old equipment	2,000
Gain	$ 600

The gain reduces the cost basis of the new asset as follows:

Cost	$22,000
Less: Gain	600
Recorded cost of new equipment	$21,400

An alternative computation of the recorded cost of the new equipment is

Book value of old equipment	$ 2,000
Add: Cash payment	19,400
Recorded cost of new equipment	$21,400

The entry to record the trade-in is

Accumulated Depreciation	18,000	
Equipment (new)	21,400	
Equipment (old)		20,000
Cash		19,400

LOSS IS RECOGNIZED

If the trade-in allowance is less than the book value of the old asset, a loss is recognized in accordance with *APB Opinion 29*. Therefore, the new asset is reflected at cost.

EXAMPLE 15 Assume the same information as in Example 14 except that the trade-in allowance is $1,200 instead of $2,600. The cash payment now required is $20,800 ($22,000 − $1,200). The journal entries to update the accumulated depreciation account and to record the trade-in are

Depreciation Expense	500	
Accumulated Depreciation		500
Accumulated Depreciation	18,000	
Equipment (new)	22,000	
Loss on Disposal of Fixed Assets	800*	
Equipment (old)		20,000
Cash		20,800

*The loss is equal to

Book Value	$2,000
Less: Trade-in Value	1,200
Loss	$ 800

In the preparation of a tax return, no gain or loss is recognized when an asset is exchanged for a similar one. In this case, the cost of the new asset is equal to the book value of the old asset plus the boot given.

10.5 INTANGIBLE ASSETS

Intangible assets lack physical substance and arise from a right granted by the government or another company. Intangibles may be acquired or developed internally. Examples of rights granted by the government are patents, copyrights, and trademarks, while an example of a privilege granted by another company is a franchise. Other types of intangibles include organization costs, leasehold improvements, and goodwill. Organization costs are the expenditures incurred in starting a new company; an example would be legal fees. Leasehold improvements are expenditures made by a tenant to his or her leased property, such as the cost of putting up new paneling. Goodwill represents the amount paid for another business in excess of the fair market value of its tangible net assets. For example, if company A paid $100,000 for company B's net assets having a fair market value of $84,000, the amount paid for goodwill is $16,000. Goodwill can be recorded only when a company *purchases* another business. The amount paid for the goodwill of a business may be based upon the acquired firm's excess earnings over other companies in the industry. Internally developed goodwill (e.g., good customer relations) is *not* recorded in the accounts.

EXAMPLE 16 The net assets of Alpha Company are $800,000, which includes intangibles of $100,000. Trans Corporation decides to acquire the business, paying book value for the net assets. It decides to capitalize the goodwill at 16 percent. Goodwill is to be based on the excess earnings over 8 percent. In prior years, net income has approximated 10 percent of net tangible assets. The amount of goodwill is equal to

Average net income ($700,000 × 0.10)	$70,000
Less: Normal net income ($700,000 × 0.08)	56,000
Excess net income	$14,000
Capitalized goodwill ($14,000/0.16)	$87,500

10.6 ACCOUNTING FOR INTANGIBLE ASSETS

APB Opinion 17 specifies the requirements for accounting for intangible assets.

Intangibles that have been acquired, such as goodwill, should be recorded at cost. In the event that an intangible is acquired for other than cash, it should be reflected at either the fair market value of the consideration given or the fair market value of the right received, whichever is more clearly evident. Intangibles should not be arbitrarily written off if they still have value.

When identifiable intangibles are internally developed (e.g., patents), they should be recorded as assets and reflected at cost. If they are *not* identifiable, they should be expensed.

Intangible assets must be *amortized* over the period benefited *not* to exceed *40 years*. Amortization is a term used to describe the systematic write-off to expense of an intangible asset's cost over its *economic* life. The straight-line method of amortization is used. The amortization entry is

Amortization Expense

Intangible Asset

The credit is made directly to the given intangible asset account. However, it would not be incorrect to credit an accumulated amortization account, if desired.

Some intangibles have a limited legal life. An example is patents, which have a legal life of 17 years.

EXAMPLE 17 On January 1, 20X1, company A paid $1,700 to obtain a patent that has a life of 17 years. The appropriate journal entry to record the amortization for 20X1 is

Amortization Expense   100
    Patents   100

An amortization expense of $100 is shown in the 20X1 income statement.

The patent account of $1,600 ($1,700 − $100) is shown under Intangible Assets in the December 31, 20X1, balance sheet.

Costs incurred in sustaining an intangible asset should be capitalized. For example, legal costs incurred in successfully defending a patent should be charged to the patent account.

If an intangible asset is suddenly deemed to be worthless, the asset account should be written off and a loss recognized. An example occurs when a company loses the (final) legal case involving its patent.

FASB 2 covers research and development costs. It requires such costs to be expensed in the year incurred.

10.7 DEFERRED CHARGES

Deferred charges are of a long-term, nonrecurring nature. They are allocated to a number of future periods. Examples are start-up costs and plant rearrangement costs.

Deferred charges are customarily listed as the last asset category in the balance sheet since their dollar value is usually insignificant relative to total assets.

10.8 OTHER ASSETS

When noncurrent assets cannot be properly placed into the asset classifications already discussed, they may be included in the Other Assets category. Placement of an item in this classification depends upon its nature and dollar magnitude. However, this classification should be used as a last resort.

Summary

(1) The allocation of the cost of a fixed asset to the periods benefited from it is called _____.

(2) The cost of a fixed asset less its accumulated depreciation is equal to the _____.

(3) The value placed on a fixed asset at the end of its useful life is known as _____.

(4) A fixed asset not subject to depreciation is _____.

(5) The depreciation method which results in equal periodic charges is the _____ method.

(6) The method which doubles the straight-line rate of depreciation and then applies it to the book value of the asset at the beginning of the year is known as the _____ method.

(7) The method whereby a series of fractions are used to depreciate the asset is referred to as the _____ method.

(8) When the use of equipment varies considerably from year to year, an appropriate method of depreciation is the _____ method.

(9) The term _____ refers to the exchange of an old fixed asset for a new one.

(10) The amount paid to purchase an item after a trade-in allowance is deducted from the price is called _____.

(11) Equipment purchased for $20,000 with a trade-in gain of $1,500 will be recorded at _____.

(12) Equipment purchased for $20,000 with a trade-in loss of $1,000 will be recorded at _____.

(13) The loss on disposal of a fixed asset is shown under _____ in the income statement.

(14) _____ assets lack physical substance and arise from a right granted by the government or another company.

(15) Acquired intangibles should be recorded as _____ at cost.

(16) Internally developed intangibles which are not specifically identifiable should be recorded as _____.

(17) Goodwill can only be recorded in a business combination accounted for under the purchase method when the cost to the acquirer _____ the fair market value of the net assets of the acquired company.

(18) Intangible assets must be amortized over their useful lives but not in excess of _____ years.

(19) A patent recorded at $20,000 has a remaining legal life of 14 years. However, its economic life is now estimated to be 10 years. The annual amortization expense will be _____ .

(20) Legal costs incurred in defending a patent should be _____ .

(21) The _____ account is charged for expenditures made in starting a company.

(22) Start-up costs are classified in the _____ section of the balance sheet.

Answers: (1) depreciation; (2) book value; (3) salvage value; (4) land; (5) straight-line; (6) double-declining-balance; (7) sum-of-the-years'-digits; (8) units-of-production; (9) trade-in; (10) boot; (11) $18,500; (12) $20,000; (13) Other Expenses; (14) Intangible; (15) assets; (16) expenses; (17) exceeds; (18) 40; (19) $2,000; (20) capitalized; (21) organization cost; (22) deferred charge

Solved Problems

10.1 Martin Company purchased a machine having a list price of $75,000. Because the machine was immediately paid for, the company was entitled to a 2 percent discount. Costs incurred to make the machine ready for use included: freight, $3,000; installation, $485; electrical wiring, $700; repair expense because the machine was improperly handled, $100; and rental of a special crane, $435. What is the acquisition cost of the machine?

SOLUTION

List Price	$75,000	
Discount ($75,000 × 2%)	1,500	$73,500
Freight		3,000
Installation		485
Electrical Wiring		700
Rental of Crane		435
Total Cost		$78,120

10.2 On January 1, 20X5, a machine was purchased for $30,000. The estimated life is six years and the salvage value is $1,500. Determine the annual depreciation using the straight-line method.

SOLUTION

$$\text{Depreciation expense} = \frac{\$30,000 - \$1,500}{6} = \$4,750$$

10.3 Using the information supplied in Problem 10.2, compute the depreciation for the first three years by the sum-of-the-years'-digits method.

SOLUTION

$$S = \frac{(N)(N+1)}{2} = \frac{6(6+1)}{2} = 21$$

Year	Fraction	× Depreciable Amount	= Depreciation
1	6/21	$28,500	$8,143
2	5/21	28,500	6,786
3	4/21	28,500	5,429

10.4 Solve Problem 10.3 using the double-declining-balance method.

SOLUTION

The double-declining rate is 1/3 [2 × (1/6)]. Salvage value is ignored in the computation.

Year	Book Value at Beginning of Year	× Rate =	Depreciation Expense	Year-end Book Value
1	$30,000	1/3	$10,000	$20,000
2	20,000	1/3	6,667	13,333
3	13,333	1/3	4,444	8,889

10.5 A printing press was purchased on January 1, 20X7, for $15,000. It has an estimated life of 14 years and a salvage value of $1,000. The straight-line depreciation method is used. How would the printing press and the related accumulated depreciation be shown on the balance sheet at (*a*) December 31, 20X7, and (*b*) December 31, 20X8?

SOLUTION

$$\text{Depreciation expense} = \frac{\$15,000 - \$1,000}{14} = \$1,000$$

(*a*)
Printing Press	$15,000
Less: Accumulated Depreciation	1,000
Book Value	$14,000

(*b*)
Printing Press	$15,000
Less: Accumulated Depreciation	2,000
Book Value	$13,000

10.6 Using the information in Problem 10.5, what would be reported in the income statement for (*a*) 20X7 and (*b*) 20X8?

SOLUTION

(*a*) Depreciation Expense, $1,000

(*b*) Depreciation Expense, $1,000

10.7 A truck was purchased on October 1, 20X5, for $10,000. The estimated life is five years and the salvage value is $500. The straight-line depreciation method is used. What would be reported on the balance sheet at (*a*) December 31, 20X5, and (*b*) December 31, 20X6?

SOLUTION

$$\text{Depreciation per year} = \frac{\$10,000 - \$500}{5} = \$1,900$$

(*a*) Depreciation for 3 months = $1,900 × 3/12 = $475

Truck	$10,000
Less: Accumulated Depreciation	475
Book Value	$ 9,525

(*b*)

Truck	$10,000
Less: Accumulated Depreciation	2,375*
Book Value	$ 7,625

*$475 + $1,900 = $2,375

10.8 Referring to Problem 10.7, what would be reported in the income statement for (*a*) 20X5 and (*b*) 20X6?

SOLUTION

(*a*) Depreciation Expense, $475

(*b*) Depreciation Expense, $1,900

10.9 On October 1, 20X4, a machine was purchased for $13,000. It has a life of five years and a salvage value of $1,000. The sum-of-the-years'-digits depreciation method is used. What is the depreciation expense for (*a*) 20X4 and (*b*) 20X5?

SOLUTION

(*a*) 10/1/X4–12/31/X4   5/15 × $12,000 = $4,000 × 3/12 = $1,000
(*b*)   1/1/X5– 9/30/X5   5/15 × $12,000 = $4,000 × 9/12 = $3,000
        10/1/X5–12/31/X5   4/15 × $12,000 = $3,200 × 3/12 =   800
                                                             $3,800

10.10 On July 1, 20X6, Carol Corporation purchased factory equipment for $25,000. Salvage value was estimated to be $1,000. The equipment will be depreciated over 10 years using the double-declining-balance method. What amount should be reported for depreciation expense in 20X7? (AICPA Adapted)

SOLUTION

Depreciation expense for the six months ended Dec. 31, 20X6, is $25,000 × 20% = $5,000 × 6/12 = $2,500. The book value at the end of 20X6 is $22,500 ($25,000 − $2,500). Depreciation expense for 20X7 is $22,500 × 20% = $4,500.

10.11 On March 19, 20X1, an auto was acquired for $10,000. It has an estimated life of eight years and a salvage value of $1,500. It is decided to depreciate the auto based upon mileage. The estimated total mileage is 85,000. The car was driven 6,000 miles in 20X1 and 11,000 miles in 20X2.

Insurance paid on the car is $700 annually. Determine the depreciation expense for (*a*) 20X1 and (*b*) 20X2.

SOLUTION

Insurance paid on the auto does *not* affect depreciation expense but rather is shown as insurance expense.

$$\text{Depreciation expense} = \frac{\$10,000 - \$1,500}{85,000 \text{ miles}} = \$0.10 \text{ per mile}$$

(*a*) $6,000 \times \$0.10 = \$\ 600$
(*b*) $11,000 \times \$0.10 = \$1,100$

10.12 A fixed asset costs $48,000 and has an estimated salvage value of $6,000. The anticipated life is 10 years. Fill in the following tables.

Sum-of-the-Years'-Digits Method

Year	Depreciation Expense	Accumulated Depreciation	Year-end Book Value
1			
2			
3			

Double-Declining-Balance Method

Year	Depreciation Expense	Accumulated Depreciation	Year-end Book Value
1			
2			
3			

SOLUTION

Sum-of-the-Years'-Digits Method

Year	Depreciation Expense	Accumulated Depreciation	Year-end Book Value
1	$7,636*	$ 7,636	$40,364
2	6,873	14,509	33,491
3	6,109	20,618	27,382

$*S = \frac{10(10+1)}{2} = 55; \ 10/55 \times \$42,000 = \$7,636$

Double-Declining-Balance Method

Year	Depreciation Expense	Accumulated Depreciation	Year-end Book Value
1	$9,600*	$ 9,600	$38,400
2	7,680**	17,280	30,720
3	6,144	23,424	24,576

*10% × 2 = 20% × $48,000 = $9,600

**20% × $38,400 = $7,680

10.13 Equipment costing $19,500 with accumulated depreciation of $12,000 is discarded. There is no salvage value. Prepare the appropriate journal entry for its disposal.

SOLUTION

Accumulated Depreciation	12,000	
Loss on Disposal of Fixed Assets	7,500	
Equipment		19,500

Since there is no salvage value, the book value of $7,500 for the asset is considered a loss.

10.14 Using the information given in Problem 10.13, prepare the entry if the equipment was sold for $9,000.

SOLUTION

Accumulated Depreciation	12,000	
Cash	9,000	
Equipment		19,500
Gain on Disposal of Fixed Assets		1,500*

*Cash received	$9,000
Book value	7,500
Gain	$1,500

10.15 Using the information in Problem 10.13, prepare the entry if the equipment was sold for $5,000.

SOLUTION

Accumulated Depreciation	12,000	
Cash	5,000	
Loss on Disposal of Fixed Assets	2,500	
Equipment		19,500

10.16 The Brentwood Company traded in an old machine for a new one priced at $4,000. A $200 trade-in allowance was given. The cost of the old machine was $3,500 and its accumulated depreciation was $3,400. Prepare the entry to record the trade-in.

SOLUTION

Accumulated Depreciation	3,400	
Machine (new)	3,900	
Machine (old)		3,500
Cash		3,800

The recorded cost of the new machine is calculated as follows:

Trade-in allowance	$200
Book value of old machine	100
Gain	$100

The gain reduces the cost basis of the new asset:

Price of new machine	$4,000
Less: Unrecognized gain	100
Cost of new machine	$3,900

An alternative computation is:

Book value of old machine	$ 100
Cash paid	3,800
Cost of new machine	$3,900

10.17 Using the same information given in Problem 10.16, prepare the entry for the trade-in, assuming an allowance of $80 is given for the old machine.

SOLUTION

Accumulated Depreciation	3,400	
Machine (new)	4,000	
Loss on Disposal on Fixed Assets	20*	
Machine (old)		3,500
Cash		3,920

*Book value	$100
Trade-in allowance	80
Loss	$ 20

10.18 A machine costing $8,000 with accumulated depreciation of $6,600 is exchanged for a new machine. The trade-in allowance given is $2,300. The price of the new machine is $10,000. Prepare the entry for the exchange of the machines.

SOLUTION

Accumulated Depreciation	6,600	
Machine (new)	9,100	
Machine (old)		8,000
Cash		7.700

The recorded cost of the new machine is calculated as follows:

Trade-in allowance	$2,300
Book value	1,400
Gain	$ 900

The gain reduces the cost basis of the new asset:

Price of new machine	$10,000
Less: Unrecognized gain	900
Cost of new machine	$ 9,100

10.19 The transactions below pertain to either the disposal or trade-in of a fixed asset. Depreciation has been recorded up to the end of the preceding year. If an item is disposed of prior to the 15th of a given month, do not depreciate the asset for that month. Prepare journal entries for each transaction.

July   5—Office equipment costing $10,000 with accumulated depreciation of $8,400 was sold for $1,800. The annual depreciation is $600.

July 31—Six typewriters costing $9,000 with accumulated depreciation of $8,000 were discarded. They had no salvage value. Annual depreciation is $1,200.

Sept. 30—An old cash register costing $800 with accumulated depreciation of $600 was traded in for a new one priced at $900. The trade-in allowance was $100. Annual depreciation is $120. A note was issued for the balance due on the new cash register.

Nov. 10—A desk costing $1,000 with accumulated depreciation of $800 was exchanged for a new one priced at $1,400. A trade-in allowance of $200 was given. Annual depreciation is $60.

SOLUTION

July 5	Depreciation Expense	300*	
	Accumulated Depreciation		300
	Accumulated Depreciation	8,700	
	Cash	1,800	
	Office Equipment		10,000
	Gain on Disposal of Fixed Assets		500
July 31	Depreciation Expense	700**	
	Accumulated Depreciation		700
	Accumulated Depreciation	8,700	
	Loss on Disposal of Fixed Assets	300	
	Office Equipment		9,000

Sept. 30	Depreciation Expense	90†	
	Accumulated Depreciation		90
	Accumulated Depreciation	690	
	Office Equipment (new)	900	
	Loss on Disposal of Fixed Assets	10††	
	Office Equipment (old)		800
	Note Payable		800
Nov. 10	Depreciation Expense	50‡	
	Accumulated Depreciation		50
	Accumulated Depreciation	850	
	Office Equipment (new)	1,350‡‡	
	Office Equipment (old)		1,000
	Cash		1,200

---

*$50 per month × 6 = $300

**$100 per month × 7 = $700

†$10 per month × 9 = $90

††Book value	$110
Trade-in allowance	100
Loss	$ 10

‡$5 per month × 10 = $50

‡‡Trade-in allowance	$200
Book value	150
Gain	$ 50
Price of new equipment	$1,400
Less: Unrecognized gain	50
Cost of new equipment	$1,350

10.20 The following costs were incurred prior to starting a new business:

Attorney's fees in connection with the organization of the company	$5,000
Improvements to leased offices prior to occupancy	8,000
Meetings of incorporators	3,000
State filing fees	1,000

What amount should be charged to the organization cost account?

SOLUTION

$$\$5,000 + 3,000 + 1,000 = \$9,000$$

Even though leasehold improvements are intangible assets, they are not included with organization costs. Rather, they are amortized over the life of the property or the lease period, whichever is shorter.

10.21 On January 3, 20X1, ABC Company opened a Burger Eatery franchise after paying a fee of $30,000. It was decided to amortize the fee over 20 years. (*a*) Prepare the appropriate annual amortization entry. (*b*) Determine the balance in the franchise fee account at December 31, 20X4.

SOLUTION

(a)

Amortization Expense	1,500*	
Franchise Fee		1,500

*30,000/20 years = $1,500

(b)

Cost	$30,000
Less: Accumulated Amortization	
($1,500 × 4)	6,000
Balance	$24,000

10.22 A patent was acquired on January 1, 20X5, for $8,500. It was decided to amortize it over 17 years. After 3 years had been amortized, the company decided that the remaining life should be 10 years rather than 14 years. Taking into account the new life, prepare the entry to record amortization expense for the fourth year.

SOLUTION

Original annual amortization expense: $8,500/17 = $500

Cost	$8,500
Less: Accumulated amortization ($500 × 3)	
Balance at the end of the 3rd year	1,500
	$7,000

Annual amortization expense after change in estimated life: $7,000/10 = $700

The journal entry in the fourth year is

Amortization Expense	700	
Patents		700

10.23 On January 2, 20X5, Hermes Corporation acquired a patent for $192,000. The patent had a remaining legal life of 12 years and an estimated useful life of 8 years. In January 20X9 Hermes paid $12,000 in legal fees in a successful defense of the patent. What should Hermes record as patent amortization for 20X9? (AICPA Adapted)

SOLUTION

Cost	$192,000
Less: Accumulated amortization	
(20X5–20X8) ($192,000 × 4/8)	96,000
Balance, December 31, 20X8	$ 96,000
Legal fees, 20X9	12,000
Balance prior to amortization	
(4 years remaining)	$108,000
Amortization expense for 20X9	
($108,000/4)	$ 27,000

10.24 In January 20X5 Tracy Corporation purchased a patent for a new consumer product for $180,000. At the time of purchase, the patent was valid for 15 years. Due to the competitive nature of the product, however, the patent was estimated to have a useful life of only 10 years. During 20X8 the product was permanently removed from the market under government order because of a potential health hazard present in the product. What amount should Tracy charge to expense during 20X8? (AICPA Adapted)

SOLUTION

Cost	$180,000
Less: Accumulated amortization	
(20X5–20X7) ($180,000 × 3/10)	54,000
Balance, December 31, 20X7	$126,000
Amortization expense for 20X8	$126,000

Since the patent is now worthless, the patent account must be written off.

10.25 Andover Company has $1,500,000 of net assets, of which $240,000 are intangibles. An investor offers to buy the business, paying book value for the net assets. Goodwill is to be capitalized at 15 percent and is to be based on the excess earnings over 12 percent. The yearly earnings of the company have averaged 14 percent of net tangible assets. Determine the amount of goodwill.

SOLUTION

Average net income ($1,260,000 × 0.14)	$176,400
Normal net income ($1,260,000 × 0.12)	151,200
Excess net income	$ 25,200
Capitalized goodwill ($25,200/0.15)	$168,000

10.26 The owners of the Zoot Suit Clothing Store are contemplating selling the business to new interests. The cumulative earnings for the past five years amounted to $450,000, including extraordinary gains of $10,000. The annual earnings based on an average rate of return on investment for this industry would have been $76,000. If excess earnings are to be capitalized at 10 percent, what is the implied goodwill? (AICPA Adapted)

SOLUTION

Cumulative earnings	$450,000
Less: Extraordinary gains	10,000
Normal earnings	$440,000
Average earnings ($440,000/5)	$ 88,000
Industry average earnings	76,000
Excess earnings	$ 12,000
Implied goodwill ($12,000/0.10)	$120,000

CHAPTER 11

Liabilities

11.1 INTRODUCTION

Liabilities are obligations of the entity that require future payment or the rendering of services. Examples are accounts payable, taxes payable, accrued expenses, unearned revenue, bonds payable, mortgages payable, and leases payable. Liabilities may be of a current or noncurrent nature.

11.2 CURRENT LIABILITIES

These are claims due within one year or the normal operating cycle of the business, whichever is greater. Current liabilities are typically paid out of current assets. Current liabilities are of five types:

1. *Accounts payable.* Obligations for goods or services that have been acquired on account.
2. *Notes payable.* Written promises to pay money at a future date.
3. *Accrued expenses.* Liabilities relating to expenses incurred but not paid such as accrued salaries and accrued interest.
4. *Withholdings.* Amounts withheld from employees' salaries that are to be remitted to federal and local tax agencies or are for employee benefits. Examples are federal and state income taxes, social security taxes (FICA), medical group insurance, and retirement plans.

EXAMPLE 1 A company's weekly payroll is $5,000. Employee withholdings are: income taxes, $1,000; social security, $300; and medical insurance, $170. The appropriate journal entry is

Salaries Expense	5,000	
Income Taxes Payable		1,000
Social Security Taxes Payable		300
Medical Insurance Payable		170
Cash		3,530

The employer must also pay his or her own payroll taxes, which consist of social security tax (the employer must match the amount withheld from employees) and federal and state unemployment insurance taxes. Assuming the federal unemployment insurance is $35 and the state unemployment insurance is $135, the entry is

Payroll Taxes Expense	470	
Social Security Taxes Payable		300
Federal Unemployment Taxes Payable		35
State Unemployment Taxes Payable		135

The employer's total payroll expense is $5,470, consisting of the wages and payroll taxes.

When the withholdings are paid by the company to the appropriate party, the payable is debited and cash is credited.

5. *Unearned (deferred) revenue.* This represents revenue received but not earned yet such as receipt of advance payments for rental income and subscription revenue. These obligations are in the form of future delivery of goods or services rather than dollars to be paid. If long-term advances are made (extending beyond one year), they are classified as noncurrent liabilities.

11.3 NONCURRENT LIABILITIES

Noncurrent liabilities are sometimes used to finance noncurrent assets. The expectation is that the return generated from the long-term asset will be sufficient to meet the interest and principal payment of the debt. Long-term liabilities include:

Bonds payable. A bond is a written promise by the company to pay the face amount at the maturity date. Periodic interest payments are required, typically on a semiannual basis. Bonds are usually stated in $1,000 denominations. Debt financing has several advantages compared to equity financing. Interest expense is tax deductible, whereas dividend payments are not. During inflation, the debt is being paid back in cheaper dollars. However, there are drawbacks to debt financing, including the risk of not being able to meet the fixed interest charges and principal at maturity, and restrictions placed on the company under the bond agreement such as minimum working capital requirements.

Long-term notes payable. When a note is issued, funds are obtained from a specific lender rather than through the issuance of bonds payable to the public at large.

Mortgage payable. A mortgage has as its security the property financed. It represents a lien on the property in case of default.

Leases. The lessee uses the property in return for periodic rental payments to the lessor. In the case of a *capital lease*, the lessee shows as a long-term liability the present value of future minimum rental payments to be made. A capital lease is one in which *one* of the following four criteria is met:

1. The lessee receives title to the property at the end of the lease term.

2. The lessee can acquire the property under a "bargain purchase option."

3. The life of the lease is 75 percent or more of the life of the property.

4. At the date of lease, the present value of the future minimum lease payments equals or exceeds 90 percent of the fair market value of the property.

If at least one of the criteria is not met, an *operating* lease is indicated. This is accounted for as a regular rental.

11.4 TYPES OF BONDS

A trustee such as a bank is selected by the company to safeguard the creditors' interest. The agreement (indenture) between the trustee and corporation spells out the particulars of the bond issue. The trustee may hold collateral as security against default on the bonds. *Collateral trust bonds* have as their collateral the firm's investments in other companies. *Sinking fund bonds* require the company to make annual deposits with the trustee. At maturity, the amount in the sinking fund (consisting of principal and interest) should be sufficient to pay the face of the bonds. *Unsecured bonds* (debentures) may be issued by credit-worthy companies. For these, no collateral is required.

There are registered and coupon bonds. A *registered bond* has the owner's name on the face of the bond and interest is paid directly to him or her. A *coupon bond* does not indicate the owner's name and interest is paid to the individual who presents a dated coupon.

Convertible bonds may be exchanged by the holder for other securities of the company at a later date. *Callable bonds* may be reacquired at the option of the issuing company prior to their maturity.

Serial bonds mature in installments rather than at a fixed maturity date.

11.5 ACCOUNTING FOR BONDS

When bonds are issued at their face value, the entry is to debit cash and credit bonds payable. The entry to record the interest each period is to debit interest expense and credit cash. Interest is equal to

$$\text{Face of bond} \times \text{Annual interest rate} \times \text{Period between last interest date and now}$$

EXAMPLE 2   On January 1, 20X1, Arco Corporation issued $50,000 10-year, 15 percent bonds. The bonds were sold at face value. Interest is payable semiannually on July 1 and January 1. The entries for 20X1 are

20X1			
Jan. 1	Cash	50,000	
	Bonds Payable		50,000
July 1	Interest Expense	3,750*	
	Cash		3,750
Dec. 31	Interest Expense	3,750	
	Interest Payable		3,750

*$50,000 × 15% × 6/12 = $3,750

Note that on January 1, 20X2, the interest payment date, the entry would be

20X2			
Jan. 1	Interest Payable	3,750	
	Cash		3,750

The market price of a bond will most likely be different than its face value (maturity value). A bond's market value depends upon a number of factors, such as its interest rate, years left to maturity, and the financial soundness of the company. For example, if a bond's interest rate is much lower than the going interest rate in the marketplace, the market price of the bond will be considerably lower than its face value.

The difference between the sales price of a bond and its face value is recorded as Premium on Bonds Payable (when issue price exceeds face value) or as Discount on Bonds Payable (when issue price is less than face value).

The face value of a bond is stated as 100 percent. Therefore, a bond issued at a premium would be sold at more than 100 percent. A bond issued at a discount would be sold at less than 100 percent.

EXAMPLE 3 The proceeds of a $1,000 bond issued at 108 would be $1,080 ($1,000 × 108%). If the bond was sold at 93, the proceeds would be $930 ($1,000 × 93%).

PREMIUM ON BONDS PAYABLE

A bond would normally be sold at a premium if its face (nominal) interest rate exceeds the current market rate for a comparable quality bond. The premium should not be considered income but rather interest received in advance that will serve to adjust the contract rate of interest. The premium account is amortized over the life of the bond as a reduction of interest expense. The entry is to debit premium on bonds payable and credit interest expense. The true interest expense (net cost of borrowing) for a given year is therefore the face interest less the adjustment for the premium amortization. In the balance sheet, the unamortized premium is added to the face value of the bonds payable in order to derive the current carrying value (present value) of the bond. At the maturity date, the carrying value of the bond will equal its face value since the principal of the bond must be paid at that time.

EXAMPLE 4 On January 1, Smith Corporation sold $50,000 10-year, 15 percent bonds at 105. Interest is payable semiannually on June 30 and December 31. The entry to record the issuance is

Jan. 1	Cash	52,500	
	Bonds Payable		50,000
	Premium on Bonds Payable		2,500

The entries for the semiannual interest payments are

June 30	Interest Expense	3,750	
	Cash		3,750
Dec. 31	Interest Expense	3,750	
	Cash		3,750

The annual premium amortization is $250 ($2,500/10). The entry is

Dec. 31	Premium on Bonds Payable	250	
	Interest Expense		250

The Interest Expense account at year's end appears below.

Interest Expense

June 30	3,750	Dec. 31	250
Dec. 31	3,750		
	7,500		

The Interest Expense account has a balance of $7,250, which represents the net borrowing cost for the year.

The balance in the premium account at year's end is $2,250:

Premium on Bonds Payable

Dec. 31	250	Jan. 1	2,500

The balance sheet at December 31 shows the carrying value of the bonds at $52,250:

Long-term Liabilities	
Bonds Payable	$50,000
Add: Premium on Bonds Payable	2,250*
Carrying Value	$52,250

*Unamortized amount.

At the end of the tenth year, the carrying value of the bonds will equal their maturity value of $50,000. The journal entry to pay the maturity value is to debit bonds payable and credit cash for $50,000.

DISCOUNT ON BONDS PAYABLE

A bond would normally be sold at a discount when its face interest is below the market interest rate. The discount is considered an incremental interest expense, which is amortized over the life of the bond. The entry is to debit interest expense and credit discount on bonds payable. The true interest expense (net borrowing cost) for a given year is therefore the face interest plus the discount amortization. In the balance sheet, the unamortized discount is subtracted from bonds payable to arrive at the current carrying value of the bond. Unamortized discount is a contra account. At maturity, the unamortized discount account will be reduced to zero and hence the carrying value of the bond will equal its face value.

EXAMPLE 5   Assume the same facts as in Example 4 except that the bonds are sold at 94. The entry to record the issuance of the bonds is

Jan. 1	Cash	47,000	
	Discount on Bonds Payable	3,000	
	Bonds Payable		50,000

At the date the bonds are issued, the carrying value of bonds payable is equal to the proceeds received for them. If a balance sheet was prepared immediately after the issuance of the bonds, the liability would be $47,000

Long-term Liabilities	
Bonds Payable	$50,000
Less: Discount on Bonds Payable	3,000
Carrying Value	$47,000

Over the life of the bonds, the carrying value increases gradually until its equals the maturity value. The entries to record the interest payments are

June 30	Interest Expense	3,750	
	Cash		3,750
Dec. 31	Interest Expense	3,750	
	Cash		3.750

The annual discount amortization is $300 ($3,000/10). The entry is

Dec. 31   Interest Expense   300
                    Discount on Bonds Payable   300

Note that interest expense has been increased, but no cash payment is involved.
The Interest Expense account at year's end follows:

Interest Expense

June 30	3,750	
Dec. 31	3,750	
Dec. 31	300	
	7,800	

The Interest Expense account equals $7,800, which is the net borrowing cost for the year.
The balance in the Discount account at year's end is $2,700, as indicated below:

Discount on Bonds Payable

| Jan. 1 | 3,000 | Dec. 31 | 300 |

The balance sheet at December 31 shows the carrying value of the bonds at $47,300:

Long-term Liabilities
Bonds Payable $50,000
Less: Discount on Bonds Payable   2,700
Carrying Value $47,300

At the end of the tenth year, the carrying value of the bonds will be the same as their face value, $50,000.

11.6   BONDS SOLD AT FACE VALUE BETWEEN INTEREST DATES

When bonds are sold between interest dates the purchaser must pay the interest that has been accrued subsequent to the last interest payment date. This is because at the next interest date the purchaser will receive the interest for the *full* period. The net effect is that the purchaser will earn the interest he or she is entitled to for the period he or she *held* the bond.

EXAMPLE 6   Bonds are sold on August 31. Interest is payable June 30 and December 31. The purchaser will have to pay for two months of accrued interest (June 30–August 31). On December 31, the purchaser will receive six months' interest (June 30–December 31). The net effect is that the purchaser has earned interest for four months (August 31–December 31).

When bonds are sold at face value between interest dates the entry on the seller's books is

Cash
      Bonds Payable
      Interest expense

EXAMPLE 7   On March 1, 20X1, a company issues $50,000 of 10-year, 15 percent bonds at face value. The bonds are dated January 1, 20X1. Interest is payable on January 1 and July 1.

The entry to record the issuance is

20X1			
March 1	Cash	51,250	
	Bonds Payable		50,000
	Interest Expense		1,250*

*Accrued interest is for 2 months (January 1–March 1): $50,000 \times 15\% \times 2/12 = \$1,250$.

The accrued interest collected from purchasers between interest dates is returned to them on the next interest payment date. On July 1, semiannual interest for the full six months is paid. The entry is

20X1			
July 1	Interest Expense	3,750*	
	Cash		3,750

*$50,000 \times 15\% \times 6/12 = \$3,750$

The Interest Expense account now appears as follows:

Interest Expense			
July 1	3,750	March 1	1,250

The $2,500 balance in the Interest Expense account represents the net interest cost to the issuer for four months (March 1–July 1).

An adjusting entry is required at year's end for the accrued interest:

20X1			
Dec. 31	Interest Expense	3,750	
	Interest Payable		3,750

When the interest is paid at the next interest date, the entry is

20X2			
Jan. 1	Interest Payable	3,750	
	Cash		3,750

EXAMPLE 8   On June 1, 20X1, a company issues $100,000 of 10-year, 16% bonds at face value. The bonds are dated March 1, 20X1. Interest is payable March 1 and September 1.

The entry to record the issuance is

20X1			
June 1	Cash	104,000	
	Bonds Payable		100,000
	Interest Expense		4,000*

*Accrued interest is for 3 months (March 1–June 1): $100,000 \times 16\% \times 3/12 = \$4,000$.

The entry on the next interest payment date is

```
20X1
Sept. 1        Interest Expense                          8,000*
                    Cash                                              8,000
```
_____

*$100,000 × 16% × 6/12 = $8,000

The Interest Expense account now shows:

Interest Expense

Sept. 1 8,000	June 1 4,000

The net interest cost to the issuer is $4,000 for the three-month period June 1–September 1. The adjusting entry at year's end is

```
20X1
Dec. 31        Interest Expense                          5,333*
                    Interest Payable                                5,333
```
_____

*Accrued interest for 4 months (September 1–December 31): $100,000 × 16% × 4/12 = $5,333 (rounded).

When the semiannual interest is paid on March 1, 20X2, the entry to record the payment is

```
20X2
March 1        Interest Expense                          2,667*
                    Interest Payable                     5,333
                    Cash                                              8,000
```
_____

*The interest expense applicable thus far for 20X2 is for 2 months (December 31, 20X1–March 1, 20X2): $100,000 × 16% × 2/12 = $2,667 (rounded).

11.7 BONDS SOLD AT A PREMIUM OR DISCOUNT BETWEEN INTEREST DATES

When bonds are sold between interest dates at a premium or discount, the entry to record the issuance reflects the accrued interest and the premium or discount. Assuming a premium is involved, the entry is

```
        Cash
                Bonds Payable
                Premium on Bonds Payable
                Interest Expense
```

The premium or discount is amortized over a period between the *issuance* date and the *maturity* date. The date of the bonds is *not* used in determining the amortization period. The amortization per year is based on the number of months that the bonds are outstanding.

EXAMPLE 9   A 5-year bond dated January 1, 20X1, is sold on March 1, 20X1, at a premium of $1,160. The amortization period is 4 years and 10 months (March 1, 20X1–December 31, 20X5), or 58 months. For 20X1, the premium amortization is for 10 months (March 1, 20X1–December 31, 20X1). The amount of the amortization is $200 ($1,160 × 10/58).

EXAMPLE 10   On May 1, 20X1, a company issues $50,000 of 10-year, 12 percent bonds at 110. The bonds are dated January 1, 20X1. Interest is payable on January 1 and July 1. The bonds will be outstanding for 9 years and 8 months, or 116 months. Appropriate journal entries are

20X1			
May 1	Cash	57,000	
	Bonds Payable		50,000
	Premium on Bonds Payable		5,000
	Interest Expense		2,000*
July 1	Interest Expense	3,000**	
	Cash		3,000
Dec. 31	Interest Expense	3,000	
	Interest Payable		3,000
	Premium on Bonds Payable	345†	
	Interest Expense		345
20X2			
Jan. 1	Interest Payable	3,000**	
	Cash		3,000

*Accrued interest is for 4 months (January 1–May 1):
$$\$50,000 \times 12\% \times 4/12 = \$2,000.$$

**$50,000 × 12% × 6/12 = $3,000

†The bonds were held for 8 months in 20X1 (May 1–December 31):
$$\$5,000 \times 8/116 = \$345 \text{ (rounded)}.$$

11.8 EARLY EXTINGUISHMENT OF BONDS

Where a callable option exists, a company may redeem its bonds prior to maturity. This may be the choice when the interest rate on the debt is considerably higher than the current market interest rate. In this case, the company will profit by issuing new bonds at a lower interest rate and use the funds to reacquire the original, higher interest bonds. The call price is usually a few points above face value.

Even if a call provision does not exist, the company may still retire its bonds early by purchasing them in the open market.

EXAMPLE 11   Charles Corporation has outstanding bonds payable of $100,000 with an unamortized premium of $5,000. The call price on the bonds is 102. If we assume that all the bonds are redeemed, the journal entry is

Bonds Payable	100,000	
Premium on Bonds Payable	5,000	
Cash		102,000
Gain on the Early Extinguishment of Debt		3,000

The Gain account is shown separately in the income statement as an extraordinary item.

EXAMPLE 12   Assume the same facts as in Example 11 except that only 20 percent of the outstanding bonds are redeemed. The journal entry is

Bonds Payable	20,000	
Premium on Bonds Payable	1,000	
Cash		20,400
Gain on the Early Extinguishment of Debt		600

11.9   BOND CONVERSION

A convertible bond gives the holder the option to convert it into stock at a later date. A conversion factor indicates how many shares of stock will be received for each $1,000 bond held. The bond conversion is likely when the market price of the stock rises considerably.

EXAMPLE 13   Convertible bonds of $100,000 are exchanged for common stock. Each bond is convertible into 10 shares of stock. Since there are 100 bonds ($100,000/$1,000), the amount of shares to be issued is 1,000 (100 bonds × 10 shares).

EXAMPLE 14   Ajax Corporation has $200,000 of convertible bonds outstanding with an unamortized discount of $12,000. The bonds are convertible at the rate of 30 shares of $20 par common stock for each bond held. The journal entry upon conversion is

Bonds Payable	200,000	
Discount on Bonds Payable		12,000
Common Stock		120,000*
Premium on Common Stock		68,000

        *200 bonds × 30 shares = 6,000 shares × $20 par = $120,000

11.10   CONTINGENT LIABILITIES

A business may face *potential* liabilities arising from previous events. However, *uncertainty* exists with regard to the amount, *if any*, of the company's liability. For example, in the *unlikely* event that the maker of a note that was discounted at the bank defaults upon it, the company will be required to make payment to the bank. Contingent liabilities may also arise from litigation, product warranties, and additional tax assessments.

FASB 5 covers accounting for contingencies. A loss from a contingency shall be accrued by a charge to income and a credit to the estimated liability if *both* of the following conditions are met:

1.   Information prior to the issuance of the financial statements indicates that it is *probable* that an asset had been impaired or a liability had been incurred at the date of the financial statements.

2.   The amount of loss can be *reasonably estimated*.

If no accrual is made because the above criteria have not been met, *disclosure* of the contingency shall be made when there is a *reasonable possibility* that a loss may have been incurred.

EXAMPLE 15   On December 6, 20X1, a lawsuit was initiated against the company. It is probable that the firm will have a legal liability of about $100,000. The entry to record the estimated liability is

Loss	100,000	
Estimated Liability		100,000

Summary

(1)   The two types of liabilities are _____ and _____ .

(2)   Current liabilities are due within one year or the normal operating cycle of the business, whichever is _____ .

(3)   _____ are long-term liabilities offered to the general public.

(4)   A key advantage of issuing bonds is that their _____ is tax deductible.

(5)   In a(n) _____ lease, the lessee records a liability for the present value of future minimum rental payments to be made.

(6)   The payroll tax expense of an employer consists of social security taxes and _____ taxes.

(7)   Most bonds are issued in _____ denominations.

(8)   When the name of the owner appears on the bond it is known as a(n) _____ bond.

(9)   A bond which does not have the name of the owner on it but has attached coupons is known as a(n) _____ bond.

(10)   A(n) _____ is an unsecured bond.

(11)   Bonds that may be exchanged for other securities under specified conditions are referred to as _____ bonds.

(12)   _____ bonds mature periodically rather than at a fixed maturity date.

(13)   The interest payment on a bond is based on its _____ .

(14)   A bond will usually be issued at a discount when the face interest rate is _____ than the market rate.

(15)   If bonds are sold at 108, they have been issued at a(n) _____ .
(16)   Premium on bonds payable appears in the balance sheet as a(n) _____ to _____ .

(17)   The amortization of bond discount will _____ interest expense.

(18)   When bonds are sold at a discount or premium, the amortization period is from the _____ date to the _____ date.

(19)   When a bond is sold at face value between interest dates, the proceeds received by the issuing company are equal to the face value of the bond plus _____ .

(20)   _____ bonds may be redeemed before maturity.

(21)   The call price of a bond is typically _____ its face value.

(22)   The gain or loss on the early extinguishment of debt is shown in the income statement as a(n) _____ item.

Answers: (1) current, noncurrent; (2) longer; (3) Bonds; (4) interest expense; (5) capital; (6) unemployment insurance; (7) $1,000; (8) registered; (9) coupon; (10) debenture; (11) convertible; (12) Serial; (13) face value; (14) lower; (15) premium; (16) addition, bonds payable; (17) increase; (18) issuance, maturity; (19) accrued interest; (20) Callable; (21) above; (22) extraordinary

Solved Problems

11.1   Gross salaries for the week total $23,000. The following amounts were withheld from employee salaries: income taxes, $3,100; social security, $1,200; and union dues, $320. Prepare the necessary journal entry to record the payment of the payroll.

SOLUTION

Salaries Expense	23,000	
Income Taxes Payable		3,100
Social Security Taxes Payable		1,200
Union Dues Payable		320
Cash		18,380

11.2   On January 1, 20X1, *The Journal of Accountancy* received three-year subscriptions totalling $60,000. Prepare all appropriate journal entries for 20X1.

SOLUTION

20X1			
Jan. 1	Cash	60,000	
	Unearned Subscription Income		60,000
Dec. 31	Unearned Subscription Income	20,000	
	Subscription Income		20,000

11.3   On January 1, 20X1, Burns Corporation issued $200,000 16 percent, 20-year bonds at 103. Interest is payable on July 1 and January 1. Prepare appropriate journal entries for 20X1 for the issuance of the bonds, recording of interest, and the amortization of premium.

SOLUTION

20X1

Jan. 1	Cash	206,000	
	Bonds Payable		200,000
	Premium on Bonds Payable		6,000
July 1	Interest Expense	16,000*	
	Cash		16,000
Dec. 31	Interest Expense	16,000	
	Interest Payable		16,000
	Premium on Bonds Payable	300**	
	Interest Expense		300

*$200,000 \times 16\% \times 6/12 = \$16,000$

**$\$6,000/20$ years $= \$300$

11.4 (a) Using the information in Problem 11.3, prepare the long-term liabilities section of the balance sheet as of December 31, 20X1.

(b) What will the carrying value of the bonds be at the maturity date?

SOLUTION

(a)   *Long-term Liabilities*

Bonds Payable	$200,000
Add: Premium on Bonds Payable	5,700
Carrying Value	$205,700

(b) $200,000

11.5 Assume that Burns Corporation in Problem 11.3 issued the bonds at 98 instead of 103. Prepare appropriate journal entries for 20X1 for the issuance of the bonds, recording of interest, and the amortization of discount.

SOLUTION

20X1

Jan. 1	Cash	196,000	
	Discount on Bonds Payable	4,000	
	Bonds Payable		200,000
July 1	Interest Expense	16,000	
	Cash		16,000
Dec. 31	Interest Expense	16,000	
	Interest Payable		16,000
	Interest Expense	200*	
	Discount on Bonds Payable		200

*$\$4,000/20$ years $= \$200$

11.6 (a) Referring to the information in Problem 11.5, prepare the long-term liabilities section of the balance sheet as of December 31, 20X1.

(b) What will be the carrying value of the bonds at the end of the 20th year?

SOLUTION

(a)   *Long-term Liabilities*

Bonds Payable	$200,000
Less: Discount on Bonds Payable	3,800
Carrying Value	$196,200

(b) $200,000

11.7 The Restman Corporation sold $200,000 of 15 percent, 10-year bonds on March 1, 20X1. The bonds are dated January 1, 20X1. Interest is payable on July 1 and January 1. The bonds were sold at face value.

(a) Prepare the journal entries for 20X1.

(b) Prepare the journal entry for January 1, 20X2.

SOLUTION

(a) 20X1

March 1	Cash	205,000	
	Bonds Payable		200,000
	Interest Expense		5,000*
July 1	Interest Expense	15,000**	
	Cash		15,000
Dec. 31	Interest Expense	15,000	
	Interest Payable		15,000

(b) 20X2

Jan. 1	Interest Payable	15,000	
	Cash		15,000

---

*Accrued interest is for 2 months (January 1–March 1):
$200,000 × 15% × 2/12 = $5,000.

**$200,000 × 15% × 6/12 = $15,000

11.8 On March 1, 20X1, Molar Corporation issued $450,000 of 15 percent, 20-year bonds at face value. The bonds are dated February 1, 20X1. On June 1, 20X1, another $300,000 of the bonds were issued at face value. Interest is payable August 1 and February 1. Prepare all appropriate entries for 20X1 and the entry on February 1, 20X2.

SOLUTION

20X1				
March 1	Cash		455,625	
		Bonds Payable		450,000
		Interest Expense		5,625*
June 1	Cash		315,000	
		Bonds Payable		300,000
		Interest Expense		15,000**
Aug. 1	Interest Expense		56,250†	
		Cash		56,250
Dec. 31	Interest Expense		46,875††	
		Interest Payable		46,875
20X2				
Feb. 1	Interest Expense		9,375‡	
	Interest Payable		46,875	
		Cash		56,250

*Accrued interest is for 1 month (February 1–March 1): $450,000 × 15% × 1/12 = $5,625.

**Accrued interest is for 4 months (February 1–June 1); $300,000 × 15% × 4/12 = $15,000.

†$750,000 × 15% × 6/12 = $56,250

††Accrued interest is for 5 months (August 1–December 31): $750,000 × 15% × 5/12 = $46,875.

‡The interest expense applicable thus far for 20X2 is for 1 month (December 31–February 1): $750,000 × 15% × 1/12 = $9,375.

11.9 Based on the following information for Caton Incorporated, prepare the appropriate journal entries for 20X7 and 20X8.

20X7

Mar. 1—Issued $200,000 of 16 percent, 20-year bonds at 103. The bonds are dated March 1, 20X7. Interest is payable on March 1 and September 1.

Sept. 1—Paid the semiannual interest

Dec. 31—Recorded the accrued interest on the bonds

Dec. 31—Recorded the amortization of the premium

20X8

Mar. 1—Paid the semiannual interest

Sept. 1—Paid the semiannual interest

Dec. 31—Recorded the accrued interest on the bonds

Dec. 31—Recorded the amortization of premium

SOLUTION

20X7				
March 1	Cash		206,000	
		Bonds Payable		200,000
		Premium on Bonds Payable		6,000
Sept. 1	Interest Expense		16,000*	
		Cash		16,000
Dec. 31	Interest Expense		10,667**	
		Interest Payable		10,667
	Premium on Bonds Payable		250†	
		Interest Expense		250
20X8				
March 1	Interest Expense		5,333††	
	Interest Payable		10,667	
		Cash		16,000
Sept. 1	Interest Expense		16,000*	
		Cash		16,000
Dec. 31	Interest Expense		10,667**	
		Interest Payable		10,667
	Premium on Bonds Payable		300‡	
		Interest Expense		300

---

*$200,000 \times 16\% \times 6/12 = \$16,000$

**Accrued interest is for 4 months (September 1–December 31): $\$200,000 \times 16\% \times 4/12 = \$10,667$ (rounded).

†The life of the bonds is 240 months (12 months $\times$ 20 years). Amortization is for 10 months (March 1–December 31): $\$6,000 \times 10/240 = \$250$.

††Accrued interest is for 2 months (December 31–March 1): $\$200,000 \times 16\% \times 2/12 = \$5,333$ (rounded).

‡Amortization is for one year: $\$6,000/20$ years $= \$300$.

11.10 With regard to Problem 11.9, prepare the long-term liabilities section of the balance sheet as of December 31, 20X8.

SOLUTION

Long-term Liabilities	
Bonds Payable	$200,000
Add: Premium on Bonds Payable	5,450*
Carrying Value	$205,450

---

*$\$6,000 - \$250 - \$300 = \$5,450$

11.11 On April 1, 20X6, $100,000 of 14 percent, 10-year bonds were sold at 98. The bonds are dated January 1, 20X6. Interest is payable on January 1 and July 1. What is the amount to be received by the company at the issuance date?

SOLUTION

Price of bonds ($100,000 × 98%)	$ 98,000
Accrued interest for 3 months ($100,000 × 14% × 3/12)	3,500
Proceeds	$101,500

11.12 On May 1, 20X1, a company issues $100,000 of 18 percent, 12-year bonds at 106. The bonds are dated March 1, 20X1. Interest is payable March 1 and September 1. Prepare journal entries for (a) 20X1 and (b) 20X2.

SOLUTION

(a)   20X1

May 1	Cash	109,000	
	Bonds Payable		100,000
	Premium on Bonds Payable		6,000
	Interest Expense		3,000*
Sept. 1	Interest Expense	9,000**	
	Cash		9,000
Dec. 31	Interest Expense	6,000†	
	Interest Payable		6,000
	Premium on Bonds Payable	338††	
	Interest Expense		338

(b)   20X2

March 1	Interest Expense	3,000*	
	Interest Payable	6,000	
	Cash		9,000
Sept. 1	Interest Expense	9,000**	
	Cash		9,000
Dec. 31	Interest Expense	6,000†	
	Interest Payable		6,000
	Premium on Bonds Payable	507‡	
	Interest Expense		507

---

*Accrued interest is for 2 months: $100,000 × 18% × 2/12 = $3,000.

**$100,000 × 18% × 6/12 = $9,000

†Accrued interest is for 4 months (September 1–December 31): $100,000 × 18% × 4/12 = $6,000.

††The bonds are outstanding for 11 years and 10 months, or 142 months. The bonds were held for 8 months in 20X1 (May 1–December 31): $6,000 × 8/142 = $338 (rounded).

‡$6,000 × 12/142 = $507 (rounded).

11.13 The Stonewall Company had the following ledger accounts prior to redeeming its bonds at 103:

Bonds Payable		Discount on Bonds Payable	
	900,000	15,000	

(a) Prepare the entry to record the redemption.

(b) Prepare the entry assuming that only 20 percent of the bonds were called.

SOLUTION

(a)	Bonds Payable	900,000	
	Loss on Early Extinguishment of Debt	42,000	
	Cash		927,000*
	Discount on Bonds Payable		15,000

(b)	Bonds Payable	180,000**	
	Loss on Early Extinguishment of Debt	8,400	
	Cash		185,400†
	Discount on Bonds Payable		3,000††

    *$900,000 × 103% = $927,000
   **$900,000 × 20% = $180,000
    †$180,000 × 103% = $185,400
   ††$15,000 × 20% = $3,000

11.14 The following ledger accounts relate to Hooper Corporation's convertible bonds:

Bonds Payable		Premium on Bonds Payable	
	900,000		10,000

Prepare the entry to record the conversion assuming that all bondholders convert their holdings at the ratio of eight shares of $100 par common stock for each bond held.

SOLUTION

Bonds Payable	900,000	
Premium on Bonds Payable	10,000	
Common Stock		720,000*
Premium on Common Stock		190,000

    *There are 900 bonds ($900,000/$1,000).
     900 bonds × 8 shares = 7,200 shares × $100 par = $720,000

11.15 There is a pending lawsuit against Ames Corporation that may possibly result in future damages of $30,000. What recognition should be given to it in the financial statements?

SOLUTION

Footnote disclosure should be given of the particulars of the pending litigation, including the possible estimated loss of $30,000.

CHAPTER 12

Corporations

12.1 INTRODUCTION

The corporation is an artificial being created by law with an *indefinite life*. It is owned by stockholders who hold shares in it. The advantages of incorporating are: (1) in the event the corporation fails, stockholders are only accountable for the amount they have invested; (2) ownership may easily be transferred by selling the shares held; (3) the corporation continues to exist even with the death of a stockholder; (4) contracts can be entered into in the corporate name; and (5) significant funds can be raised through the sale of stock to the public. The disadvantages of the corporate form are: (1) high taxes; (2) annual fees paid to the state in which the company operates; (3) *double taxation* in that the source of dividends, corporate income, is subject to corporate income taxes and the dividends received by stockholders are themselves subject to personal income taxes; (4) the cost of printing stock certificates; (5) governmental regulation over corporate affairs; and (6) the filing of financial reports, as required by the Securities and Exchange Commission, that may disclose vital information to creditors.

12.2 TERMINOLOGY

A *stockholder* is an owner of the company and as such is entitled to vote, share in earnings through the receipt of dividends, share in the disposition of assets after creditors if the company becomes bankrupt, sell his or her ownership interest, and invest in additional shares on a proportionate basis if the company increases the amount of shares outstanding (preemptive right). Stockholders elect a *board of directors* who make corporate policy decisions and appoint corporate officers.

Shares of stock are issued as evidence of ownership in the company. The *stock certificate* typically has a *par value* printed on it. This represents an arbitrary amount assigned to it as per the corporation's charter. The market price of the stock is what the stock is currently selling for on the stock exchange.

Authorized shares are the maximum amount that can be issued according to the articles of incorporation. However, the company may apply at a later date to the state for permission to increase the number of authorized shares. *Issued shares* are the amount of authorized shares that have been sold to the public. The difference between the authorized shares and the issued shares represents the *unissued shares*. *Treasury stock* represents the issued shares that have been reacquired by the company. *Outstanding shares* are those shares being *held by stockholders*. Outstanding shares equal issued shares less treasury stock. Dividends are based on outstanding shares. *Subscribed shares* are those shares under contract at a specified price for which a down payment has been given. The shares will not be issued until full payment is received from the subscriber.

EXAMPLE 1 ABC Company has an authorization for 100,000 shares. During 20X1, 82,000 shares were issued. During the year, the company bought back 5,000 shares. The outstanding shares at year's end are determined as follows:

Issued Shares	82,000
Less: Treasury Stock	5,000
Outstanding Shares	77,000

Dividends will be based on the outstanding shares of 77,000.

12.3 TYPES OF STOCK

The two types of stock are common and preferred. If a company only has one class of stock, it is known as *common stock*. An owner of common stock has voting rights. *Preferred stock* does not have voting rights but does have preference over common stock in the event of liquidation and in the distribution of dividends. However, the amount of dividends paid to preferred stockholders is typically limited to a given percentage of par value. Most preferred stock is *cumulative*, which means that if no dividends are paid in a given year those dividends accumulate (dividends in arrears). The preferred stockholders must receive the dividends in arrears before common stockholders can receive any dividends. *Noncumulative* preferred stock means that omitted dividends are lost. Preferred stock is typically *nonparticipating*, which means it does not receive dividends in excess of the fixed percentage rate. *Participating* preferred stock, which is rarely issued, means that in addition to the regular specified dividend it will participate with common stock in any additional dividends paid.

EXAMPLE 2 Charles Corporation has 10,000 shares of cumulative, nonparticipating preferred stock paying dividends of $2 per share. There are 35,000 shares of common stock. In 20X1 and 20X2, no dividends were paid. In 20X3, dividends of $82,000 were paid. The dividend distribution in 20X3 is

Preferred Stock (10,000 shares × $2 = $20,000 dividends per year × 3 years)	$60,000
Common Stock ($82,000 − $60,000)	22,000
Total Dividend	$82,000

12.4 STOCKHOLDERS' EQUITY

The stockholders' equity section of the balance sheet consists of capital stock, paid-in capital, retained earnings, and total stockholders' equity.

Capital stock. This section shows the *par value* of the stock issued. Preferred stock is listed before common stock because of its preference in liquidation.

Paid-in capital. This section shows the amount received over the par value of the stock issued.

Retained earnings. This represents the accumulated earnings of the company since inception less the dividends declared.

Total stockholders' equity. This is the sum of the above.

12.5 ISSUANCE OF STOCK

An entry is made when shares are issued by the company to stockholders. However, when one stockholder sells his or her shares to another stockholder, no entry is made on the company's books since the entity is not involved in the transaction. All that will happen as far as the company is concerned is the mailing of the dividend check to the new shareholder.

When stock is issued at par value, cash is debited and the particular security (common stock or preferred stock) is credited.

EXAMPLE 3 Altman Corporation issued at par 1,000 shares of $10 par value common stock. The journal entry is

Cash	10,000	
Common Stock		10,000

The market price of a company's stock will inevitably be different from its par value. Possible reasons include inflation, financial strength of the entity, business conditions, and the trend in dividends.

When stock is sold at an issuance price that is different than par value, cash is debited for the amount received and the particular security (common stock or preferred stock) is credited at par value. The difference will represent either a premium or a discount.

When stock is sold above par value, the excess is called a premium. The premium account is shown under the paid-in capital section of stockholders' equity because it relates to the issuance of the company's stock. It is *not* an income statement account since the company earns profits by selling goods and services to outsiders, *not* by issuing shares of stock.

In the case where the issuance price is less than par value, a discount account ensues. This is shown under paid-in capital as a reduction. The issuance of stock at a discount is very rare. In many states, it is prohibited.

EXAMPLE 4 Western Corporation issued 5,000 shares of $10 par value preferred stock for $16 a share. The journal entry is

Cash	80,000	
Preferred Stock		50,000
Premium on Preferred Stock		30,000

EXAMPLE 5 Western Corporation issued 10,000 shares of $20 par value common stock for $19 a share. The journal entry is

Cash	190,000	
Discount on Common Stock	10,000	
Common Stock		200,000

EXAMPLE 6 Using the information in Examples 4 and 5 and assuming Western Corporation's retained earnings balance is $40,000, we can show the company's stockholders' equity section as follows:

Balance Sheet (partial)

Stockholders' Equity		
Capital Stock		
Preferred Stock, $10 par value, issued and outstanding 5,000 shares	$ 50,000	
Common Stock, $20 par value, issued and outstanding 10,000 shares	200,000	$250,000
Paid-in Capital		
Premium on Preferred Stock	$ 30,000	
Premium on Common Stock	(10,000)	20,000
Retained Earnings		40,000
Total Stockholders' Equity		$310,000

If stock is issued for other than cash, the asset received is recorded at its fair market value.

EXAMPLE 7   Lorkin Corporation issues 1,000 shares of $5 par value common stock in exchange for land valued at $5,500. The journal entry is

Land	5,500	
Common Stock		5,000
Premium on Common Stock		500

12.6   SUBSCRIBED STOCK

Stock may be acquired under an installment plan. The journal entry for the down payment is

Cash (down payment)
Subscriptions Receivable (balance due)
    Common Stock Subscribed (par value)
    Premium on Common Stock (subscription price over par value)

Subscriptions receivable is a current asset. Common stock subscribed is shown under capital stock in the stockholders' equity section.

The journal entry for each payment made by the subscriber is

Cash
    Subscriptions Receivable

When *full* payment has been received, the subscribed stock will be issued. The journal entries are

Cash
    Subscriptions Receivable

Common Stock Subscribed
    Common Stock

EXAMPLE 8   On March 5, Hart Corporation received subscriptions for 10,000 shares of $15 par value common stock. The subscription price is $18 per share. A down payment of 40 percent was made. On June 12, the balance due from the subscribers was received. The appropriate journal entries are

March 5	Cash	72,000	
	Subscriptions Receivable	108,000	
	Common Stock Subscribed		150,000
	Premium on Common Stock		30,000
June 12	Cash	108,000	
	Subscriptions Receivable		108,000
	Common Stock Subscribed	150,000	
	Common Stock		150,000

If a subscriber defaults on his or her subscription, the company must account for it in accordance with the laws of the state of its incorporation. Some states require the subscriber to forfeit the amount he or she has paid. Other states require that shares be issued based upon a percentage of the amount paid by the subscriber.

12.7 TREASURY STOCK

Treasury stock represents issued stock that has been reacquired by the company. The reasons for the reacquisition include having shares available for a stock option plan or for the acquisition of another company, and attempting to support the market price of stock. Shares of stock held in the treasury are not entitled to dividends or voting rights. Treasury stock is shown in the balance sheet as a reduction to stockholders' equity since in essence the company is returning capital to stockholders.

The most common method of accounting for treasury stock is to record it at cost. The par value and the market price at which the stock was originally sold is *not* considered. The journal entry is

Treasury Stock

Cash

When treasury stock is resold, the difference between the selling price and the cost is reflected in an account called Paid-in Capital—Treasury Stock. If the selling price exceeds the purchase price, the journal entry is

Cash

Treasury Stock

Paid-In Capital—Treasury Stock

EXAMPLE 9 Drake Company's stockholders' equity section of its balance sheet as of December 31, 20X0, appears below.

Balance sheet (partial)
December 31, 20X0

Stockholders' Equity	
Capital Stock	
Common Stock, $10 par value, authorized 40,000 shares; issued and outstanding 20,000 shares	$200,000
Paid-in Capital	
Premium on Common Stock	15,000
Retained Earnings	20,000
Total Stockholders' Equity	$235,000

The company had the following transactions during 20X1:

April   7—Purchased 1,000 shares of outstanding common stock at $18 per share

Aug. 16—Sold 400 shares of treasury stock at $20 per share

Dec.   6—Sold 250 shares of treasury stock at $16 per share

The appropriate journal entries for the above transactions are

April 7	Treasury Stock	18,000	
	Cash		18,000
Aug. 16	Cash	8,000	
	Treasury Stock		7,200*
	Paid-in Capital—Treasury Stock		800
Dec. 6	Cash	4,000	
	Paid-in Capital—Treasury Stock	500	
	Treasury Stock		4,500**

*400 shares $\times$ $18 = $7,200

**250 shares $\times$ $18 = $4,500

Assume the net income for the year was $3,000. The stockholders' equity section of the balance sheet at December 31, 20X1, follows:

Balance Sheet (partial)
December 31, 20X1

Stockholders' Equity
   Capital Stock
      Common Stock, $10 par value, authorized 40,000 shares;
         issued and outstanding 20,000 shares $200,000

Stockholders' Equity		
Capital Stock		
Common Stock, $10 par value, authorized 40,000 shares; issued and outstanding 20,000 shares		$200,000
Paid-In Capital		
Premium on Common Stock	$15,000*	
Paid-in Capital—Treasury Stock	300	15,300
Retained Earnings		23,000
Subtotal		$238,300
Less: Treasury Stock (350 shares at cost)		6,300**
Total Stockholders' Equity		$232,000

_____

*$800 − $500 = $300
**$18,000 − $7,200 − $4,500 = $6,300

When a company experiences financial problems, stockholders may donate shares back to the company so that they may be resold. At the date of donation, *no entry* is made since there is no cost to the company in obtaining the shares. All that is required is a *memorandum* disclosing the amount of shares donated. When the donated treasury stock is subsequently sold, the journal entry is

                 Cash
                    Paid-in Capital—Donation

The Paid-in Capital account is shown under stockholders' equity in the balance sheet.

EXAMPLE 10   On February 7, Harris Corporation received 1,000 shares of donated common stock having a par value of $15. On April 9, it sold the shares for $23,000. The journal entries are

     Feb. 7   Memorandum: Received 1,000 shares of $15
               par value common stock as a donation.

     April 9   Cash   23,000
                Paid-in Capital—Donation   23,000

12.8   DIVIDENDS

Dividends are a reduction of retained earnings and are usually in the form of cash or stock. When a dividend is declared, it becomes a legal liability of the company. Three important dates associated with dividends are:

1. *Declaration date.* The date upon which a dividend is declared by the board of directors.
2. *Date of record.* The date upon which a stockholder must hold the stock in order to be entitled to receive the dividend.
3. *Payment date.* The date the stockholder receives the dividend.

Journal entries are made on the declaration and payment dates. No entry is made on the date of record.

CASH DIVIDENDS

The usual type of dividend is in the form of cash. A cash dividend is typically expressed on a dollar-and-cents-per-share basis. However, with preferred stock, the dividend is sometimes expressed as a percentage of par value.

EXAMPLE 11   On November 15, 20X1, a cash dividend of $1.50 per share was declared on 10,000 shares of $10 par value common stock. The record date is December 20, 20X1. Payment is to be made on January 15, 20X2. The journal entries are

20X1			
Nov. 15	Retained Earnings	15,000*	
	Cash Dividends Payable		15,000
Dec. 20	No Entry		
20X2			
Jan. 15	Cash Dividends Payable	15,000	
	Cash		15,000

*10,000 shares × $1.50 = $15,000

Note that cash dividends payable is a Current Liability account.

EXAMPLE 12   Jones Corporation has outstanding 20,000 shares of $10 par value, 12 percent preferred stock. On October 15, 20X1, a cash dividend was declared to holders of record as of December 15, 20X1. The payment date is January 15, 20X2. The journal entries are

20X1			
Oct. 15	Retained Earnings	24,000*	
	Cash Dividends Payable		24,000
Dec. 15	No Entry		
20X2			
Jan. 15	Cash Dividends Payable	24,000	
	Cash		24,000

*20,000 shares × $10 par = $200,000 par value × 12% dividend rate = $24,000

STOCK DIVIDENDS

A stock dividend involves the issuance of additional shares to stockholders. A stock dividend may be declared when the cash position of the firm is inadequate and/or when the firm wishes to prompt more trading by reducing the market price of stock.

A *small* stock dividend (when amounts to be distributed are *less* than 20–25 percent of the outstanding stock) requires the following entry when the dividend is declared:

> Retained Earnings (based on the market value of the shares)
>   Stock Dividend Distributable (based on the par value of the shares)
>   Premium on Common Stock

A *large* stock dividend (when amounts to be distributed are *more* than 20–25 percent of the outstanding stock) requires the following entry when the dividend is declared:

> Retained Earnings (based on the par value of the shares)
>   Stock Dividend Distributable (based on the par value of the shares)

The entry for the actual stock issuance is the *same* whether there is a small or large stock dividend:

> Stock Dividend Distributable
>   Common Stock

The Stock Dividend Distributable account is shown under the capital stock section of stockholders' equity. It should be noted that the capital stock section shows not only the par value of the stock issued but also the par value of securities that will become issued stock at a later date. Examples are stock dividends and stock subscribed. Stock dividend distributable is *not a liability* since there is no obligation to pay cash.

EXAMPLE 13   Laim Corporation has 40,000 shares of $10 par value common stock outstanding. On December 7, 20X1, it declared a 5 percent stock dividend to the shareholders of record on January 7, 20X2. On December 7, the market price of the stock was $25 per share. The issuance date is February 6, 20X2. Appropriate journal entries follow:

20X1			
Dec. 7	Retained Earnings	50,000*	
	Common Stock Dividend Distributable		20,000**
	Premium on Common Stock		30,000
20X2			
Jan. 7	No Entry		
Feb. 6	Common Stock Dividend Distributable	20,000	
	Common Stock		20,000

———————————

    *40,000 shares × 5% = 2,000 shares × $25 = $50,000

    **2,000 shares × $10 = $20,000

As can be seen from the journal entries, there is no effect on stockholders' equity for a stock dividend since all the accounts involved are stockholder equity accounts. Retained earnings has decreased, but common stock and premium on common stock have increased by the same total amount. A stock dividend therefore provides *no* income for shareholders. It increases the shares held but the proportionate interest of each stockholder in the company remains the same. In other words, if a stockholder had a 2 percent interest in the company before a stock dividend, he or she will have the same 2 percent interest after the stock dividend.

EXAMPLE 14   Mr. X owns 200 shares of Company X. Outstanding shares are 10,000. He thus has a 2 percent interest. A stock dividend of 10 percent is issued. Mr. X will now have 220 shares out of 11,000 issued shares. His proportionate interest has remained at 2 percent (220/11,000).

PROPERTY DIVIDENDS

In rare cases, a property dividend may be declared which calls for the distribution of noncash assets. When a company is going to liquidate, for example, it may decide to distribute a property dividend. The journal entry at the declaration date is

Retained Earnings
Property Dividends Payable

At the payment date, the entry is

Property Dividends Payable
Asset

Property dividends payable is a current liability.

12.9 STOCK SPLITS

A stock split involves issuing a substantial amount of additional shares and reducing the par value of the stock on a proportionate basis. *No entry* is made because the company's accounts do not change. However, there should be a *memorandum* describing the stock split. A stock split is often prompted by a desire to reduce the market price per share in order to stimulate investor buying.

EXAMPLE 15   Smith Corporation has 1,000 shares of $20 par value common stock. The total par value is thus $20,000. A four-for-one stock split is issued. There will now be 4,000 shares at a $5-par value. The total par value remains at $20,000. Theoretically, the market price per share of the stock should also drop to one-fourth of what it was before the split.

12.10 RETAINED EARNINGS

Retained earnings is the accumulated earnings of the business that have not been distributed to stockholders. A profitable business will have a credit balance. However, if accumulated losses exceed accumulated earnings, the account will have a debit balance (deficit). Retained earnings is shown in the stockholders' equity section.

Retained earnings may be either *unappropriated* (free for dividend distribution) or *appropriated* (reserved and unavailable for dividend distribution). When an appropriation is made, unappropriated retained earnings is reduced and the specific appropriated retained earnings account comes into being. The total retained earnings of the company therefore consist of the balance in the unappropriated retained earnings account and the balances in the appropriated retained earnings accounts. Different kinds of appropriations may exist, such as appropriations for contingencies, plant expansion, bond indebtedness, and treasury stock. When an appropriation is established, the following entry is made:

Retained Earnings
Appropriation of Retained Earnings

When the appropriation is no longer needed, the above entry is reversed:

Appropriation of Retained Earnings
Retained Earnings

EXAMPLE 16   Pulsa Corporation has a balance in retained earnings of $80,000. The company decides to establish a reserve for plant expansion of $15,000. The entry is

| Retained Earnings | 15,000 | |
| Appropriation for Plant Expansion | | 15,000 |

The company acquires $5,000 of treasury stock. The entry for the appropriation is

| Retained Earnings | 5,000 | |
| Appropriation for Treasury Stock | | 5,000 |

Many states require that an appropriation of retained earnings be established that is equal to the cost of the treasury stock on hand. This restriction on retained earnings is designed to protect creditors.

Treasury stock costing $3,000 is sold. The entry to reverse part of the appropriation that is no longer needed is

| Appropriation for Treasury Stock | 3,000 | |
| Retained Earnings | | 3,000 |

Under the stockholders' equity section, retained earnings would be broken down as follows:

Balance Sheet (partial)

Unappropriated Retained Earnings		$63,000*
Appropriated Retained Earnings:		
For Plant Expansion	$15,000	
For Treasury Stock	2,000**	17,000
Total Retained Earnings		$80,000

*$80,000 − $15,000 − $5,000 + $3,000 = $63,000
**$5,000 − $3,000 = $2,000

In conclusion, retained earnings is increased by net income but reduced by a net loss, dividends, and appropriations.

12.11 COMPREHENSIVE STOCKHOLDERS' EQUITY SECTION

In order to review the material covered in this chapter, it would be beneficial to prepare a stockholders' equity section containing the accounts already discussed.

EXAMPLE 17 Selected ledger accounts of Jones Corporation as of December 31, 20X5, appear below:

Common Stock, $10 par value, authorized 60,000 shares; issued 40,000 shares, outstanding 39,620 shares	$400,000
Preferred Stock, 15%, $20 par value, authorized 30,000 shares; issued and outstanding 10,000 shares	200,000
Common Stock Dividend Distributable, 2,000 shares	20,000
Common Stock Subscribed, 5,000 shares	50,000
Paid-in Capital—Donation	10,000
Premium on Preferred Stock	15,000
Premium on Common Stock	50,000
Paid-in Capital—Treasury Stock	12,000
Unappropriated Retained Earnings	80,000
Appropriation for Treasury Stock	4,200
Appropriation for Contingencies	20,000
Treasury Stock (380 shares of common stock)	4,200

The stockholders' equity section of the balance sheet as of December 31, 20X5, appears below:

Balance Sheet (partial)

Stockholders' Equity

Capital Stock			
Preferred Stock, 15%, $20 par value, authorized 30,000 shares; issued and outstanding 10,000 shares		$200,000	
Common Stock, $10 par value, authorized 60,000 shares, issued 40,000 shares, outstanding 39,620 shares		400,000	
Common Stock Subscribed, 5,000 shares		50,000	
Common Stock Dividend Distributable, 2,000 shares		20,000	$670,000
Paid-in Capital			
Premium on Preferred Stock		$ 15,000	
Premium on Common Stock		50,000	
Paid-in Capital—Donation		10,000	
Paid-in Capital—Treasury Stock		12,000	$ 87,000
Retained Earnings			
Unappropriated		$ 80,000	
Appropriated			
For Contingencies	$20,000		
For Treasury Stock	4,200	24,200	104,200
Subtotal			$861,200
Less: Treasury Stock (380 shares of common stock)			4,200
Total Stockholders' Equity			$857,000

Summary

(1) The supervision of the corporation is in the hands of the _____ .

(2) The _____ is the evidence of ownership in the corporation.

(3) Limited liability in the event of dissolution is one of the chief advantages of a(n) _____ .

(4) When a corporation is organized, the _____ will specify how many shares of common and preferred stock are authorized.

(5) When only one class of stock is issued, it is called _____ stock.

(6) An arbitrary amount assigned to each share of stock at the date of incorporation is called _____ value.

(7) With _____ preferred stock, shareholders are entitled to dividends in arrears.

(8) When stock is issued above par value it is sold at a(n) _____ .

(9) _____ stock is equal to _____ stock less treasury stock.

(10) _____ stock exists when an individual makes a down payment on shares.

(11) The account Common Stock Subscribed is shown under _____ in the stockholders' equity section.

(12) Treasury stock is recorded at _____ .

(13) Treasury stock is shown in the balance sheet as a reduction of _____ .

(14) When treasury stock is sold above cost, the excess is credited to _____ .

(15) The decision to reduce the par value of a company's stock and issue a proportionate number of shares is known as a(n) _____ .

(16) The accumulated earnings of a company less the dividends is recorded in the _____ account.

(17) A(n) _____ in retained earnings exists when net losses exceed net profits.

(18) A stockholder is entitled to dividends if he or she holds shares on the date of _____ .

(19) When a dividend is declared, regardless of whether the dividend is cash or stock, the _____ account is debited.

(20) A(n) _____ dividend is a pro rata distribution of stock to shareholders.

(21) As a result of a stock dividend, stockholders' equity _____ .

(22) A(n) _____ of retained earnings means that the appropriated amount is unavailable for dividends.

Answers: (1) board of directors; (2) stock certificate; (3) corporation; (4) charter; (5) common; (6) par; (7) cumulative; (8) premium; (9) Outstanding, issued; (10) Subscribed; (11) capital stock; (12) cost; (13) stockholders' equity; (14) paid-in capital—treasury stock; (15) split; (16) Retained Earnings; (17) deficit; (18) record; (19) Retained Earnings; (20) stock; (21) remains the same; (22) appropriation

Solved Problems

12.1 On January 1, Heather Corporation started business. It was authorized to issue 50,000 shares of common stock and 40,000 shares of preferred stock. On January 1, it issued 6,000 shares of $10 par value common stock for cash. On June 20, the company issued an additional 5,000 shares of common stock and also 1,500 shares of 5 percent, $100 par value preferred stock. All shares were issued at par value. Prepare the appropriate journal entries.

SOLUTION

Jan. 1	Cash		60,000	
	Common Stock			60,000
June 20	Cash		200,000	
	Common Stock			50,000
	Preferred Stock			150,000

12.2 Referring to Problem 12.1, prepare the stockholders' equity section of the balance sheet as of June 30.

SOLUTION

Balance Sheet (partial)

Stockholders' Equity

    Capital Stock

        Preferred Stock, 5%, $100 par value, authorized

           40,000 shares; issued and outstanding 1,500 shares $150,000

        Common Stock, $10 par value, authorized 50,000 shares;

           issued and outstanding 11,000 shares   110,000

    Total Stockholders' Equity $260,000

12.3 Brent Corporation is authorized to issue 20,000 shares of preferred stock and 30,000 shares of common stock. The company issued 3,000 shares of 5 percent, $70 par value preferred stock at $68 and 4,000 shares of $35 par value common stock at $40.

    (*a*) Prepare appropriate journal entries.

    (*b*) Prepare the stockholders' equity section of the balance sheet.

SOLUTION

(*a*)	Cash	204,000	
	Discount on Preferred Stock	6,000	
	Preferred Stock		210,000
	Cash	160,000	
	Common Stock		140,000
	Premium on Common Stock		20,000

(b)   **Balance Sheet (partial)**

Stockholders' Equity

  Capital Stock

    Preferred Stock, 5%, $70 par value, authorized 20,000

      shares; issued and outstanding 3,000 shares $210,000

    Common Stock, $35 par value, authorized 30,000

      shares; issued and outstanding 4,000 shares   140,000

                                                                   $350,000

  Paid-in Capital

    Discount on Preferred Stock $ (6,000)

    Premium on Common Stock   20,000   14,000

  Total Stockholders' Equity $364,000

12.4   Kelly Corporation issued 12,000 shares of $8 par value common stock in exchange for equipment valued at $120,000. Prepare the appropriate journal entry.

        SOLUTION

Equipment	120,000	
Common Stock		96,000*
Premium on Common Stock		24,000

           *12,000 shares × $8 = $96,000

12.5   Jacoby Corporation purchased the fixed assets listed below in exchange for 4,500 shares of $100 par value preferred stock.

Asset	Cost	Fair Market Value
Land	$125,000	$108,750
Building	250,000	217,500
Equipment	70,000	60,900
Machinery	140,000	108,950

        Prepare the appropriate journal entry.

        SOLUTION

Land	108,750	
Building	217,500	
Equipment	60,900	
Machinery	108,950	
Preferred Stock		450,000
Premium on Preferred Stock		46,100

12.6   On February 1, the Riverhead Corporation received subscriptions to 40,000 shares of $25 par value common stock at $28 per share. Of the subscription price, 50 percent was collected. On May 1, the balance was paid and the stock was issued. Prepare the necessary journal entries.

SOLUTION

Feb. 1	Cash		560,000	
	Subscriptions Receivable		560,000	
		Common Stock Subscribed		1,000,000
		Premium on Common Stock		120,000
May 1	Cash		560,000	
	Subscriptions Receivable			560,000
	Common Stock Subscribed		1,000,000	
		Common Stock		1,000,000

12.7 Dial Corporation has an authorization to issue 15,000 shares of common stock. To date, it has issued 9,000 shares. The par value is $25. Prepare entries for the following transactions:

Feb. 1—The company received 3,000 shares of donated common stock from its stockholders.

April 1—1,800 shares of treasury stock were sold at $45 per share.

June 1—The remaining shares of treasury stock were sold at $30 per share.

SOLUTION

Feb. 1	Memorandum: Received 3,000 shares of donated common stock having a par value of $25.		
April 1	Cash	81,000	
	Paid-in Capital—Donation		81,000
June 1	Cash	36,000	
	Paid-in Capital—Donation		36,000

12.8 Based on the information in Problem 12.7, prepare the stockholders' equity section of the balance sheet as of (*a*) February 28, (*b*) April 30, and (*c*) June 30.

SOLUTION

(*a*)   *Stockholders' Equity*
   Capital Stock
      Common Stock, $25 par value, authorized 15,000 shares;
         issued 9,000 shares, oustanding 6,000 shares $225,000
   Total Stockholders' Equity $225,000

(*b*)   *Stockholders' Equity*
   Capital Stock
      Common Stock, $25 par value, authorized 15,000 shares;
         issued 9,000 shares, outstanding 7,800 shares $225,000
   Paid-in Capital
      Paid-in Capital—Donation   81,000
   Total Stockholders' Equity $306,000

(c)   *Stockholders' Equity*
  Capital Stock
   Common Stock, $25 par value, authorized 15,000 shares;
    issued and outstanding 9,000 shares $225,000
  Paid-in Capital
   Paid-in Capital—Donation   117,000
  Total Stockholders' Equity $342,000

12.9   Referring to Problem 12.7, prepare the entries if the 3,000 shares of treasury stock were bought for $120,000 instead of being donated.

SOLUTION

Feb. 1	Treasury Stock		120,000	
	Cash			120,000
April 1	Cash		81,000	
	Treasury Stock			72,000*
	Paid-in Capital—Treasury Stock			9,000
June 1	Cash		36,000	
	Paid-in Capital—Treasury Stock		12,000	
	Treasury Stock			48,000**

*$120,000/3,000 shares = $40 per share × 1,800 shares = $72,000

**1,200 shares × $40 = $48,000

12.10   XYZ Company's stockholders' equity section of the balance sheet as of January 1 follows:

Balance Sheet (partial)

Stockholders' Equity
 Capital Stock
  Preferred Stock, 5%, $100 par value, authorized 30,000 shares;
   issued and outstanding 18,000 shares $1,800,000
  Common Stock, $50 par value, authorized 120,000 shares;
   issued and outstanding 80,000 shares   4,000,000 $5,800,000
 Paid-in Capital
  Premium on Preferred Stock $ 40,000
  Premium on Common Stock   100,000   140,000
 Retained Earnings   600,000
 Total Stockholders' Equity $6,540,000

Selected transactions follow:

April 8—Received subscriptions to 6,000 shares of preferred stock at $104. A down payment of 50 percent was made.

July 10—Purchased 10,000 shares of treasury common for $400,000.

Sept. 8—Received payment from the subscribers equal to 40 percent of the subscription price.

Oct. 20—Sold 5,000 shares of treasury common for $250,000.

Dec. 8—After the balance due from the subscribers was received, the shares were issued.

Dec. 15—Sold 3,000 shares of treasury common for $102,000.

Dec. 31—Net income for the year was $30,000.

Prepare journal entries for the above transactions.

SOLUTION

April 8	Cash		312,000	
	Subscriptions Receivable		312,000	
		Preferred Stock Subscribed		600,000
		Premium on Preferred Stock		24,000
July 10	Treasury Stock		400,000*	
		Cash		400,000
Sept. 8	Cash		249,600	
		Subscriptions Receivable		249,600
Oct. 20	Cash		250,000	
		Treasury Stock		200,000**
		Paid-in Capital—Treasury Stock		50,000
Dec. 8	Cash		62,400	
		Subscriptions Receivable		62,400
	Preferred Stock Subscribed		600,000	
		Preferred Stock		600,000
15	Cash		102,000	
	Paid-in Capital—Treasury Stock		18,000	
		Treasury Stock		120,000†
31	Income Summary		30,000	
		Retained Earnings		30,000

---

*Cost per share = $400,000/10,000 shares = $40

**5,000 shares × $40 = $200,000

†3,000 shares × $40 = $120,000

12.11 Using the information from Problem 12.10, prepare the stockholders' equity section of the balance sheet as of December 31.

SOLUTION

Balance Sheet (partial)

Stockholders' Equity

Capital Stock

Preferred Stock, 5%, $100 par value, authorized 30,000 shares;
issued and outstanding 24,000 shares $2,400,000

Common Stock, $50 par value, authorized 120,000 shares;
issued and outstanding 80,000 shares   4,000,000 $6,400,000

Paid-in Capital

Premium on Preferred Stock $ 64,000

Premium on Common Stock   100,000

Paid-in Capital—Treasury Stock   32,000   196,000

Retained Earnings   630,000

Subtotal $7,226,000

Less: Treasury Stock (2,000 common shares at cost)   80,000

Total Stockholders' Equity $7,146,000

12.12 Wilson Corporation has 30,000 shares of cumulative, nonparticipating preferred stock paying dividends of $0.50 per share. There are 50,000 shares of common stock. In 20X1 and 20X2, no dividends were paid. In 20X3, dividends of $70,000 were paid. What is the dividend distribution in 20X3?

SOLUTION

Preferred Stock (30,000 shares × $0.50 = $15,000
dividends per year × 3 years) $45,000

Common Stock ($70,000 − $45,000)   25,000

Total Dividend $70,000

12.13 The Dover Corporation has 10,000 shares of common stock outstanding. On March 5, the company declared a cash dividend of $5 per share payable to stockholders of record on April 5. Payment of the dividend was made on June 1. Prepare appropriate journal entries.

SOLUTION

March 5	Retained Earnings	50,000	
	Cash Dividends Payable		50,000
April 5	No Entry		
June 1	Cash Dividends Payable	50,000	
	Cash		50.000

12.14 The Benson Corporation's stockholders' equity section of its balance sheet as of December 31, 20X1, appears below:

Balance Sheet (partial)
December 31, 20X1

Stockholders' Equity
   Capital Stock
      Common Stock, $120 par value, authorized 12,000 shares;

issued and outstanding 9,000 shares	$1,080,000
Paid-in Capital	
Premium on Common Stock	40,000
Retained Earnings	220,000
Total Stockholders' Equity	$1,340,000

During 20X2, the following transactions occurred:

March   4—A cash dividend of $8 per share was declared.

May   15—A 10 percent stock dividend was declared. The fair market value of the stock is $124 per share.

July   9—The stock dividend was issued.

(*a*)   Prepare appropriate journal entries for the above.

(*b*)   Prepare the stockholders' equity section of the balance sheet as of December 31, 20X2.

SOLUTION

(*a*)

March 4	Retained Earnings	72,000*	
	Cash Dividends Payable		72,000
May 15	Retained Earnings	111,600**	
	Common Stock Dividend Distributable		108,000†
	Premium on Common Stock		3,600
July 9	Common Stock Dividend Distributable	108,000	
	Common Stock		108,000

---

*9,000 shares × $8 = $72,000

**9,000 shares × 10% = 900 shares × $124 = $111,600

†900 shares × $120 = $108,000

(b)   *Balance Sheet (partial)*
                                      December 31, 20X2

    Stockholders' Equity
      Capital Stock
        Common Stock, $120 par value, authorized 12,000 shares;
          issued and outstanding 9,900 shares $1,188,000
      Paid-in Capital
        Premium on Common Stock   43,600
      Retained Earnings   36,400*
      Total Stockholders' Equity $1,268,000

*$220,000 − $72,000 − $111,600 = $36,400

12.15 Referring to Problem 12.14, assume that on February 15, 20X3, the company reacquired 1,200 shares of common stock at $126 per share. Also assume that on April 12, 20X3, when the market price of the stock was $130, a 5 percent stock dividend was declared. Prepare appropriate journal entries.

SOLUTION

20X3			
Feb. 15	Treasury Stock	151,200*	
	Cash		151,200
April 12	Retained Earnings	56,550**	
	Common Stock Dividend Distributable		52,200†
	Premium on Common Stock		4,350

*1,200 shares × $126 = $151,200
**9,900 − 1,200 = 8,700 outstanding shares × 5% = 435 shares × $130 = $56,550
†435 shares × $120 par value = $52,200

12.16 The Simpson Company has 50,000 shares of common stock having a par value of $12 per share. The board of directors decided on a two-for-one stock split. The market price of the stock was $20 before the split.

(a) Record the stock split.

(b) What will the market price per share be immediately after the split?

SOLUTION

(a) No entry is needed since the company's account balances remain the same. However, there should be a memorandum to the effect that there are now 100,000 shares having a par value of $6 per share.

(b) $10 ($20/2).

12.17 The Boswell Corporation shows the following Retained Earnings accounts:

Unappropriated	$210,000
Appropriation for Treasury Stock	100,000
Appropriation for Self-insurance	140,000

During the period, the following transactions occurred:

(*a*) Declared a cash dividend of $80,000.

(*b*) Reduced the appropriation for self-insurance by $20,000.

(*c*) Set up an account for appropriation for plant expansion and made a deposit of $18,000.

(*d*) Increased the appropriation for treasury stock by $23,000.

Journalize the foregoing transactions.

SOLUTION

(*a*)	Retained Earnings	80,000	
	Cash Dividends Payable		80,000
(*b*)	Appropriation for Self-insurance	20,000	
	Retained Earnings		20,000
(*c*)	Retained Earnings	18,000	
	Appropriation for Plant Expansion		18,000
	Plant Expansion Fund	18,000	
	Cash		18,000
(*d*)	Retained Earnings	23,000	
	Appropriation for Treasury Stock		23,000

12.18 The Donald Corporation's Retained Earnings accounts are as follows:

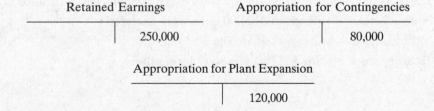

Retained Earnings	Appropriation for Contingencies
250,000	80,000

Appropriation for Plant Expansion
120,000

Journalize the following transactions.

(*a*) Reduced the appropriation for plant expansion to $58,000.

(*b*) Increased the appropriation for contingencies by $22,000.

(*c*) Established an appropriation for bonded indebtedness account for $10,000.

(*d*) Declared a cash dividend of $80,000.

SOLUTION

(a)	Appropriation for Plant Expansion	62,000	
	Retained Earnings		62,000
(b)	Retained Earnings	22,000	
	Appropriation for Contingencies		22,000
(c)	Retained Earnings	10,000	
	Appropriation for Bonded Indebtedness		10,000
(d)	Retained Earnings	80,000	
	Cash Dividends Payable		80,000

12.19 Based upon the answer to Problem 12.18, prepare a schedule of retained earnings.

SOLUTION

Unappropriated Retained Earnings		$200,000
Appropriated Retained Earnings		
For Contingencies	$102,000	
For Plant Expansion	58,000	
For Bonded Indebtedness	10,000	170,000
Total Retained Earnings		$370,000

12.20 Prepare a schedule of retained earnings for the Carol Company based on the following information for the year ended December 31, 20X7.

(a) As of January 1, 20X7, the Unappropriated Retained Earnings account had a balance of $250,000. The appropriation for Treasury Stock account had a balance of $125,000.

(b) Four quarterly dividends of $12,000 each were declared.

(c) Net income for the year was $56,000.

(d) Treasury stock costing $25,000 was sold during the year.

SOLUTION

Unappropriated Retained Earnings	$258,000
Appropriation for Treasury Stock	100,000
Total Retained Earnings	$358,000

12.21 For each of the accounts listed below, identify the appropriate account category by writing an **X** in the correct column.

Account	Asset	Liability	Stockholders' Equity Capital Stock	Paid-in Capital	Retained Earnings
Common Stock					
Subscriptions Receivable					
Common Stock Subscribed					
Discount on Preferred Stock					
Donated Capital					
Organization Costs					
Premium on Preferred Stock					
Appropriation for Plant Expansion					
Paid-in Capital—Treasury Stock					

SOLUTION

Account	Asset	Liability	Stockholders' Equity Capital Stock	Paid-in Capital	Retained Earnings
Common Stock			X		
Subscriptions Receivable	X				
Common Stock Subscribed			X		
Discount on Preferred Stock				X	
Donated Capital				X	
Organization Costs	X				
Premium on Preferred Stock				X	
Appropriation for Plant Expansion					X
Paid-in Capital—Treasury Stock				X	

12.22 Indicate the effect of each of the following items on the stockholders' equity categories.

	Capital Stock	Paid-in Capital	Retained Earnings
A stock subscription in excess of par value			
Receipt of a donation			
Receipt of a subscription to stock at par			
Declaration of a stock dividend where market price exceeds par value			
Issuance of a stock dividend			
Increasing an appropriation for contingencies			
Declaration of a cash dividend			

SOLUTION

	Capital Stock	Paid-in Capital	Retained Earnings
A stock subscription in excess of par value	Increase	Increase	None
Receipt of a donation	None	Increase	None
Receipt of a subscription to stock at par	Increase	None	None
Declaration of a stock dividend where market price exceeds par value	Increase	Increase	Decrease
Issuance of a stock dividend	None	None	None
Increasing an appropriation for contingencies	None	None	None
Declaration of a cash dividend	None	None	Decrease

12.23 The ledger accounts of Trans Corporation as of December 31, 20X3, appear below:

Common Stock, $10 par value, authorized 100,000 shares; issued 60,000 shares, outstanding 56,000 shares	$600,000
Common Stock Dividend Distributable, 3,000 shares	30,000
Paid-in Capital—Donation	12,000
Preferred Stock, 12%, $15 par value, authorized 70,000 shares; issued and outstanding 20,000 shares	300,000
Common Stock Subscribed, 4,000 shares	40,000
Premium on Preferred Stock	60,000
Premium on Common Stock	75,000
Paid-in Capital—Treasury Stock	35,000
Treasury Stock (4,000 shares of common stock)	48,000
Appropriation for Plant Expansion	50,000
Unappropriated Retained Earnings	150,000

Prepare the stockholders' equity section of the balance sheet as of December 31, 20X3.

SOLUTION

Balance Sheet (partial)
December 31, 20X3

Stockholders' Equity

Capital Stock			
Preferred Stock, 12%, $15 par value, authorized 70,000 shares; issued and outstanding 20,000 shares		$300,000	
Common Stock, $10 par value, authorized 100,000 shares; issued 60,000 shares, outstanding 56,000 shares		600,000	
Common Stock Subscribed, 4,000 shares		40,000	
Common Stock Dividend Distributable, 3,000 shares		30,000	$ 970,000
Paid-in Capital			
Premium on Preferred Stock		$ 60,000	
Premium on Common Stock		75,000	
Paid-in Capital—Donation		12,000	
Paid-in Capital—Treasury Stock		35,000	182,000
Retained Earnings			
Unappropriated		$150,000	
Appropriated			
For Treasury Stock	$48,000		
For Plant Expansion	50,000	98,000	248,000
Subtotal			$1,400,000
Less: Treasury Stock (4,000 shares of common stock)			48,000
Total Stockholders' Equity			$1,352,000

1. On January 1, 20X1, Larkin Corporation acquired a machine costing $45,000. The estimated life is five years and the salvage value is $3,000. Determine the depreciation expense for the first two years using the (*a*) straight-line method, (*b*) sum-of-the-years'-digits method, and (*c*) double-declining-balance method.

2. On July 1, 20X1, Pearson Corporation acquired equipment costing $120,000. The estimated life is 10 years and the salvage value is $10,000. Determine the depreciation expense for 20X1 and 20X2 using the sum-of-the-years'-digits method.

3. With regard to Problem 2, show how the equipment would be reported on the balance sheet on (*a*) December 31, 20X1, and (*b*) December 31, 20X2.

4. On March 31, 20X5, a machine costing $45,000 with accumulated depreciation of $16,000 as of December 31, 20X4, is sold for $30,000. The annual straight-line depreciation rate is 10 percent. There was an original salvage value of $5,000. Prepare the appropriate journal entries on March 31, 20X5.

5. The following information relates to a trade-in:

Old Equipment	
Cost	$30,000
Accumulated depreciation as of December 31 of the previous year	20,000
Depreciation expense for the current year up to the time of trade-in	2,000
New Equipment	
Cost	38,000
Trade-in allowance on old equipment	7,000

Assuming an exchange of similar equipment, prepare appropriate journal entries for the trade-in.

6. According to *APB Opinion 17*, what is the maximum period over which intangible assets may be amortized?

7. The net assets of Arjay Corporation are $500,000, which includes intangibles of $80,000. Maxwell Corporation decides to buy the business, paying book value for the net assets. It decides to capitalize goodwill at 15 percent. Goodwill is to be based on the excess earnings over 10 percent. In previous years, net income has averaged 14 percent of net tangible assets. Determine the amount of the goodwill.

8. On January 1, 20X1, Jones Corporation sold $100,000 of 10-year, 16 percent bonds at 106. Interest is payable semiannually on June 30 and December 31. Prepare the appropriate journal entries for 20X1.

9. With regard to Problem 8, how will the bonds payable be reported in the balance sheet as of December 31, 20X2? What will be the carrying value of the bonds at the maturity date?

10. On June 1, 20X1, a company issues $400,000 of 5-year, 18 percent bonds at face value. The bonds are dated March 1, 20X1. Interest is payable March 1 and September 1. Prepare appropriate journal entries from June 1, 20X1, to March 1, 20X2.

11. On April 1, 20X1, Alex Corporation issues $500,000 of 20-year, 16 percent bonds at 95. The bonds are dated January 1, 20X1. Interest is payable June 30 and December 31. Prepare the appropriate journal entries for 20X1.

12. Western Corporation has bonds payable outstanding of $200,000 with an unamortized premium of $15,000. The call price on the bonds is 103. It is decided to redeem 40 percent of the outstanding bonds. Prepare the appropriate journal entry for the redemption.

13. Record the following transactions:

    (a) Issued 1,000 shares of $10 par value common stock for $25 a share

    (b) Issued 2,000 shares of $20 par value preferred stock in exchange for land valued at $45,000

14. On April 7, Winston Corporation received subscriptions for 3,000 shares of $15 par value common stock. The subscription price was $22 per share. A 10 percent down payment was made. On May 9, an additional $30,000 was received. On June 10, the balance due from the subscribers was remitted. Prepare appropriate journal entries.

15. Record the following transactions:

    (a) Purchased 2,000 shares of $10 par value outstanding common stock at $16 per share

    (b) Sold 500 shares of treasury stock at $18 per share

    (c) Sold 300 shares of treasury stock at $15 per share

    (d) Received a donation of 900 shares of common stock

    (e) Sold the donated treasury stock for $17,100

16. Wilder Corporation has 10,000 shares of $15 par value, 14 percent, preferred stock. On November 6, 20X1, a cash dividend is declared to holders of record as of December 9, 20X1. The market price of the stock on November 6, 20X1, was $25. The payment date is January 20, 20X2. Prepare appropriate journal entries.

17. Porter Corporation has 50,000 shares of $10 par value common stock outstanding. On December 12, 20X1, it declared a 10 percent stock dividend to the shareholders of record on January 4, 20X2. On December 12, the market price of the stock was $24 per share. The issuance date is February 9, 20X2. Prepare appropriate journal entries.

Answers to Examination IV

1. (a) $\dfrac{\text{Cost} - \text{Salvage value}}{\text{Number of years of useful life}} = \dfrac{\$45,000 - \$3,000}{5} = \dfrac{\$42,000}{5} = \$8,400 \text{ per year}$

(b) $\dfrac{\text{Remaining years of useful life}}{\text{Sum of the years of useful life*}} \times (\text{Cost} - \text{Salvage value}) = \text{Depreciation}$

$*S = \dfrac{(N)(N+1)}{2} = \dfrac{5(5+1)}{2} = 15$

Year	Fraction × Depreciable Amount = Depreciation Expense		
20X1	5/15	$42,000	$14,000
20X2	4/15	42,000	11,200

(c) Straight-line rate $= \dfrac{\$8,400}{42,000} = 20\%$

Double-declining rate $= 2 \times 20\% = 40\%$
Salvage value is ignored.

Year	Book Value at Beginning of Year	× Rate =	Depreciation Expense	Year-end Book Value
20X1	$45,000	40%	$18,000	$27,000
20X2	27,000	40%	10,800	16,200

2. $(S) = \dfrac{(N)(N+1)}{2} = \dfrac{10(11)}{2} = 55$

20X1

July 1–December 31 $\quad \dfrac{10}{55} \times \$110,000 = \$20,000 \times \dfrac{6}{12} = \$10,000$

20X2

January 1–June 30 $\dfrac{10}{55} \times \$110,000 = \$20,000 \times \dfrac{6}{12} = \$10,000$ (or $\$20,000 - \$10,000$)

July 1–December 31 $\dfrac{9}{55} \times \$110,000 = \$18,000 \times \dfrac{6}{12} = \dfrac{9,000}{\$19,000}$

3. (*a*)

Equipment	$120,000	
Less: Accumulated Depreciation	10,000	
Book Value	$110,000	

(*b*)

Equipment	$120,000	
Less: Accumulated Depreciation	19,000	
Book Value	$101,000	

4. 20X5

March 31	Depreciation Expense	1,000*	
	Accumulated Depreciation		1,000
	Cash	30,000	
	Accumulated Depreciation	17,000	
	Machinery		45,000
	Gain on Disposal of Fixed Assets		2,000

*10% $\times$ \$40,000 = \$4,000 $\times$ 3/12 = \$1,000

5.

Depreciation Expense	2,000	
Accumulated Depreciation		2,000
Accumulated Depreciation	22,000	
Equipment (new)	39,000	
Equipment (old)		30,000
Cash		31,000*

*\$38,000 $-$ \$7,000 = \$31,000

6. 40 years

7.

Average Net Income (\$420,000 $\times$ 0.14)	$ 58,800
Normal Net Income (\$420,000 $\times$ 0.10)	42,000
Excess Net Income	$ 16,800
Capitalized Goodwill (\$16,800/0.15)	$112,000

8. 20X1

Jan. 1	Cash	106,000	
	Bonds Payable		100,000
	Premium on Bonds Payable		6,000

| June 30 | Interest Expense | 8,000* | |
| | Cash | | 8,000 |

| Dec. 31 | Interest Expense | 8,000 | |
| | Cash | | 8,000 |

| | Premium on Bonds Payable | 600** | |
| | Interest Expense | | 600 |

---

*$100,000 × 16% × 6/12 = $8,000

**$6,000/10 = $600

9.

Balance Sheet (partial)
December 31, 20X2

Long-term Liabilities

Bonds Payable	$100,000
Add: Premium on Bonds Payable	4,800*
Carrying Value	$104,800

---

*Premium on Bonds Payable

12/31/X1	600	1/1/X1	6,000
12/31/X2	600	Balance	4,800
	1,200		

At the maturity date, the carrying value of the bonds will be their face value, $100,000.

10.

20X1

June 1	Cash	418,000	
	Bonds Payable		400,000
	Interest Expense		18,000*

| Sept. 1 | Interest Expense | 36,000** | |
| | Cash | | 36,000 |

| Dec. 31 | Interest Expense | 24,000† | |
| | Interest Payable | | 24,000 |

20X2

March 1	Interest Expense	12,000††	
	Interest Payable	24,000	
	Cash		36,000

---

*Accrued interest is for 3 months (March 1–June 1): $400,000 × 18% × 3/12 = $18,000.

**$400,000 × 18% × 6/12 = $36,000

†Accrued interest is for 4 months (September 1–December 31): $400,000 × 18% × 4/12 = $24,000.

††The interest expense applicable thus far for 20X2 is for 2 months (December 31, 20X1–March 1, 20X2): $400,000 × 18% × 2/12 = $12,000.

11.

	20X1			
	April 1	Cash	495,000	
		Discount on Bonds Payable	25,000	
		Bonds Payable		500,000
		Interest Expense		20,000*
	June 30	Interest Expense	40,000**	
		Cash		40,000
	Dec. 31	Interest Expense	40,000	
		Cash		40,000
		Interest Expense	949†	
		Discount on Bonds Payable		949

*Accrued interest is for 3 months (January 1–April 1): $500,000 \times 16\% \times 3/12 = \$20,000$.

**$500,000 \times 16\% \times 6/12 = \$40,000$

†The bonds will be outstanding for 19 years and 9 months, or 237 months. The bonds were held for 9 months in 20X1 (April 1–December 31). The amortization is: $\$25,000 \times 9/237 = \$949$ (rounded).

12.

Bonds Payable	80,000	
Premium on Bonds Payable	6,000	
Cash		82,400
Gain on Early Extinguishment of Debt		3,600

13. (*a*)

Cash	25,000	
Common Stock		10,000
Premium on Common Stock		15,000

(*b*)

Land	45,000	
Preferred Stock		40,000
Premium on Preferred Stock		5,000

14.

	April 7	Cash	6,600	
		Subscriptions Receivable	59,400	
		Common Stock Subscribed		45,000
		Premium on Common Stock		21,000
	May 9	Cash	30,000	
		Subscriptions Receivable		30,000
	June 10	Cash	29,400	
		Subscriptions Receivable		29,400
		Common Stock Subscribed	45,000	
		Common Stock		45,000

15. (*a*)

Treasury Stock		32,000	
Cash			32,000

(*b*)

Cash		9,000	
Treasury Stock			8,000
Paid-in Capital—Treasury Stock			1,000

(*c*)

Cash		4,500	
Paid-in Capital—Treasury Stock		300	
Treasury Stock			4,800

(*d*)   Memorandum: Received 900 shares of $10 par value common stock as a donation.

(*e*)

Cash		17,100	
Paid-in Capital—Donation			17,100

16.

20X1				
Nov. 6	Retained Earnings		21,000*	
	Cash Dividends Payable			21,000
Dec. 9	No Entry			
20X2				
Jan. 20	Cash Dividends Payable		21,000	
	Cash			21,000

---

*10,000 shares × $15 par value = $150,000 par value × 14% dividend rate = $21,000

17.

20X1				
Dec. 12	Retained Earnings	120,000*		
	Common Stock Dividend Distributable		50,000**	
	Premium on Common Stock		70,000	
20X2				
Jan. 4	No Entry			
Feb. 9	Common Stock Dividend Distributable		50,000	
	Common Stock			50,000

---

*50,000 shares × 10% = 5,000 shares × $24 = $120,000

**5,000 shares × $10 par value = $50,000

CHAPTER 13

Partnerships

13.1 FEATURES OF THE PARTNERSHIP

According to the Uniform Partnership Act, a partnership is defined as an association of two or more individuals who carry on as co-owners a business for profit. In general, accounting for a partnership follows the same rules as for a sole proprietorship with the exception that there are separate drawing and capital accounts for each partner. Partnerships are quite often formed in order to bring together different skills or talents, and to bring together necessary capital in order to operate an enterprise. The major characteristics of the partnership form of business are summarized below.

Limited life.   A partnership, unlike a corporation, does not have an unlimited life. A partnership may come to an end by the withdrawal or death of any member of the business, mutual agreement between the partners, completion of the goal for which the partnership was formed, bankruptcy, or court order.

Ease of formation.   Unlike a corporation, a partnership can be formed without any formal proceedings. Although not necessary, a formal partnership agreement spelling out the rights and responsibilities of all the partners is recommended. In cases where the written agreement is silent, the Uniform Partnership Act governs. As a minimum, the partnership agreement should cover the initial capital contributions by each member, withdrawal of funds, distributional percentages of profits and losses, admission of new partners, withdrawal of partners, and the accounting for the eventual dissolution of the business.

Ownership of property.   The property contributed to the partnership by a given partner and the property purchased by the partnership become *jointly* owned by the partners. No partner owns any particular piece of partnership property. Each partner's interest in partnership property is based on his or her proportionate capital balance.

Unlimited liability.   Unlike the corporate form of business, in a partnership each individual member is held *personally* liable for all the debts of the firm. Partnership obligations can be satisfied not only with partnership assets but also with the personal holdings of each partner. However, a newly admitted partner may or may not elect to assume the debts of the partnership existing prior to his or her admission. When a partner withdraws from the firm he or she should give sufficient notice to the public. If the person does not, he or she may be held liable for all partnership liabilities incurred *after* withdrawal. Those partners who retire or withdraw continue to remain liable for partnership obligations existing at the time of withdrawal unless a *novation* exists. A novation is a creditor's consent to release a given partner's liability for partnership debt.

Allocation of net income or net loss.   Profits and losses are divided among the partners in conformity with the terms of the partnership agreement. If nothing is expressly stated, profits and losses are distributed equally.

Mutual agency. Each partner acts as an *agent* for the others. The partnership is legally held responsible for the acts of any partner as long as those acts relate to normal partnership activity. However, the partnership is not bound by acts committed beyond the scope of partnership business.

13.2   INITIAL PARTNERSHIP INVESTMENTS

When an investment is made by a partner the journal entry is

Asset

Capital

When a noncash asset is invested it should be recorded at its *fair market value* at the date of transfer to the partnership.

An obligation assumed by the partnership is credited to the specific liability account involved.

EXAMPLE 1   Enright and Geller form a partnership. Enright, who was previously the sole proprietor, brings the following into the partnership:

	Ledger Balance	Fair Market Value
Cash	$12,000	$12,000
Accounts Receivable	7,000	7,000
Inventory	20,000	18,000
Auto	7,000	5,500
Accumulated Depreciation, Auto	2,000	
Accounts Payable	9,000	9,000
Allowance for Uncollectible Accounts	600	600

The following entry is made to record Enright's initial investment:

Cash	12,000	
Accounts Receivable	7,000	
Inventory	18,000	
Auto	5,500	
Allowance for Uncollectible Accounts		600
Accounts Payable		9,000
Enright, Capital		32,900

Depreciation on the auto on the partnership books will be based on the assigned value of $5,500. Investments made subsequent to the formation of the partnership are credited to the capital accounts.

EXAMPLE 2   Enright invests $5,000 cash and Geller invests office supplies of $1,000. The entry is

Cash	5,000	
Office Supplies	1,000	
Enright, Capital		5,000
Geller, Capital		1,000

13.3 PARTNER DRAWING ACCOUNTS

The partner's drawing account is treated the same way as the drawing account of the owner in the single proprietorship. A personal withdrawal by a partner represents a disinvestment in the business and requires the following journal entry:

Mr./Ms. X, Drawing
Cash

If an asset other than cash is withdrawn (e.g., furniture), that specific asset is credited.

13.4 ALLOCATING NET INCOME OR LOSS TO PARTNERS

Partnership net income or loss is divided in the manner specified in the partnership agreement. Usually, the division is based upon the proportionate capital interest of each partner.

DIVISION BASED ON CAPITAL INTEREST

In this case, net income is allocated based upon the ratio of the partners' capital balances.

EXAMPLE 3 Nelson and Levine have capital balances of $40,000 and $10,000, respectively. The net income for the year is $5,000, which is to be divided based upon the capital balances. The journal entry is

Income Summary	5,000	
Nelson, Capital		4,000*
Levine, Capital		1,000**

$$* \frac{\$40,000}{\$50,000} \times \$5,000 = \$4,000$$

$$** \frac{\$10,000}{\$50,000} \times \$5,000 = \$1,000$$

DIVISION BASED EQUALLY

In this case, each partner gets an equal amount of profit regardless of any other factor (e.g., capital balance, services rendered).

EXAMPLE 4 Assume the same facts as in Example 3 except that profit is to be shared equally. The entry is

Income Summary	5,000	
Nelson, Capital		2,500
Levine, Capital		2,500

DIVISION BASED PARTIALLY ON SALARY

In this case, partners are given credit for services rendered and the remaining profit is allocated on some specific basis.

EXAMPLE 5   Assume the same facts as in Example 3 except that Nelson and Levine are assigned salary allowances of $2,000 and $800, respectively. The remaining net income is to be allocated based on their capital balances. The computation is

	Nelson	Levine	Total
Salary	$2,000	$ 800	$2,800
Balance	1,760*	440**	2,200
Total	$3,760	$1,240	$5,000

$$ * \frac{\$40,000}{\$50,000} \times \$2,200 = \$1,760 $$

$$ ** \frac{\$10,000}{\$50,000} \times \$2,200 = \$440 $$

The journal entry is

Income Summary	5,000	
Nelson, Capital		3,760
Levine, Capital		1,240

DIVISION BASED PARTIALLY ON INTEREST

In this case, each partner receives interest on his or her capital balance and the remaining net income is allocated on some specified basis.

EXAMPLE 6   Assume the same facts as in Example 3 except that each partner is to receive 8 percent interest on his or her capital balance and the remaining earnings are to be divided equally. The computation is

	Nelson	Levine	Total
Interest on Capital Balance	$3,200	$ 800	$4,000
Balance	500	500	1,000
Total	$3,700	$1,300	$5,000

The journal entry is

Income Summary	5,000	
Nelson, Capital		3,700
Levine, Capital		1,300

DIVISION BASED PARTIALLY ON SALARY AND INTEREST

Each partner may get a salary, interest on his or her capital balance, and the remainder of the profit on some basis.

EXAMPLE 7   Assume the same facts as in Example 3 except that Nelson and Levine are to get salaries of $1,000 and $600, respectively, receive 5 percent interest on capital, and divide the remainder of the profit equally. The computation is

	Nelson	Levine	Total
Salary	$1,000	$ 600	$1,600
Interest	2,000	500	2,500
Balance	450	450	900
Total	$3,450	$1,550	$5,000

The journal entry is

Income Summary	5,000	
Nelson, Capital		3,450
Levine, Capital		1,550

It is possible that in some cases the net income may be less than the salary and/or interest allowances for the partners. If so, the remaining negative balance should be allocated to the partners as if it were a loss.

EXAMPLE 8   Assume that in Example 7 the interest rate on the capital balances was 9 percent. The computation is

	Nelson	Levine	Total
Salary	$1,000	$ 600	$1,600
Interest	3,600	900	4,500
	$4,600	$1,500	$6,100
Balance	−550	−550	−1,100
Total	$4,050	$ 950	$5,000

The journal entry is

Income Summary	5,000	
Nelson, Capital		4,050
Levine, Capital		950

13.5 ADMITTING A NEW PARTNER

Under the Uniform Partnership Act a partner has the option to sell all or part of his or her interest in the partnership without the consent of the others. The individual who acquires the selling partner's interest obtains the right to share in profits. However, unless admitted to the firm, the individual does not have the right to vote or participate in partnership affairs.

ADMISSION BY ACQUIRING AN INTEREST

A new partner who buys an interest from an old partner pays the purchase price *directly* to the old partner. An entry is made on the partnership books to transfer only the capital from the old partner to the new one. All other accounts are left intact.

EXAMPLE 9   Simon and Davis have capital balances of $60,000 and $40,000, respectively. Smith purchases half of Simon's interest for $33,000. The entry to transfer the capital balances is

Simon, Capital	30,000	
Smith, Capital		30,000

Note that $30,000, half of Simon's capital, has been transferred to Smith. The extra $3,000 paid by Smith to Simon is not reflected in the partnership books. Rather the $3,000 is in the nature of a *personal* benefit to Simon.

ADMISSION BY CONTRIBUTING ASSETS

The new partner may contribute assets to the firm. The entry is

Asset
　　Capital

EXAMPLE 10   Assume the same facts as in Example 9 except that Smith contributes $25,000 for a one-fifth interest in the new partnership. The journal entry is

Cash	25,000	
Smith, Capital		25,000

Smith now has a one-fifth interest ($25,000/$125,000).

In the prior two examples, we assumed that the book value of the assets of the partnership were reflective of their fair market value at the time that Smith was admitted. Hence, no adjustments to the recorded values were needed. However, in most cases, partnership assets have to be revalued or goodwill recognized prior to the admission of a new partner.

Asset revaluation.   Prior to admitting a new partner, certain assets of the partnership have to be adjusted from book value to fair market value. The net effect of this revaluation is allocated to the existing partners based on the profit-sharing ratio.

EXAMPLE 11   Simon and Davis share profits equally. Prior to the admission of Smith, it is decided that equipment having a book value of $6,000 is worth $7,500. The entry for the revaluation is

Equipment	1,500	
Simon, Capital		750
Davis, Capital		750

When many assets require revaluation, a temporary account called Asset Revaluation may be established to reflect the adjustments. The account would then be closed to the partners' capital accounts.

Recording goodwill.   When a partnership earns *excess* earnings over other similar firms it has goodwill associated with it. Goodwill may arise because of a number of factors, such as the business talents of the partners, better goods or services provided, and an established "name." When a new partner is admitted, he or she may have to pay for the goodwill of the partnership. In such a case, the goodwill account is debited and the capital accounts of the old partners are credited based on the profit-and-loss ratio.

EXAMPLE 12   Simon and Davis have capital balances of $60,000 and $40,000, respectively. Net income is shared equally. Smith gains admission to the partnership by contributing $30,000 for a one-fifth interest. While the total capital of the partnership prior to Smith's admission is $100,000, the parties agree that the firm is worth $120,000. The $20,000 excess represents goodwill that must be divided equally between the old partners. The journal entry to record goodwill is

Goodwill	20,000	
Simon, Capital		10,000
Davis, Capital		10,000

The entry to admit the new partner is

Cash	30,000	
Smith, Capital		30,000

Note that Smith now has a one-fifth interest in the partnership ($30,000/$150,000).

Goodwill may be associated with the incoming partner if, for example, the new partner has a good customer following. If the old partners agree to give the new partner recognition for his or her goodwill, the goodwill account is debited and the new partner's capital account is credited.

EXAMPLE 13   Simon and Davis have capital balances of $60,000 and $40,000, respectively. Smith gains admittance into the partnership by making an investment of $40,000. Smith is granted goodwill recognition of $10,000. The journal entry is

Cash	40,000	
Goodwill	10,000	
Smith, Capital		50,000

13.6   LIQUIDATING A PARTNERSHIP

To discontinue a partnership, the following steps are required: (1) the accounts are adjusted and closed; (2) assets are sold; (3) liabilities are paid; and (4) the remaining cash is distributed to the partners based on their *remaining capital balances*.

EXAMPLE 14   Liquidation at a Gain
Tyler, Simpson, and White terminate their partnership. The partnership books have been adjusted and all the accounts have been closed. The following is the post-closing trial balance:

Cash	$40,000	
Noncash Assets	25,000	
Liabilities		$15,000
Tyler, Capital		5,000
Simpson, Capital		10,000
White, Capital		35,000
	$65,000	$65,000

The partners share profits and losses equally. The necessary journal entries if the noncash assets are sold for $40,000 follow.

(a)   *For the sale of assets*

Cash	40,000	
Noncash Assets		25,000
Tyler, Capital		5,000
Simpson, Capital		5,000
White, Capital		5,000

(b)   *For the payment to creditors*

Liabilities	15,000	
Cash		15,000

(c)   *For the cash distribution*

Tyler, Capital	10,000	
Simpson, Capital	15,000	
White, Capital	40,000	
Cash		65,000

Notice that the final cash distribution is based on the partners' ending capital balances.

EXAMPLE 15   Liquidation at a Loss

The partnership of Sanders, Candby, and Rogers has ceased operations. All accounts have been adjusted and closed. The following is the post-closing trial balance:

Cash	$ 50,000	
Noncash Assets	75,000	
Liabilities		$ 20,000
Sanders, Capital		25,000
Candby, Capital		30,000
Rogers, Capital		50,000
	$125,000	$125,000

The partners share profits and losses equally. The necessary journal entries if the noncash assets are sold for $60,000 follow.

(a)   *For the sale of assets*

Cash	60,000	
Sanders, Capital	5,000	
Candby, Capital	5,000	
Rogers, Capital	5,000	
Noncash Assets		75,000

(b)   *For the payment to creditors*

Liabilities	20,000	
Cash		20,000

(c)   *For the cash distribution*

Sanders, Capital	20,000	
Candby, Capital	25,000	
Rogers, Capital	45,000	
Cash		90,000

Summary

(1)   A partner can be held _____ liable for the debts of the partnership.

(2)   Partnership property is _____ owned by the partners.

(3)   In a case where the written agreement is silent on a particular partnership right, the _____ governs.

(4)   If the partnership agreement does not specify how net income or loss is to be divided, it should be shared _____ by the partners.

(5)   A(n) _____ releases a withdrawing partner from liability for the debts of the partnership.

(6)   When a partnership is formed, noncash assets that are contributed by a partner are recorded at their _____ .

(7)   When a new partner purchases an interest from an old partner, the entry on the partnership books is to transfer the _____ between the partners.

(8)   When a new partner contributes inventory to the partnership, the entry is to debit _____ and credit the partner's _____ .

(9)   _____ refers to the superior earning power of the partnership.

(10)   Alberni has a capital balance of $50,000. Winston purchases 40 percent of Alberni's interest for $22,000. On the partnership books, Alberni's capital will be reduced by _____ .

(11)   When a new partner is admitted and must pay for the goodwill of the partnership, the _____ account is debited and the _____ accounts of the old partners are credited based on the _____ ratio.

(12)   When a partnership is terminated, the cash left after assets have been sold and liabilities have been paid is distributed to the partners according to their _____ balances.

Answers: (1) personally; (2) jointly; (3) Uniform Partnership Act; (4) equally; (5) novation; (6) fair market value; (7) capital; (8) inventory, capital; (9) Goodwill; (10) $20,000; (11) goodwill, capital, profit-and-loss; (12) remaining capital

Solved Problems

13.1   Barry and Robbins form a partnership. Barry contributes the following to the partnership:

	Ledger Balance	Fair Market Value
Cash	$25,000	$25,000
Notes Receivable	5,000	5,000
Inventory	9,000	7,000
Machinery	6,000	4,000*
Accumulated Depreciation	1,400	
Accounts Payable	13,000	13,000

*Note that fair market value is different from book value.

Robbins contributes $23,000 in cash to the partnership. Prepare the necessary journal entries.

SOLUTION

Cash	25,000	
Notes Receivable	5,000	
Inventory	7,000	
Machinery	4,000	
Accounts Payable		13,000
Barry, Capital		28,000
Cash	23,000	
Robbins, Capital		23,000

13.2   After the formation of a partnership, Jones invests $3,000 cash and Harris invests office equipment of $2,000. Prepare the appropriate journal entry.

SOLUTION

Cash	3,000	
Office Equipment	2,000	
Jones, Capital		3,000
Harris, Capital		2,000

13.3 Hornung and List have capital balances of $30,000 and $20,000, respectively. The net income for the year is $4,000. Prepare the appropriate journal entry for each of the following cases:

(a) Net income is shared equally.

(b) Net income is shared based upon the capital balances.

(c) Hornung and List are to be given salary allowances of $500 and $800, respectively. The remaining net income is to be divided equally.

(d) Each partner is to receive interest of 5 percent on his or her capital balance. The remaining net income is to be divided based upon their capital balances.

SOLUTION

(a)
Income Summary		4,000	
Hornung, Capital			2,000
List, Capital			2,000

(b)
Income Summary		4,000	
Hornung, Capital			2,400
List, Capital			1,600

(c)

	Hornung	List	Total
Salary	$ 500	$ 800	$1,300
Balance	1,350	1,350	2,700
Total	$1,850	$2,150	$4,000

Income Summary		4,000	
Hornung, Capital			1,850
List, Capital			2,150

(d)

	Hornung	List	Total
Interest on Capital Balance	$1,500	$1,000	$2,500
Balance	900	600	1,500
Total	$2,400	$1,600	$4,000

Income Summary		4,000	
Hornung, Capital			2,400
List, Capital			1,600

13.4 Carey and Reid are partners with capital balances of $12,000 and $18,000, respectively. Landry is admitted to the partnership. Prepare the appropriate journal entry for each of the following:

(a) Landry purchases a 20 percent partnership interest for $7,000.

(b) Landry contributes $10,000 for a 25 percent partnership interest.

(c) Landry contributes an amount to obtain a $33\frac{1}{3}$ percent partnership interest.

SOLUTION

(*a*)
Carey, Capital		2,400	
Reid, Capital		3,600	
Landry, Capital			6,000

Since 20 percent of $30,000 is $6,000, Carey and Reid received $1,000 from Landry as a personal benefit (see Example 9). Note that the partners' capital balances determine the basis for distributing the $6,000 (40 percent for Carey and 60 percent for Reid).

(*b*)
Cash	10,000	
Landry, Capital		10,000

(*c*) To determine the amount Landry contributed, we first state the problem in mathematical terms. We know that Landry's contribution is one-third of the total capital. We can therefore write

$$X = 1/3 \text{ (Existing capital} + X)$$

where X is Landry's contribution. The existing capital is $30,000, so

$$X = 1/3 \, (\$30,000 + X)$$
$$X = \$10,000 + 1/3X$$
$$2/3X = \$10,000$$
$$X = \$15,000$$

The journal entry therefore is

Cash	15,000	
Landry, Capital		15,000

13.5 The following is the balance sheet of the Smith–Henry partnership:

Smith–Henry Partnership
Balance Sheet
June 30, 20X2

ASSETS		LIABILITIES AND OWNERS' EQUITY	
Current Assets	$ 75,000	Accounts Payable	$ 85,000
Noncurrent Assets	160,000	Smith, Capital	90,000
Total Assets	$235,000	Henry, Capital	60,000
		Total Liabilities and Owners' Equity	$235,000

On July 1, 20X2, Carsen is admitted to the partnership.
Prepare the appropriate journal entry for each of the following:

(*a*) Carsen purchases $33\frac{1}{3}$ percent of Smith's interest for $35,000.

(*b*) Carsen contributes $50,000 to obtain a 25 percent interest in the firm.

SOLUTION

(*a*)
Smith, Capital	30,000	
Carsen, Capital		30,000

(*b*)
Cash	50,000	
Carsen, Capital		50,000

13.6 Watson and Wilson are partners who share profits equally. Watson's capital is $18,000 and Wilson's capital is $12,000. Williams is admitted to the partnership but is not required to make a capital investment; however, Williams does receive a 25 percent interest in the business. It is agreed that after the admission of Williams, profits will continue to be shared equally.

Prepare the appropriate journal entry for the admission of the new partner.

SOLUTION

Watson, Capital	3,750	
Wilson, Capital	3,750	
Williams, Capital		7,500

13.7 The capital balances of Smith and Jones are $60,000 and $80,000, respectively. The partners agree to admit Brown, who will contribute $60,000 for a 25 percent interest. Prepare the necessary journal entries for the admission of Brown.

SOLUTION

Goodwill	40,000	
Smith, Capital		20,000
Jones, Capital		20,000
Cash	60,000	
Brown, Capital		60,000

We know goodwill must be a consideration since a $60,000 contribution would in these circumstances result in a 30 percent interest [$60,000 ÷ ($60,000 + $80,000 + $60,000)]. To calculate the goodwill we write

$$\text{Brown's contribution} = 25\% \ (\text{Total Capital} + \text{Goodwill})$$
$$\$60,000 = 25\% \ (\$200,000 + \text{Goodwill})$$
$$\$240,000 = \$200,000 + \text{Goodwill}$$
$$\$40,000 = \text{Goodwill}$$

13.8 Schwartz and Hoyt have capital balances of $60,000 and $30,000, respectively. Logan gains admission into the partnership by making an investment of $20,000. Logan is given goodwill recognition of $4,000. Prepare the appropriate journal entry.

SOLUTION

Cash	20,000	
Goodwill	4,000	
Logan, Capital		24,000

13.9 The partnership of Fox, Johnson, and Taylor decides to liquidate. All accounts have been adjusted and closed. The following is the post-closing trial balance:

Cash	$ 60,000	
Noncash Assets	100,000	
Liabilities		$ 50,000
Fox, Capital		20,000
Johnson, Capital		35,000
Taylor, Capital		55,000
	$160,000	$160,000

The noncash assets are sold for $91,000, and the partners share profits and losses equally. Prepare the appropriate journal entries.

SOLUTION

Cash	91,000	
Fox, Capital	3,000	
Johnson, Capital	3,000	
Taylor, Capital	3,000	
Noncash Assets		100,000
Liabilities	50,000	
Cash		50,000
Fox, Capital	17,000	
Johnson, Capital	32,000	
Taylor, Capital	52,000	
Cash		101.000

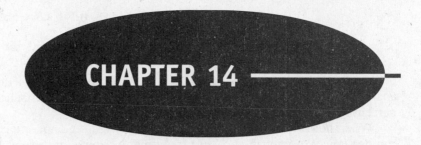

CHAPTER 14

Financial Statement Analysis

14.1 INTRODUCTION

The financial statements of an enterprise present the raw data of its assets, liabilities, and equities in the balance sheet and its revenue and expenses in the income statement. Without subjecting these data to analysis, many fallacious conclusions might be drawn concerning the financial condition of the enterprise.

Financial statement analysis is undertaken by creditors, investors, and other financial statement users in order to determine the credit worthiness and earning potential of an entity. This chapter explores the various measuring instruments that can be used to evaluate the financial health of a business, including horizontal, vertical, and ratio analysis.

It is important for the analyst to examine trends in accounts and ratios over the years, and to make comparisons with other firms in the industry. The analyst must be reasonably sure that the data given in different years within an enterprise, or within the industry, are comparable. Conclusions drawn from comparing the inventory of a company using LIFO valuation with the inventory of a company using FIFO valuation might have little validity. Also, when two companies use different methods of depreciation, it will be difficult to compare their relative profitability and fixed asset balances.

14.2 HORIZONTAL ANALYSIS

Horizontal analysis looks at the trend in the accounts in dollar and percentage terms over the years. A $3-million profit year looks very good following a $1-million profit year, but much less desirable after a $4-million profit year. Horizontal analysis is usually shown in comparative financial statements (see Examples 1 and 2). In annual reports, companies often show comparative financial data for five years.

Horizontal analysis stresses the trends of the various accounts in the financial statements. It is then an easy matter to identify areas of wide divergence that require further analysis. In the income statement shown in Example 2, the large increase in sales returns and allowances coupled with the decrease in sales for the period 20X2–20X3 should cause concern. One might compare these results with those of competitors. The problem might be industry wide, or just within the company.

It is important to show both the dollar amount of change and the percentage of change because using either one alone might cause misleading conclusions. For example, because the increase of 100 percent in the interest expense from 20X1 to 20X2 resulted from a difference of only $1,000, no further analysis might be warranted. On the other hand, a large numerical change might result in only a small percentage change, indicating no cause for concern.

When horizontal analysis is used over many years, comparative financial statements might be too cumbersome. Another method of presenting horizontal analysis is by looking at trends relative to a base year. A year that is representative of the firm's activity is chosen as the base. Each account of the base year is assigned an index of 100. An index for an account in a succeeding year is found by dividing the account's amount by the base year amount and multiplying by 100. Referring to Example 1, if we let 20X1 be the base year in the balance sheet, Accounts Receivable would be given the index of 100. In 20X2, the index would be 150 ($15/10 \times 100$), and in 20X3 it would be 200 ($20/10 \times 100$). A *condensed* form of the balance sheet using *trend analysis* is shown in Example 3.

EXAMPLE 1

The Ratio Company
Comparative Balance Sheet
(In Thousands of Dollars)
December 31, 20X3, 20X2, and 20X1

ASSETS	20X3	20X2	20X1	Increase or (Decrease) 20X3−20X2	Increase or (Decrease) 20X2−20X1	Percentage of Increase or (Decrease) 20X3−20X2	Percentage of Increase or (Decrease) 20X2−20X1
Current Assets							
Cash	$ 30.0	$ 35	$ 35	$(5.0)	—	(14.3%)	—
Accounts Receivable	20.0	15	10	5.0	$ 5	33.3	50.0%
Marketable Securities	20.0	15	5	5.0	10	33.3	200.0
Inventory	50.0	45	50	5.0	(5)	11.1	(10.0)
Total Current Assets	$120.0	$110	$100	$10.0	$10	9.1	10.0
Plant Assets	100.0	90	85	10.0	5	11.1	5.9
Total Assets	$220.0	$200	$185	$20.0	$15	10.0	8.1
LIABILITIES							
Current Liabilities	$ 55.4	$ 50	$ 52	$ 5.4	$(2)	10.8	(3.8)
Long-term Liabilities	80.0	75	70	5.0	5	6.7	7.1
Total Liabilities	$135.4	$125	$122	$10.4	$ 3	8.3	2.5
STOCKHOLDERS' EQUITY							
Common Stock, 4,500 shares $10 par value	$ 45.0	$ 45	$ 45	—	—	—	—
Retained Earnings	39.6	30	18	$ 9.6	$12	32.0	66.7
Total Stockholders' Equity	$ 84.6	$ 75	$ 63	$ 9.6	$12	12.8	19.0
Total Liabilities and Stockholders' Equity	$220.0	$200	$185	$20.0	$15	10.0	8.1

EXAMPLE 2

The Ratio Company
Comparative Income Statement
(In Thousands of Dollars)
For the Years Ended December 31, 20X3, 20X2, and 20X1

	20X3	20X2	20X1	Increase or (Decrease) 20X3−20X2	Increase or (Decrease) 20X2−20X1	Percentage of Increase or (Decrease) 20X3−20X2	Percentage of Increase or (Decrease) 20X2−20X1
Sales	$100.0	$110	$50	$(10.0)	$60	(9.1%)	120.0%
Sales Returns and Allowances	20.0	8	3	12.0	5	150.0	166.7
Net Sales	$ 80.0	$102	$47	$(22.0)	$55	(21.6)	117.0
Cost of Goods Sold	50.0	60	25	(10.0)	35	(16.7)	140.0
Gross Profit	$ 30.0	$ 42	$22	$(12.0)	$20	(28.6)	90.9
Operating Expenses							
Selling Expenses	$ 11.0	$ 13	$ 8	$ (2.0)	$ 5	(15.4)	62.5
General Expenses	4.0	7	4	(3.0)	3	(42.9)	75.0
Total Operating Expenses	$ 15.0	$ 20	$12	$ (5.0)	$ 8	(25.0)	66.7
Income from Operations	$ 15.0	$ 22	$10	$ (7.0)	$12	(31.8)	120.0
Nonoperating Income	3.0	0	1	3.0	(1)	—	(100.0)
Income before Interest Expense and Taxes	$ 18.0	$ 22	$11	$ (4.0)	$11	(18.2)	100.0
Interest Expense	2.0	2	1	—	1	—	100.0
Income before Taxes	$ 16.0	$ 20	$10	$ (4.0)	$10	(20.0)	100.0
Income Taxes (40% rate)	6.4	8	4	(1.6)	4	(20.0)	100.0
Net Income	9.6	12	6	(2.4)	6	(20.0)	100.0

EXAMPLE 3

The Ratio Company
Trend Analysis of the Balance Sheet
December 31, 20X3, 20X2, and 20X1

	20X3	20X2	20X1
ASSETS			
Current Assets	120.0	110.0	100
Plant Assets	117.6	105.9	100
Total Assets	118.9	108.1	100
LIABILITIES			
Current Liabilities	106.5	96.2	100
Long-term Liabilities	114.3	107.1	100
Total Liabilities	111.0	102.5	100
STOCKHOLDERS' EQUITY			
Common Stock	100.0	100.0	100
Retained Earnings	220.0	166.7	100
Total Stockholders' Equity	134.3	119.0	100
Total Liabilities and Stockholders' Equity	118.9	108.1	100

14.3 VERTICAL ANALYSIS

In *vertical analysis*, a significant item on a financial statement is used as a base value, and all other items on the financial statement are compared to it. In performing vertical analysis for the balance sheet, total assets is assigned 100 percent. Each asset account is expressed as a percentage of total assets. Total liabilities and stockholders' equity is also assigned 100 percent. Each liability and equity account is then expressed as a percentage of total liabilities and stockholders' equity. In the income statement, net sales is given the value of 100 and all other accounts are evaluated in comparison to net sales. The resulting figures are then given in a common size statement. The common size analysis of Ratio Company's income statement is shown in Example 4.

EXAMPLE 4

The Ratio Company
Income Statement and
Common Size Analysis
(In Thousands of Dollars)
For the Years Ended December 31, 20X3 and 20X2

	20X3		20X2	
	Amount	Percent	Amount	Percent
Sales	$100.00	125.0	$110.0	107.8
Sales Returns and Allowances	20.0	25.0	8.0	7.8
Net Sales	$ 80.0	100.0	$102.0	100.0
Cost of Goods Sold	50.0	62.5	60.0	58.8
Gross Profit	$ 30.0	37.5	$ 42.0	41.2
Operating Expenses				
Selling Expenses	$ 11.0	13.8	$ 13.0	12.7
General Expenses	4.0	5.0	7.0	6.9
Total Operating Expenses	$ 15.0	18.8	$ 20.0	19.6
Income from Operations	$ 15.0	18.8	$ 22.0	21.6
Nonoperating Income	3.0	3.8		
Income before Interest Expense and Taxes	$ 18.0	22.5	$ 22.0	21.6
Interest Expense	2.0	2.5	2.0	2.0
Income before Taxes	$ 16.0	20.0	$ 20.0	19.6
Income Taxes	6.4	8.0	8.0	7.8
Net Income	$ 9.6	12.0	$ 12.0	11.8

The common size analysis shown in Example 4 gives the percentage of each account to net sales. The analyst should compare these figures from year to year in order to identify areas requiring further attention.

Vertical analysis tends to exhibit the internal structure of the enterprise. It indicates the relative amount of each income statement account to revenue. It shows the mix of assets that produces the income and the mix of the sources of capital, whether provided by current or long-term liabilities, or by equity funding.

The vertical percentages of a company should be compared to its competitors or to industry percentages so that one may ascertain the firm's relative position.

As in horizontal analysis, vertical analysis is not the end of the process. The analyst must be prepared to probe deeper into the areas that either horizontal or vertical analysis, or both, indicates as being possible problem areas.

14.4 RATIO ANALYSIS

Horizontal and vertical analysis compares one figure to another within the same category. It is also essential to compare two figures applicable to different categories. This is accomplished through *ratio analysis*. There are many ratios that the analyst can use, depending upon what he or she considers as being important *relationships*. There is no point in computing ratios of unrelated items. For example, there is no interest in the ratio of sales returns and allowances to income taxes.

14.5 LIQUIDITY RATIOS

Liquidity is the company's ability to convert noncash assets into cash or to obtain cash in order to meet current liabilities. Liquidity applies to the short term, which is typically viewed as a time span of one year or less.

Liquidity is essential to the proper carrying out of business activity, particularly in times of adversity such as when the business is shut down by a strike. The firm would be required to satisfy current liabilities before current assets could be realized. In times of recession, operating losses may ensue. If liquidity is insufficient to cushion such losses, serious financial difficulty may be in store. Poor liquidity is analogous to a person having a fever in that both are a symptom of a fundamental problem.

Analyzing corporate liquidity is especially important to creditors. If a company has a poor liquidity position, it may lead to a delay in receiving interest and principal payments or even losses on the amounts due.

A description of various liquidity measures follows.

WORKING CAPITAL

Working capital is equal to current assets less current liabilities. It is a safety cushion to creditors. A greater balance is required when the entity has difficulty borrowing on short notice.

The Ratio Company had a working capital of $64,600 in 20X3 ($120,000 − $55,400) and $60,000 in 20X2. The increase in working capital is a favorable sign.

CURRENT RATIO

The current ratio is equal to current assets divided by current liabilities. It is used to measure the ability of an enterprise to meet its current liabilities out of current assets. The limitation of the ratio is that it may rise just prior to financial distress because of a company's desire to improve its cash position by, for example, selling fixed assets. Such dispositions, while resulting in a more favorable current ratio, will have a detrimental effect upon production capacity. Another limitation of the current ratio is that it will be excessively high when inventory is carried on the LIFO basis.

The Ratio Company's current ratio for 20X3 was 2.17 ($120,000/$55,400; see Example 1) and for 20X2 it was 2.2. The ratio has remained fairly constant over the years.

QUICK (ACID-TEST) RATIO

The quick ratio is a stringent test of liquidity. It is found by dividing the most liquid current assets (cash, marketable securities, and accounts receivable) by current liabilities. Inventory is not included in this ratio because it usually takes a long time to convert inventory into cash. Prepaid expenses are also not included because they are not convertible into cash, and as such are not capable of covering current liabilities.

The Ratio Company had a quick ratio of 1.3 in 20X2 and 1.26 in 20X3, computed as ($30,000 + $20,000 + $20,000) ÷ $55,400. The ratio has been fairly constant over the years.

ACCOUNTS RECEIVABLE RATIOS

Accounts receivable ratios consist of the accounts receivable turnover and the collection period, which is the number of days the receivables are held. The *accounts receivable turnover* gives the number of times accounts receivable are collected during the year. The turnover is found by dividing net credit sales (if not available, then total sales) by the average accounts receivable. Average accounts receivable is typically found by adding the beginning accounts receivable to the ending accounts receivable and dividing by two. However, average accounts receivable may be computed more accurately on a monthly or quarterly basis, but this information is usually known only to management. Using data from the shortest period available will give the most accurate ratio. The higher the accounts receivable turnover, the better since this means the company is collecting quickly from customers. These funds can then be invested for a return. Ratio Company's average accounts receivable for 20X3 is $17,500 ($15,000 plus $20,000, divided by two) and the accounts receivable turnover is 4.57 times ($80,000/$17,500). For 20X2, the accounts receivable turnover is 8.16. The drop in the accounts receivable turnover ratio is significant, indicating a serious problem in collecting from customers. It implies that a careful analysis of the company's credit policy is required.

The *collection period*, or the number of days sales remain in accounts receivable, is found by dividing the accounts receivable turnover into 365 days. In 20X3, the Ratio Company's collection period was 79.9 days (365/4.57). This means that it took almost 80 days for a sale to be converted to cash. In 20X2, the collection period was 44.7 days. The materially higher collection period in 20X3 indicates a danger that customer balances may become uncollectible. Perhaps the company is now selling to highly marginal customers.

INVENTORY RATIOS

If a company is holding excess inventory, it means that funds are being tied up in inventory that could be invested elsewhere for a return. In addition, there will be high carrying costs to store the goods. The risk of obsolescence also exists. Two major ratios to look at are the inventory turnover and the number of days inventory is held.

Inventory turnover is computed by dividing the cost of goods sold by the average inventory. Average inventory is determined by adding the beginning and ending inventories and dividing by two. The inventory turnover for Ratio Company in 20X3 was 1.05 times ($50,000/$47,500) and in 20X2 it was 1.26 times.

The decline in the inventory turnover indicates the stocking of more goods. An attempt should be made to determine whether specific inventory categories are not selling well and the reasons therefor. However, a decline in the turnover rate would not cause concern if it was primarily due to the introduction of a new product line in which the advertising effects were not felt yet.

The number of days inventory is held is computed by dividing 365 days by the turnover rate. The result indicates the length of time needed to buy, sell, and replace inventory. For Ratio Company, the average age of inventory in 20X3 was 347.6 days (365/1.05) and in 20X2 it was 289.7 days. The increase in the holding period implies greater risk of obsolescence.

OPERATING CYCLE

The operating cycle of the business is the number of days it takes to convert inventory to cash. It is found by adding the collection period to the average age of inventory. In 20X3, it took Ratio Company 427.5 days (79.9 + 347.6) to convert the inventory into cash. In 20X2, the operating cycle was 334.4 days. The increase from 20X2 to 20X3 indicates an unfavorable trend since more money is being tied up in noncash assets.

A short operating cycle is desirable because cash is collected faster and the cash can then be invested for a return.

SUMMARY

A summary of the liquidity measures follows:

Working capital = Current assets − Current liabilities

$$\text{Current ratio} = \frac{\text{Current assets}}{\text{Current liabilities}}$$

$$\text{Quick (acid-test) ratio} = \frac{\text{Cash} + \text{Marketable securities} + \text{Accounts receivable}}{\text{Current liabilities}}$$

Accounts receivable

1. $\text{Accounts receivable turnover} = \dfrac{\text{Net credit sales}}{\text{Average accounts receivable}}$

2. $\text{Collection period} = \dfrac{365}{\text{Accounts receivable turnover}}$

Inventory

1. $\text{Inventory turnover} = \dfrac{\text{Cost of goods sold}}{\text{Average inventory}}$

2. $\text{Inventory age} = \dfrac{365}{\text{Inventory turnover}}$

Operating cycle = Number of days inventory is held + Number of days receivables are held

14.6 SOLVENCY RATIOS

Solvency is the entity's ability to meet its long-term obligations as they become due. The analysis concentrates on the long-term financial and operating structure of the business. The degree of long-term debt in the capital structure is also considered. Further, solvency is dependent upon profitability since in the long run a firm will not be able to meet its debts unless it is profitable.

RATIO OF STOCKHOLDERS' EQUITY TO TOTAL LIABILITIES

Stockholders' equity compared to total liabilities is a significant measure of solvency since a high degree of debt in the capital structure may make it difficult for the company to meet interest charges and principal at maturity. Further, with a high debt position comes the risk of running out of cash under conditions of adversity. Also, excessive debt will result in less financial flexibility in the sense that it will be difficult to obtain funds during tight money markets. For Ratio Company the ratio was 0.62 in 20X3 ($84,600/$135,400) and 0.6 in 20X2. The ratio remained fairly constant. A desired ratio depends on many variables, including the ratios of other companies in the industry, the access for further debt financing, and the stability of earnings.

RATIO OF STOCKHOLDERS' EQUITY TO LONG-TERM LIABILITIES

Another indicator of solvency is the ratio of stockholders' equity to long-term liabilities. The 20X3 ratio for Ratio Company was 1.06 ($84,600/$80,000). In 20X2, it was 1.0. The slight improvement in the ratio is primarily due to the greater percentage increase in stockholders' equity than in long-term debt.

RATIO OF PLANT ASSETS TO LONG-TERM LIABILITIES

The ratio of plant assets to long-term liabilities reflects the degree to which plant assets are financed by long-term creditors. A low ratio indicates that creditors have a significant claim on the firm's assets. The ratio also gives an indication of the extent to which additional long-term borrowing is possible. The ratio for our company was 1.25 in 20X3 ($100,000/$80,000) and 1.2 in 20X2. Therefore, there was improved coverage of long-term debt in 20X3.

INTEREST COVERAGE RATIO

The interest coverage ratio (number of times interest is earned) reflects the number of times before-tax earnings cover interest expense. This is found by dividing income before interest and taxes by the interest expense. It is a safety margin indicator in the sense that it shows how much of a decline in earnings a company can absorb. In 20X3, interest of Ratio Company was covered 9 times ($18,000/$2,000), while in 20X2 it was covered 11 times. The decline in the coverage is a negative indicator since less earnings are available to meet interest charges.

14.7 PROFITABILITY RATIOS

An indication of good financial health is the company's ability to earn a satisfactory profit and return on investment. Investors will be reluctant to associate themselves with an entity that has poor earning potential since the market price of stock and dividend potential will be adversely affected. Creditors will shy away from companies with deficient profitability since the amounts owed to them may not be paid.

Some major ratios that measure operating results are summarized below.

PROFIT MARGIN

The ratio of net income to net sales is termed the profit margin. It indicates the profitability generated from revenue and hence is an important operating performance measure. In 20X3 the ratio for our company was 0.12 ($9,600/$80,000) and in 20X2 it was 0.12. The profit margin was constant, indicating that the earning power of the business remained static.

RETURN ON INVESTMENT

Return on investment is a key measure because it looks at the earnings achieved by the investment made in the business. Basically, two ratios evaluate the return on investment. One is the return on total assets and the other is the return on owners' equity.

The return on total assets indicates the efficiency with which management has used its available resources to generate income. It is found by dividing the sum of the net income and the interest expense adjusted for the tax rate by the average total assets. In 20X3, the return on total assets for Ratio Company was 0.05 {$9,600 + $2,000 (0.6) ÷ [($220,000 + $200,000)/2]}. In 20X2, the return was 0.07. The productivity of assets in deriving income deteriorated in 20X3.

The return on owners' equity measures the return applicable to stockholders after the deduction of interest payments to creditors. It is found by dividing the net income by the average stockholders' equity. In 20X3, Ratio Company's return on owners' equity was 0.12 {$9,600 ÷ [($84,600 + $75,000)/2} and in 20X2 it was 0.17. There has been a significant drop in the return earned by the owners of the business.

RATIO OF NET SALES TO AVERAGE TOTAL ASSETS

This ratio is helpful in appraising a company's ability to efficiently utilize its asset base in generating revenue. The ratio for our company in 20X3 was 0.38 ($80,000/$210,000) and in 20X2 it was 0.53 ($102,000/$192,500). The company's utilization of assets significantly declined. Perhaps the assets are getting older and should be replaced, or inadequate repairs are being made.

EARNINGS PER SHARE

Earnings per share indicates what the earnings are for each common share held. When preferred stock is included in the capital structure, net income must be reduced by the preferred dividends to determine the amount applicable to common stock. When preferred stock does not exist, as is the case with the Ratio Company, earnings per share is equal to net income divided by common shares outstanding. Earnings per share is a useful indicator of the operating performance of the company, as well as of the dividends that may be expected. In 20X3, earnings per share for Ratio Company was $2.13 ($9,600/4,500 shares). In 20X2, it was $2.67. The decline in earnings per share should be of concern to investors.

All of the aforementioned profitability ratios have declined for Ratio Company in 20X3 relative to 20X2. This is a very negative sign.

PRICE/EARNINGS RATIO

Some ratios appraise the enterprise's relationship with its stockholders. The often quoted P/E ratio, or price/earnings ratio, is equal to the market price per share of stock divided by the earnings per share. A high P/E ratio is good because it indicates that the investing public considers the company in a favorable light.

EXAMPLE 5   Let us assume that the market price per share of Ratio Company's stock was $20 on December 31, 20X3, and $22 on December 31, 20X2. Therefore, the P/E ratio in 20X3 was 9.39 ($20/$2.13) and the ratio in 20X2 was 8.24 ($22/$2.67). The decline in the P/E multiple indicates that the stock market had a lower opinion of the company in 20X3, possibly due to the company's declining profitability.

DIVIDEND RATIOS

Many stockholders are primarily interested in receiving dividends. The dividend yield of a stock is the dividends per share divided by the market price per share. Another ratio is the dividend payout, which is equal to the dividends per share divided by the earnings per share. A decline in dividends will cause concern on the part of stockholders.

14.8 SUMMARY

Financial statement analysis is an attempt to work with the reported financial figures in order to ascertain the entity's financial strengths and weaknesses.

Most analysts tend to favor certain ratios. They may leave out some of those mentioned and include some that were not discussed here. The perspective of the analyst as investor, stockholder, or creditor is the deciding factor for which ratios to include in the analysis of an enterprise.

Once a ratio is computed, it is then compared to related ratios of the company, ratios of previous years, and ratios of competitors. The comparisons aid in showing trends over a period of time, and in showing the ability of an enterprise to compete with others in the industry. These comparisons do not mark the end of the analysis, but rather indicate areas needing further attention.

Summary

(1)   Horizontal analysis compares an account to _____ .

(2)   In a common size income statement, _____ is given the value of 100.

(3)   _____ is the ability of a company to meet its current liabilities out of current assets.

(4) The current ratio is equal to _____ divided by _____ .

(5) _____ is included in computing the current ratio but not the quick ratio.

(6) The accounts receivable turnover is equal to _____ divided by _____ .

(7) The number of days for inventory sold on credit to convert to cash is found by adding the _____ to the _____ .

(8) The ratio of _____ to long-term liabilities looks at the degree of debt in the capital structure.

(9) The number of times interest is earned is equal to _____ divided by _____ .

(10) Return on owner's equity is found by dividing _____ by _____ .

(11) The price/earnings ratio is equal to the _____ per share divided by the _____ per share.

(12) Two measures that are of interest to stockholders in evaluating the dividend policy of the firm are the dividend _____ and the dividend _____ ratios.

(13) When the comparison of ratios indicates a significant change in financial position, the analyst should _____ .

Answers: (1) the same account of a prior year; (2) net sales; (3) Liquidity; (4) current assets, current liabilities; (5) Inventory; (6) net credit sales, average accounts receivable; (7) collection period, average age of inventory; (8) stockholders' equity; (9) income before interest and taxes, interest expense; (10) net income, average stockholders' equity; (11) market price, earnings; (12) yield, payout; (13) investigate further

Solved Problems

14.1 Smith Corporation provides the following comparative income statement:

Smith Corporation
Comparative Income Statement
For the Years Ended December 31, 20X3 and 20X2

	20X3	20X2	Percentage of Increase or (Decrease)
Sales	$570,000	$680,000	
Cost of Goods Sold	200,000	170,000	
Gross Profit	$370,000	$510,000	
Operating Expenses	100,000	210,000	
Net Income	$270,000	$300,000	

(a) Using horizontal analysis, fill in the percentage change.

(b) Evaluate the results.

SOLUTION

(a)
Smith Corporation
Comparative Income Statement
For the Years Ended December 31, 20X3 and 20X2

	20X3	20X2	Percentage of Increase or (Decrease)
Sales	$570,000	$680,000	(16.2)
Cost of Goods Sold	200,000	170,000	(17.6)
Gross Profit	$370,000	$510,000	(27.5)
Operating Expenses	100,000	210,000	(52.4)
Net Income	$270,000	$300,000	(10.0)

(b) Gross profit declined 27.5 percent due to the combined effects of lower sales and higher cost of sales. However, operating expenses were sharply cut. This kept the decline in net income to only 10 percent.

14.2 Jones Corporation reports the following for the period 20X1–20X3:

	20X3	20X2	20X1
Current Liabilities	$34,000	$25,000	$20,000
Long-term Liabilities	60,000	45,000	50,000

The base year is 20X1. Using trend analysis, determine the appropriate index numbers.

SOLUTION

	20X3	20X2	20X1
Current Liabilities	170	125	100
Long-term Liabilities	120	90	100

14.3 The Lyons Corporation reported the following income statement data:

	20X2	20X1
Net Sales	$400,000	$250,000
Cost of Goods Sold	280,000	160,000
Operating Expenses	75,000	56,000

(a) Prepare a comparative income statement for 20X2 and 20X1 by using vertical analysis.

(b) Evaluate the results.

SOLUTION

(a)

The Lyons Corporation
Income Statement and
Common Size Analysis
For the Years Ended December 31, 20X2 and 20X1

	20X2		20X1	
	Amount	Percent	Amount	Percent
Net Sales	$400,000	100.0	$250,000	100.0
Cost of Goods Sold	280,000	70.0	160,000	64.0
Gross Profit	$120,000	30.0	$ 90,000	36.0
Operating Expenses	75,000	18.8	56,000	22.4
Net Income	$ 45,000	11.3	$ 34,000	13.6

(b) Cost of goods sold has risen, possibly due to the higher cost of buying merchandise. Operating expenses have dropped, possibly due to better cost control. Overall, there has been a decline in profitability.

14.4 Charles Corporation's balance sheet at December 31, 20X7, shows the following:

Current Assets	
Cash	$ 4,000
Marketable Securities	8,000
Accounts Receivable	100,000
Inventories	120,000
Prepaid Expenses	1,000
Total Current Assets	$233,000

Current Liabilities	
Notes Payable	$ 5,000
Accounts Payable	150,000
Accrued Expenses	20,000
Income Taxes Payable	1,000
Total Current Liabilities	$176,000
Long-term Liabilities	$340,000

Determine (a) working capital, (b) current ratio, and (c) quick ratio.

SOLUTION

(a) Current assets − Current liabilities = Working capital
$233,000 − $176,000 = $57,000

(b) Current ratio $= \dfrac{\text{Current assets}}{\text{Current liabilities}} = \dfrac{\$233,000}{\$176,000} = 1.32$

(c) Quick ratio $= \dfrac{\text{Cash + Marketable securities + Accounts receivable}}{\text{Current liabilities}} = \dfrac{\$4,000 + \$8,000 + \$100,000}{\$176,000}$

$= \dfrac{\$112,000}{\$176,000} = 0.64$

14.5 Based upon the answers to Problem 14.4, does Charles Corporation have good or poor liquidity if the industry averages are a current ratio of 1.29 and a quick ratio of 1.07?

SOLUTION

While the company's current ratio is slightly better than the industry norm, its quick ratio is significantly below the norm. Charles Corporation has more in current liabilities than in highly liquid assets. It therefore has a poor liquidity position.

14.6 The Rivers Company reports the following data relative to accounts receivable:

	20X2	20X1
Average Accounts Receivable	$ 400,000	$ 416,000
Net Credit Sales	2,600,000	3,100,000

The terms of sale are net 30 days. (*a*) Compute the accounts receivable turnover and the collection period. (*b*) Evaluate the results.

SOLUTION

(*a*) $\text{Accounts receivable turnover} = \dfrac{\text{Net credit sales}}{\text{Average accounts receivable}}$

20X2: $\dfrac{\$2,600,000}{\$400,000} = 6.5$ times; 20X1: $\dfrac{\$3,100,000}{\$416,000} = 7.45$ times

$\text{Collection period} = \dfrac{365 \text{ days}}{\text{Accounts receivable turnover}}$

20X2: $\dfrac{365}{6.5} = 56.2$ days; 20X1: $\dfrac{365}{7.45} = 49$ days

(*b*) The company's management of accounts receivable is poor. In both years, the collection period exceeded the terms of net 30 days. The situation is getting worse, as is indicated by the significant increase in the collection period in 20X2 relative to 20X1. The company has significant funds tied up in accounts receivable that could be invested for a return. A careful evaluation of the credit policy is needed. Perhaps sales are being made to marginal customers.

14.7 Utica Company's net accounts receivable were $250,000 at December 31, 20X8, and $300,000 at December 31, 20X9. Net cash sales for 20X9 were $100,000. The accounts receivable turnover for 20X9 was 5.0. What were Utica's total net sales for 20X9? (AICPA Adapted)

SOLUTION

$\text{Average accounts receivable} = \dfrac{\text{Beginning accounts receivable} + \text{Ending accounts receivable}}{2}$

$= \dfrac{\$250,000 + \$300,000}{2} = \$275,000$

$\text{Accounts receivable turnover} = \dfrac{\text{Net credit sales}}{\text{Average accounts receivable}}$

$5 = \dfrac{\text{Net credit sales}}{\$275,000}$

Net credit sales $= 5 \times \$275,000 = \$1,375,000$

Since the cash sales were $100,000, the total net sales must be $1,475,000.

14.8 On January 1, 20X6, the River Company's beginning inventory was $400,000. During 20X6, River purchased $1,900,000 of additional inventory. On December 31, 20X6, River's ending inventory was $500,000.

(a) What is the inventory turnover and the age of inventory for 20X6?

(b) If the inventory turnover in 20X5 was 3.3 and the age of the inventory was 110.6 days, evaluate the results for 20X6.

SOLUTION

(a)

Cost of Goods Sold	
Beginning Inventory	$ 400,000
Purchases	1,900,000
Cost of Goods Available	$2,300,000
Ending Inventory	500,000
Cost of Goods Sold	$1,800,000

$$\text{Average Inventory} = \frac{\text{Beginning inventory} + \text{Ending inventory}}{2}$$

$$= \frac{\$400,000 + \$500,000}{2} = \$450,000$$

$$\text{Inventory turnover} = \frac{\text{Cost of goods sold}}{\text{Average inventory}} = \frac{\$1,800,000}{\$450,000} = 4$$

$$\text{Age of inventory} = \frac{365 \text{ days}}{\text{Inventory turnover}} = \frac{365}{4} = 91.3 \text{ days}$$

(b) River Company's inventory management improved in 20X6, as evidenced by the higher turnover rate and decrease in the days that inventories were held. As a result, there is less liquidity risk. Further, the company's profitability will benefit by the increased turnover of merchandise.

14.9 Based on your answer to Problem 14.8, what is the operating cycle in 20X6 if we assume that the collection period is 42 days?

SOLUTION

Number of days inventory is held	91.3
Number of days receivables are held	42.0
Operating cycle	133.3 days

14.10 A condensed balance sheet and other financial data for Alpha Company appear below.

Alpha Company
Balance Sheet
December 31, 20X1

ASSETS

Current Assets	$100,000
Plant Assets	150,000
Total Assets	$250,000

LIABILITIES AND STOCKHOLDERS' EQUITY

Current Liabilities	$100,000
Long-term Liabilities	75,000
Total Liabilities	$175,000
Stockholders' Equity	75,000
Total Liabilities and Stockholders' Equity	$250,000

Income Statement Data

Net Sales	$375,000
Interest Expense	4,000
Net Income	22,500

The following account balances existed at December 31, 20X0: Total assets, $200,000; Stockholders' Equity, $65,000. The tax rate is 35 percent.

Industry Norms as of December 31, 20X1

Stockholders' equity to total liabilities	0.57
Stockholders' equity to long-term liabilities	1.15
Plant assets to long-term liabilities	2.40
Profit margin	0.12
Return on total assets	0.15
Return on stockholders' equity	0.30
Net sales to average total assets	1.71

Calculate and evaluate the following ratios for Alpha Company as of December 31, 20X1.

(*a*) Stockholders' equity to total liabilities

(*b*) Stockholders' equity to long-term liabilities

(*c*) Plant assets to long-term liabilities

(*d*) Profit margin

(*e*) Return on total assets

(*f*) Return on stockholders' equity

(*g*) Net sales to average total assets

SOLUTION

(*a*) $\dfrac{\text{Stockholders' equity}}{\text{Total liabilities}} = \dfrac{\$75,000}{\$175,000} = 0.43$

Alpha's percentage of stockholders' equity to total liabilities is considerably below the industry norm, indicating a solvency problem. Excessive debt may make it difficult for the firm to meet its obligations during a downturn in business. A high debt position will also make it difficult for the entity to obtain financing during a period of tight money supply.

(*b*) $\dfrac{\text{Stockholders' equity}}{\text{Long-term liabilities}} = \dfrac{\$75,000}{\$75,000} = 1$

The company's ratio is again below the industry norm, which means it is less solvent than other companies in the industry.

(c) $\dfrac{\text{Plant assets}}{\text{Long-term liabilities}} = \dfrac{\$150,000}{\$75,000} = 2$

Because Alpha's ratio is lower than the industry norm, we can infer that long-term creditors have a greater than normal claim on the firm's plant assets. Alpha's long-term borrowing capacity is therefore more limited than that of its competition.

(d) $\text{Profit margin} = \dfrac{\text{Net income}}{\text{Net sales}} = \dfrac{\$22,500}{\$375,000} = 0.06$

Alpha's profit margin is far below the industry norm. This indicates that the operating performance of the entity is poor because the profitability generated from revenue sources is low.

(e) $\text{Return on total assets} = \dfrac{\text{Net income} + \text{Interest expense (net of tax)}}{\text{Average total assets}}$

$$= \dfrac{\$22,500 + \$4,000(1 - 0.35)}{(\$200,000 + \$250,000)/2}$$

$$= \dfrac{\$\ 25,100}{\$225,000} = 0.11$$

Alpha's ratio is below the industry norm. Therefore, the company's efficiency in generating profit from assets is low. Profit generation is, of course, different from revenue (sales) generation because for the former, corporate expenses are deducted from sales.

(f) $\text{Return on stockholders' equity} = \dfrac{\text{Net income}}{\text{Average stockholders' equity}}$

$$= \dfrac{\$22,500}{(\$65,000 + \$75,000)/2}$$

$$= \dfrac{\$22,500}{\$70,000} = 0.32$$

Since the return earned by Alpha's stockholders is slightly more than the industry norm, investment in the firm relative to competition was advantageous to existing stockholders. This may be due to a currently low stockholders' equity investment in the firm.

(g) $\dfrac{\text{Net sales}}{\text{Average total assets}} = \dfrac{\$375,000}{\$225,000} = 1.67$

Alpha's ratio is about the same as the industry norm. Therefore, the company's ability to utilize its assets in obtaining revenue is similar to the competition's. The utilization of assets has a bearing upon the ultimate profitability to stockholders.

14.11 The Format Company reports the following balance sheet data:

Current Liabilities	$280,000
Bonds Payable, 16%	120,000
Preferred Stock, 14%, $100 par value	200,000
Common Stock, $25 par value, 16,800 shares	420,000
Premium on Common Stock	240,000
Retained Earnings	180,000

Income before taxes is $160,000. The tax rate is 40 percent. Common stockholders' equity in the previous year was $800,000. The market price per share of common stock is $35. Calculate (*a*) net income, (*b*) preferred dividends, (*c*) return on common stock, (*d*) interest coverage, (*e*) earnings per share, and (*f*) price/earnings ratio.

SOLUTION

(*a*)

Income before taxes	$160,000
Taxes (40% rate)	64,000
Net income	$ 96,000

(*b*)   14% × $200,000 = $28,000

(*c*)   Common stockholders' equity:

Common Stock	$420,000
Premium on Common Stock	240,000
Retained Earnings	180,000
Common Stockholders' Equity	$840,000

$$\text{Return on common stock} = \frac{\text{Net income} - \text{Preferred dividends}}{\text{Average common stockholders' equity}}$$

$$= \frac{\$96,000 - \$28,000}{(\$800,000 + \$840,000)/2} = \frac{\$68,000}{\$820,000} = 0.08$$

(*d*)   Income before interest and taxes equals:

Income before taxes	$160,000
Interest expense (16% × $120,000)	19,200
Income before interest and taxes	$179,200

$$\text{Interest coverage} = \frac{\text{Income before interest and taxes}}{\text{Interest expense}} = \frac{\$179,200}{\$19,200} = 9.33 \text{ times}$$

(*e*) $$\text{Earnings per share} = \frac{\text{Net income} - \text{Preferred dividends}}{\text{Common stock outstanding}} = \frac{\$96,000 - \$28,000}{16,800 \text{ shares}} = \$4.05$$

(*f*) $$\text{Price/earnings ratio} = \frac{\text{Market price per share}}{\text{Earnings per share}} = \frac{\$35.00}{\$4.05} = 8.64 \text{ times}$$

14.12 Wilder Corporation's common stock account for 20X3 and 20X2 showed $45,000 of common stock at $10 par value. Additional data are

	20X3	20X2
Dividends	$2,250.00	$3,600.00
Market Price Per Share	20.00	22.00
Earnings Per Share	2.13	2.67

(*a*) Calculate the dividends per share, dividend yield, and dividend payout.

(*b*) Evaluate the results.

SOLUTION

(a) Dividends per share = $\dfrac{\text{Dividends}}{\text{Outstanding shares}}$

20X3: $\dfrac{\$2,250}{4,500 \text{ shares}} = \$0.50$; 20X2: $\dfrac{\$3,600}{4,500 \text{ shares}} = \$0.80$

Dividend yield = $\dfrac{\text{Dividends per share}}{\text{Market price per share}}$

20X3: $\dfrac{\$0.50}{\$20.00} = 0.03$; 20X2: $\dfrac{\$0.80}{\$22.00} = 0.04$

Dividend payout = $\dfrac{\text{Dividends per share}}{\text{Earnings per share}}$

20X3: $\dfrac{\$0.50}{\$2.13} = 0.23$; 20X2: $\dfrac{\$0.80}{\$2.67} = 0.30$

(b) The decline in dividends per share, dividend yield, and dividend payout from 20X2 to 20X3 will cause concern to stockholders.

14.13 Jones Corporation's financial statements appear below.

Jones Corporation
Balance Sheet
December 31, 20X1

ASSETS

Current Assets		
Cash	$100,000	
Marketable Securities	200,000	
Inventory	300,000	
Total Current Assets		$ 600,000
Noncurrent Assets		
Plant Assets		500,000
Total Assets		$1,100,000

LIABILITIES AND STOCKHOLDERS' EQUITY

Current Liabilities	$200,000	
Long-term Liabilities	100,000	
Total Liabilities		$ 300,000
Stockholders' Equity		
Common Stock, $1 par value, 100,000 shares	$100,000	
Premium on Common Stock	500,000	
Retained Earnings	200,000	
Total Stockholders' Equity		800,000
Total Liabilities and Stockholders' Equity		$1,100,000

Jones Corporation
Income Statement
For the Year Ended December 31, 20X1

Net Sales	$10,000,000
Cost of Goods Sold	6,000,000
Gross Profit	$ 4,000,000
Operating Expenses	1,000,000
Income before Taxes	$ 3,000,000
Income Taxes (50% rate)	1,500,000
Net Income	$ 1,500,000

Additional information available is a market price of $150 per share of stock and total dividends of $600,000 for 20X1, and $250,000 of inventory as of December 31, 20X0. Compute the following ratios:

(a) Current ratio

(b) Quick ratio

(c) Inventory turnover

(d) Age of inventory

(e) Stockholders' equity to total liabilities

(f) Plant assets to long-term liabilities

(g) Operating expenses to net sales

(h) Earnings per share

(i) Price/earnings ratio

(j) Dividends per share

(k) Dividend payout

SOLUTION

(a) Current ratio $= \dfrac{\text{Current assets}}{\text{Current liabilities}} = \dfrac{\$600,000}{\$200,000} = 3$

(b) Quick ratio $= \dfrac{\text{Cash} + \text{Marketable securities}}{\text{Current liabilities}} = \dfrac{\$300,000}{\$200,000} = 1.5$

(c) Inventory turnover $= \dfrac{\text{Cost of goods sold}}{\text{Average inventory}} = \dfrac{\$6,000,000}{(\$250,000 + \$300,000)/2} = 21.82$

(d) Age of inventory $= \dfrac{365}{\text{Inventory turnover}} = \dfrac{365}{21.82} = 16.7 \text{ days}$

(e) $\dfrac{\text{Stockholders' equity}}{\text{Total liabilities}} = \dfrac{\$800,000}{\$300,000} = 2.67$

(f) $\dfrac{\text{Plant assets}}{\text{Long-term liabilities}} = \dfrac{\$500,000}{\$100,000} = 5$

(g) $\dfrac{\text{Operating expenses}}{\text{Net sales}} = \dfrac{\$1,000,000}{\$10,000,000} = 0.1$

(h) Earnings per share $= \dfrac{\text{Net income}}{\text{Outstanding common shares}} = \dfrac{\$1,500,000}{100,000 \text{ shares}} = \$15$

(*i*)   Price/earnings ratio $= \dfrac{\text{Market price per share}}{\text{Earnings per share}} = \dfrac{\$150}{\$15} = 10$

(*j*)   Dividends per share $= \dfrac{\text{Dividends}}{\text{Outstanding shares}} = \dfrac{\$600,000}{100,000 \text{ shares}} = \$6$

(*k*)   Dividend payout $= \dfrac{\text{Dividends per share}}{\text{Earnings per share}} = \dfrac{\$6}{\$15} = 0.4$

CHAPTER 15

Statement of Cash Flows

15.1 INTRODUCTION

The statement of cash flows shows the sources and uses of cash, which is a basis for cash flow analysis for financial managers. The statement aids in answering vital questions such as "Where was money obtained?" and "Where was money put and for what purpose?" The following provides a list of specific questions that can be answered by the statement of cash flows and cash flow analysis:

1. Is the company growing or just maintaining its competitive position?
2. Will the company be able to meet its financial obligations?
3. Where did the company obtain funds?
4. What use was made of net income?
5. How much of the required capital was generated internally?
6. How was the expansion in plant and equipment financed?
7. Is the business expanding faster than it can generate funds?
8. Is the company's dividend policy in balance with its operating policy?
9. Is the company's cash position sound, and what effect will it have on the market price of stock?

Cash is vital to the operation of every business. How management utilizes the flow of cash can determine a firm's success or failure. Financial managers must control their company's cash flow so that bills can be paid on time and extra dollars can be put into the purchase of inventory and new equipment or invested to generate additional earnings.

15.2 FASB REQUIREMENTS

Management and external interested parties have always recognized the need for a cash flow statement. Therefore, in recognition of the fact that cash flow information is an integral part of both investment and credit decisions, the Financial Accounting Standards Board (FASB) has issued *Statement No. 95*, "Statement of Cash Flows." This pronouncement requires that enterprises include a statement of cash flows as part of the financial statements. A statement of cash flows reports the cash receipts, payments, and net change in cash on hand resulting from the *operating*, *investing*, and *financing* activities of an enterprise during a given period. The presentation reconciles beginning and ending cash balances.

15.3   ACCRUAL BASIS OF ACCOUNTING

Under Generally Accepted Accounting Principles (GAAP), most companies use the accrual basis of accounting. This method requires that revenue be recorded when earned and that expenses be recorded when incurred. Revenue may include credit sales that have not yet been collected in cash and expenses incurred that may not have been paid in cash. Thus, under the accrual basis of accounting, net income will generally not indicate the net cash flow from operating activities. To arrive at net cash flow from operating activities, it is necessary to report revenues and expenses on a cash basis. This is accomplished by eliminating those transactions that did not result in a corresponding increase or decrease in cash on hand.

EXAMPLE 1   During 20X1, the Eastern Electric Supply Corporation earned $2,100,000 in credit sales, of which $100,000 remained uncollected as of the end of the calendar year. Cash that was actually collected by the corporation in 20X1 can be calculated as follows:

Credit sales	$2,100,000
Less: Credit sales uncollected at year end	100,000
Actual cash collected	$2,000,000

15.4   CASH AND CASH EQUIVALENTS

FASB 95 also requires that the cash flow statement explain the changes during the period in cash and cash equivalents. The latter are defined as short-term, highly liquid investments both readily convertible to known amounts of cash and so near maturity that it is appropriate to refer to them as being the equivalent of cash. Investments may or may not meet the definition of a cash equivalent. The statement indicates that only those investments with remaining maturities of three months or less at the date of their acquisition can qualify as cash equivalents.

For example, if a company bought a three-month U.S. Treasury bill two months ago, it would be treated as a cash equivalent because it was purchased within three months of its maturity date. However, a one-year bill purchased a year ago does not become a cash equivalent when its remaining maturity becomes three months or less. Other items commonly considered to be cash equivalents include commercial paper and money market funds.

15.5   PRESENTATION OF NONCASH INVESTING AND FINANCING TRANSACTIONS

A statement of cash flows focuses only on transactions involving the cash receipts and disbursements of a company. Noncash investing and financing transactions, such as the acquisition of land in return for the issuance of either bonds, preferred stock, or common stock, should not be presented in the body of the statement. These noncash transactions must, however, be disclosed elsewhere in the cash flow statement.

15.6   OPERATING, INVESTING, AND FINANCING ACTIVITIES

A statement of cash flows focuses only on transactions involving the cash receipts and disbursements of a company. As stated previously, the statement of cash flows classifies cash receipts and cash payments into operating, investing, and financing activities.

OPERATING ACTIVITIES

Operating activities include all transactions that are not investing or financing activities. They relate only to income statement items. Thus cash received from the sale of goods or services, including the collection or sale of trade accounts and notes receivable from customers, interest received on loans, and dividend income, is to be treated as cash from operating activities. Cash paid to acquire materials for the manufacture of goods for resale, rental payments to landlords, payments to employees as compensation, and interest paid to creditors are classified as cash outflows for operating activities.

EXAMPLE 2   For the year ended December 31, 20X2, the net income of the Forbes Picture Frame Corporation was $60,000. Depreciation on plant assets for the year was $25,000. The balances of the current assets and current liability accounts at the beginning and end of 20X2 are as follows:

	Beginning	End
Cash	$ 70,000	$ 65,000
Short-term Investments	-0-	9,000
Accounts Receivables	90,000	100,000
Inventories	155,000	145,000
Prepaid Expenses	9,500	7,500
Accounts Payable	59,000	51,000

What is the amount to be reported for cash flows from operating activities for 20X2?

Net income		$60,000
Add: Depreciation	$25,000	
Decrease in Inventories	10,000	
Decrease in Prepaid Expenses	2,000	37,000
Deduct: Increase in Short-term Investments	$ 9,000	
Increase in Accounts Receivable	10,000	
Decrease in Accounts Payable	8,000	27,000
Cash Inflows from Operating Activities		$70,000

INVESTING ACTIVITIES

Investing activities include cash inflows from the sale of property, plant, and equipment used in the production of goods and services, debt instruments or equity of other entities, and the collection of principal on loans made to other enterprises. Cash outflows under this category may result from the purchases of plant and equipment and other productive assets, debt instruments or equity of other entities, and the making of loans to other enterprises.

EXAMPLE 3   During 20X2, the Zandex Altimeter Corporation sold its plant and equipment for $9,000,000 and sold all of its stock investment in Trunk Realty Corporation, an unrelated entity, for $8,000,000. It bought a new plant for $7,000,000 and made a loan of $5,500,000 to another company. Net cash provided by the corporation's investing operations for the year 20X2 is calculated as follows:

Cash received:		
Sale of plant and equipment	$9,000,000	
Sale of stock investment	8,000,000	
Total		$17,000,000
Cash paid:		
Purchase of new plant	$7,000,000	
Loan to another entity	5,500,000	
Total		12,500,000
Net cash provided by investing activities		$ 4,500,000

FINANCING ACTIVITIES

The financing activities of an enterprise involve the sale of a company's own preferred and common stock, bonds, mortgages, notes, and other short- or long-term borrowings. Cash outflows classified as financing activities include the repayment of short- and long-term debt, the reacquisition of treasury stock, and the payment of cash dividends.

EXAMPLE 4 In 20X2, the Hanniford Ore Processing Corporation sold 2,000 shares of its own common stock for $2,000,000 cash and $10,000,000 of its 10 percent, 10-year bonds. It also issued another $50,000,000 in preferred stock in return for land and buildings. Hanniford then reacquired 10,000 shares of its own common stock for $8,800,000 and paid a cash dividend of $4,000,000. Net cash provided by the corporation's investing operations for the year 20X2 is calculated as follows:

Cash received:		
Sale of common stock	$ 2,000,000	
Sale of bonds	10,000,000	
Total		$12,000,000
Cash paid:		
Reacquisition of common stock	$ 8,800,000	
Cash dividend paid	4,000,000	
Total		12,800,000
Net cash used in financing activities		$ 800,000

The issuance of the preferred stock in exchange for the land and buildings is a noncash transaction that would be disclosed in supplementary form at the end of the statement.

15.7 PRESENTATION OF THE CASH FLOW STATEMENT—DIRECT AND INDIRECT METHODS

A cash flow statement can be presented in either the *direct* or *indirect* format. The investing and financing sections will be the same under either format. However, the operating section will be different.

DIRECT METHOD

Enterprises that utilize the direct method should report separately the following classes of operating cash receipts and payments:

1. Cash collected from customers, including lessees, licensee, and other similar items
2. Interest and dividends received
3. Other operating cash receipts, if any
4. Cash paid to employees and other suppliers of goods or services, including supplies, insurance, advertising, and other similar expenses
5. Interest paid
6. Income taxes paid
7. Other operating cash payments, if any

Companies that use the direct method must provide a reconciliation of net income to net cash flow from operating activities in a separate schedule in the financial statements.

INDIRECT METHOD

The indirect method starts with net income and reconciles it to net cash flow from operating activities. The cash flow from operating activities is found by adjusting net income for (1) changes in current assets and current liabilities and (2) depreciation expense. Depreciation expense is not a cash flow. Because it decreases net income, it is added back to net income in order to arrive at the operating cash flow. The following summarizes the process:

Change	Adjustment to Net Income
Decrease in a current asset	Add
Increase in a current asset	Subtract
Decrease in a current liability	Subtract
Increase in a current liability	Add

The indirect method is more widely used, because it shows the relationship between the income statement and the balance sheet and therefore aids in the analysis of these statements.

EXAMPLE 5   A comparative balance sheet and income statement of Engel Cord Corporation for the year ended December 31, 20X1, was presented as follows:

Engel Cord Corporation
Comparative Balance Sheet
December 31, 20X2

	20X2	20X1	Change Increase/Decrease
ASSETS			
Cash	$ 74,000	$ 98,000	$ 24,000 Decrease
Accounts Receivable	52,000	72,000	20,000 Decrease
Prepaid Expenses	12,000	-0-	12,000 Increase
Long-term Investments	1,000	2,000	1,000 Decrease
Land	140,000	-0-	140,000 Increase
Building	400,000	-0-	400,000 Increase
Accumulated Depreciation—Building	(22,000)	-0-	22,000 Increase
Equipment	136,000	-0-	136,000 Increase
Accumulated Depreciation—Equipment	(20,000)	-0-	20,000 Increase
Total	$773,000	$172,000	

	20X2	20X1	Change Increase/Decrease
LIABILITIES AND STOCKHOLDERS' EQUITY			
Accounts Payable	$ 81,000	$ 12,000	$ 69,000 Increase
Bonds Payable	300,000	-0-	300,000 Increase
Common Stock	120,000	120,000	-0-
Retained Earnings	272,000	40,000	232,000 Increase
Total	$773,000	$172,000	

Engel Cord Corporation
Income Statement
For the Year Ended December 31, 20X2

Revenues		$984,000
Operating Expenses (excluding depreciation)	$538,000	
Depreciation Expense	42,000	580,000
Income from Operations		404,000
Income Tax Expense		136,000
Net Income		$268,000

During 20X2, Engel Cord paid $36,000 in cash dividends. Prepare a statement of cash flows using (a) the direct method and (b) the indirect method.

(a) The statement of cash flows, using the *direct method*, would be presented as follows:

Engel Cord Corporation
Statement of Cash Flows
For the Year Ended December 31, 20X2

Cash Flows from Operating Activities:		
Cash Received from Customers	$ 1,004,000	
Cash Payments for Operating Expenses	(469,000)	
Cash Payments for Prepaid Expenses	(12,000)	
Cash Payments for Taxes	(136,000)	
Net Cash Provided by Operating Activities		$ 387,000
Cash Flows from Investing Activities:		
Cash Paid to Purchase Land	$ (140,000)	
Cash Paid to Purchase Building	(400,000)	
Cash Paid to Purchase Equipment	(136,000)	
Sale of Long-term Investment	1,000	
Net Cash Used in Investing Activities		(675,000)
Cash Flows from Financing Activities:		
Cash Received from the Issuance of Bonds	$ 300,000	
Cash Paid for Dividends	(36,000)	
Net Cash Provided by Financing Activities		264,000
Net Decrease in Cash and Cash Equivalents		(24,000)
Cash and Cash Equivalents at the Beginning of the Year		98,000
Cash and Cash Equivalents at the End of the Year		$ 74,000

Under this method, the $1,004,000 in cash received from customers represents $984,000 in sales increased by a reduction in accounts receivable of $20,000. Accounts receivable was reduced due to a conversion into cash. The cash outflow of $469,000 was determined by reducing the $538,000 in expenses by the increase to accounts payable of $69,000. All other amounts were obtained directly from either the balance sheet or the income statement.

Under the direct method, a separate schedule reconciling net income to net cash would be presented as follows:

Engel Cord Corporation
Statement of Cash Flows
For the Year Ended December 31, 20X2

Cash Flows from Operating Activities:		
Net Income		$268,000
Add: Adjustments to Reconcile Net Income to Net Cash:		
Depreciation Expense	$ 42,000	
Decrease in Accounts Receivable	20,000	
Increase in Prepaid Expenses	(12,000)	
Increase in Accounts Payable	69,000	119,000
Net Cash Provided by Operating Activities		$387,000

(b)   If the indirect method were utilized, the cash flow statement would be presented as follows:

Engel Cord Corporation
Statement of Cash Flows
For the Year Ended December 31, 20X2

Cash Flows from Operating Activities:		
Net Income		$ 268,000
Add: Adjustments to Reconcile Net Income to Net Cash Earnings:		
Depreciation Expense	$ 42,000	
Decrease in Accounts Receivable	20,000	
Increase in Prepaid Expenses	(12,000)	
Increase in Accounts Payable	69,000	119,000
Net Cash Flow Provided by Operating Activities		$ 387,000
Cash Flows from Investing Activities:		
Cash Paid to Purchase Land	$(140,000)	
Cash Paid to Purchase Building	(400,000)	
Cash Paid to Purchase Equipment	(136,000)	
Sale of Long-term Investments	1,000	
Net Cash Used in Investing Activities		(675,000)
Cash Flows from Financing Activities:		
Cash Received from the Issuance of Bonds	$ 300,000	
Cash Paid for Dividends	(36,000)	
Net Cash Provided by Financing Activities		264,000
Net Decrease in Cash Equivalents		(24,000)
Cash and Cash Equivalents at the Beginning of the Year		98,000
Cash and Cash Equivalents at the End of the Year		$ 74,000

Summary

(1)   The statement of cash flows seeks to explain the changes in _____ and _____ rather than ambiguous terms such as _____ .

(2)   In recognition of the fact that cash flow information is an integral part of both investment and credit decisions, the _____ has issued *Statement No. 95*, "Statement of Cash Flows."

(3) Depreciation expense is one of the items that must be _____ to net income to determine the cash flows from _____ .

(4) The three major categories of the statement of cash flows are cash flows associated with _____ activities, investing activities, and _____ activities.

(5) A stock dividend (is/is not) shown in the statement of cash flows.

(6) Under _____ , most companies use the _____ basis of accounting.

(7) _____ are defined as short-term, highly liquid investments both readily convertible to known amounts of cash.

(8) A cash flow statement can be presented in either the _____ or _____ format. The _____ and _____ sections will be the same under either format.

(9) Companies that use _____ provide a reconciliation of net income to net cash flow from operating activities in a separate schedule in the financial statements.

(10) _____ is more widely used, because it shows the relationship between the income statement and the balance sheet and therefore aids in the analysis of these statements.

Answers: (1) cash, cash equivalents, funds; (2) Financial Accounting Standards Board (FASB); (3) added back, operating activities; (4) operating, financing; (5) is not; (6) Generally Accepted Accounting Principles (GAAP), accrual; (7) Cash equivalents; (8) direct, indirect, investing, financing; (9) the direct method; (10) The indirect method

Solved Problems

15.1 Classify each of the following transactions as an operating activity, an investing activity, or a financing activity. Also indicate whether the activity is a source of cash or a use of cash.

(*a*) A plant was sold for $550,000.

(*b*) A profit of $75,000 was reported.

(*c*) Long-term bonds were retired.

(*d*) Cash dividends of $420,000 were paid.

(*e*) Four hundred thousand shares of preferred stock were sold.

(*f*) A new high-tech robotics unit was purchased.

(*g*) A long-term note payable was issued.

(*h*) A 50 percent interest in a company was purchased.

(*i*) A loss for the year was reported.

(*j*) Additional common stock was sold.

SOLUTION

(*a*) Investing—source of cash

(*b*) Operating—source of cash

(*c*) Financing—use of cash

(*d*) Financing—use of cash

(*e*) Financing—source of cash

(*f*) Investing—use of cash

(*g*) Financing—source of cash

(*h*) Investing—use of cash

(*i*) Operating—use of cash

(*j*) Financing—source of cash

15.2 Indicate whether each of the events described below will be added to or deducted from net income in order to compute cash flow from operations.

(*a*) Gain on sale of an asset

(*b*) Increase in accounts receivable

(*c*) Decrease in prepaid insurance

(*d*) Depreciation expense

(*e*) Increase in accounts payable

(*f*) Uncollectible accounts expense

(*g*) Decrease in wages payable

(*h*) Increase in inventory

(*i*) Amortization of a patent

SOLUTION

(*a*) Deducted from

(*b*) Deducted from

(*c*) Added to

(*d*) Added to

(*e*) Added to

(*f*) Added to

(*g*) Deducted from

(*h*) Deducted from

(*i*) Added to

15.3 Classify each transaction in the first three columns by its correct cash flow activity.

	Types of Activity			
	Operating	Investing	Financing	Not Applicable
Payments to acquire materials for manufacturing				
Payments to acquire stock of other companies				
Proceeds from the issuance of equity instruments				
Acquisition of land for the corporation's common stock				
Receipt of interest and dividends				
Payment of dividends				
Issuance of corporate bonds				
Issuance of corporate mortgage				
Receipts from sale of corporate plant				
Exchange of corporate bonds for the corporation's preferred stock				

SOLUTION

	Types of Activity			
	Operating	Investing	Financing	Not Applicable
Payments to acquire materials for manufacturing	X			
Payments to acquire stock of other companies		X		
Proceeds from the issuance of equity instruments			X	
Acquisition of land for the corporation's common stock				X
Receipt of interest and dividends	X			
Payment of dividends			X	
Issuance of corporate bonds			X	
Issuance of corporate mortgage			X	
Receipts from sale of corporate plant		X		
Exchange of corporate bonds for the corporation's preferred stock				X

15.4 McBride Bus and Terminal Lines, Inc.'s transactions for the year ended December 31, 20X2, included the following:

(1)   Purchased real estate for $500,000, which was borrowed from a bank

(2)   Sold investment securities worth $600,000

(3) Paid dividends of $300,000

(4) Issued 500 shares of common stock for $350,000

(5) Purchased machinery and equipment for $175,000

(6) Paid $750,000 toward a bank loan

(7) Accounts receivable outstanding of $100,000 were paid

(8) Accounts payable were increased by $190,000

Calculate McBride's net cash used in (*a*) its investing activities and (*b*) its financing activities.

SOLUTION

(*a*) Investing activities:

Cash Inflows:		
Sale of Investment Securities		$600,000
Less Cash Outflows:		
Purchase of Real Estate	$500,000	
Purchase of Machinery and Equipment	175,000	675,000
Net Cash Used in Investing Activities		$(75,000)

(*b*) Financing activities:

Cash Inflows:		
Borrowed from Bank to Purchase Real Estate		$ 500,000
Issued Common Stock		350,000
		$ 850,000
Less Cash Outflows:		
Paid Dividends	$(300,000)	
Paid Bank Loan	(750,000)	1,050,000
Net Cash Used in Investing Activities		$(200,000)

15.5 Beta Pipeline and Transmission Corporation's transactions for the year ended December 31, 20X2, included the following:

(1) Cash sales of $2,300,000

(2) Taxes, fines, and penalties of $80,000

(3) Sold investment securities for $980,000

(4) Borrowed $330,000 in cash from a bank

(5) Paid cash for inventory totalling $940,000

(6) Issued 10,000 shares of its preferred stock for land with a fair market value of $750,000

(7) Purchased a secret formula for $100,000

(8) Purchased land for $230,000

(9) Paid $225,000 toward a bank loan

(10) Sold 600 of its 10 percent debenture bonds due in the year 20X2 for $600,000

Calculate Beta's net cash inflows or outflows for (*a*) operating, (*b*) investing, and (*c*) financing activities. (*d*) Which of the transactions are not reported as part of the operating, investing, or financing activities of the corporation but, rather, are reported separately on the statement of cash flows?

SOLUTION

(*a*) Operating activities:

Cash Inflows:

Cash Sales		$2,300,000
Less: Cash Outflows:		
Cash Paid for Inventory	$(940,000)	
Taxes, Fines, and Penalties	(80,000)	1,020,000
Net Cash Inflows from Operating Activities		$1,280,000

(*b*) Investing activities:

Cash Inflows:

Sold Investment Securities		$ 980,000
Less: Cash Outflows:		
Purchase of Secret Formula	$(100,000)	
Purchase of Land	(230,000)	330,000
Net Cash Inflows from Investing Activities		$(650,000)

(*c*) Financing activities:

Cash Inflows:

Borrowing from Bank	$ 330,000
Sale of Debenture Bonds	600,000
Less: Cash Outflows:	$(930,000)
Paid Bank Loan	(225,000)
Net Cash Inflow from Investing Activities	$(705,000)

(*d*) The issuance of 10,000 shares of Beta's preferred stock for land with a fair market value of $750,000 does not involve an exchange of cash and must be reported separately on the statement of cash flows.

15.6 Seal Beach Steam Corporation's balance sheet accounts as of December 31, 20X1, and December 31, 20X2, and the information relating to the 20X1 activities are presented below:

	December 31	
	20X2	20X1
ASSETS		
Cash	$ 230,000	$100,000
Short-term Investments	300,000	-0-
Accounts Receivable (net)	550,000	550,000
Inventory	680,000	600,000
Long-term Investments	200,000	300,000
Plant Assets	1,700,000	1,000,000
Accumulated Depreciation	(450,000)	(450,000)
Goodwill	90,000	100,000
Total Assets	$3,300,000	$2,200,000

	December 31	
	20X2	20X1
LIABILITIES AND STOCKHOLDERS' EQUITY		
Accounts Payable	$ 825,000	$ 720,000
Long-term Debt	325,000	-0-
Common Stock, $1 par	800,000	700,000
Additional Paid-in Capital	370,000	250,000
Retained Earnings	980,000	530,000
Total Liabilities and Stockholders' Equity	$3,300,000	$2,200,000

Information relating to 20X2 activities is as follows:

(1) Net income for 20X2 was $700,000

(2) Purchase of short-term investments for $300,000, which will mature on June 30, 20X3

(3) Cash dividends declared and paid in 20X2 worth $250,000

(4) Equipment costing $400,000, having accumulated depreciation of $250,000, was sold in 20X2 for $150,000

(5) Plant assets worth $1,100,000 were purchased for cash

(6) A long-term investment costing $100,000 was sold for $135,000

(7) 100,000 shares of $1 par value common stock were sold for $2.20 a share

(8) Amortization of goodwill for 20X2 was $10,000

Calculate Seal Beach's net cash inflows or outflows for (a) operating, (b) investing, and (c) financing activities. Discuss whether or not the short-term investments are cash equivalents.

SOLUTION

(a) Operating activities:

Net Income	$ 700,000
Depreciation	250,000
Increase in Inventory	(80,000)
Increase in Accounts Payable	105,000
Gain on Sale of Investment	(35,000)
Amortization of Goodwill	10,000
Total Cash Provided from Operating Activities	$ 950,000

(b) Investing activities:

Sale of Equipment	$ 150,000
Sale of Investment	135,000
Purchase of Short-term Investments	(300,000)
Purchase of Plant Assets	(1,100,000)
Total Cash Used for Investing Activities	$(1,100,000)

(c) Financing activities:

Dividends Paid	$ (250,000)
Long-term Debt	325,000
Common Stock Issued	220,000
Total Cash Provided from Financing Activities	$ 295,000

Only short-term investments acquired within three months of their maturity date may be treated as cash equivalents. The short-term investments acquired by Seal Beach are due at the end of six months and are therefore not cash equivalents.

15.7 Cerritos Manufacturing has provided the following financial statements:

Cerritos Manufacturing
Comparative Balance Sheets
For the Years Ended December 31, 20X1 and 20X2

	20X1	20X2
ASSETS		
Cash	$ 112,500	$ 350,000
Accounts Receivable	350,000	281,250
Inventories	125,000	150,000
Plant and Equipment	1,000,000	1,025,000*
Accumulated Depreciation	(500,000)	(525,000)
Land	500,000	718,750
Total Assets	$1,587,500	$2,000,000
LIABILITIES AND EQUITY		
Accounts Payable	$ 300,000	$ 237,500
Mortgage Payable	—	250,000
Common Stock	75,000	75,000
Contributed Capital in Excess of Par	300,000	300,000
Retained Earnings	912,500	1,137,500
Total Liabilities and Equity	$1,587,500	$2,000,000

*Beginning Equipment	$1,000,000
Purchases	250,000
Less Sales	(225,000)
Ending Equipment	$1,025,000

Income Statement
For the Year Ended December 31, 20X2

Revenues	$1,200,000
Gain on Sale of Equipment	50,000
Less: Cost of Goods Sold	(640,000)
Less: Depreciation Expense	(125,000)
Less: Interest Expense	(35,000)
Net Income	$ 450,000

Other information:

(a) Equipment with a book value of $125,000 was sold for $175,000 (original cost was $225,000).

(b) Dividends of $225,000 were declared and paid.

Prepare a statement of cash flows.

SOLUTION

Cerritos Manufacturing
Statement of Cash Flows
For the Year Ended December 31, 20X2

Cash Flows from Operating Activities:

Net Income	$ 450,000	
Add (Deduct) Adjusting Items:		
Gain on Sale of Equipment	(50,000)	
Decrease in Accounts Receivable	68,750	
Increase in Inventory	(25,000)	
Depreciation Expense	125,000	
Decrease in Accounts Payable	(62,500)	
Net Operating Cash		$ 506,250
Cash Flows from Investing Activities:		
Sale of Equipment	$ 175,000	
Purchase of Equipment	(250,000)	
Purchase of Land	(218,750)	
Net Cash from Investing Activities		$(293,750)
Cash Flows from Financing Activities:		
Mortgage Received	$ 250,000	
Dividends	(225,000)	
Net Cash from Financing Activities		25,000
Net Increase in Cash		$ 237,500

CHAPTER 16

Accounting for Multinational Operations

16.1 INTRODUCTION: ACCOUNTING DIMENSIONS OF INTERNATIONAL BUSINESS

As we enter the twenty-first century, the world economy has become truly internationalized and globalized. Advances in information technology, communications, and transportation have enabled businesses to service a world market. Many U.S. companies, both large and small, are now heavily engaged in international trade. The foreign operations of many large U.S. multinational corporations now account for a major percentage (10 to 50 percent) of their sales and/or net income.

The basic business functions (i.e., finance/accounting, production, management, marketing) take on a new perspective when conducted in a foreign environment. There are different laws, economic policies, political frameworks, and social/cultural factors, which all have an effect on how business is conducted in that foreign country. From an accounting standpoint, global business activities are faced with three realities:

1. Accounting standards and practices differ from country to country. Accounting is a product of its own economic, legal, political, and sociocultural environment. Since this environment changes from country to country, the accounting system of each country is unique and different from all others.

2. Each country has a strong "accounting nationalism": it requires business companies operating within its borders to follow its own accounting standards and practices. Consequently, a foreign company operating within its borders must maintain its books and records and prepare its financial statements in the local language, using the local currency as a unit of measure, and in accordance with local accounting standards and procedures. In addition, the foreign company must comply with the local tax laws and government regulations.

This chapter was coauthored by Loc T. Nguyen, LL.M., MBA, CPA, Assistant Professor, California State University, Long Beach.

3. Cross-border business transactions often involve receivables and payables denominated in foreign currencies. During the year, these foreign currencies must be translated (converted) into the local currencies for recording in the books and records. At year-end, the foreign currency financial statements must be translated (restated) into the parent's reporting currency for purposes of consolidation. Both the recording of foreign currency transactions and the translation of financial statements require the knowledge of the exchange rates to be used and the accounting treatment of the resulting translation gains and losses.

The biggest mistake a company can make in international accounting is not to be aware of or, even worse, to ignore these realities. It should know that differences in accounting standards, tax laws, and government regulations do exist; and that these differences need to be an integral part of formulating their international business plan.

16.2 FOREIGN CURRENCY EXCHANGE RATES

Exchange rates are used to convert one currency into another currency. An exchange rate is the price of one currency in terms of another currency, i.e., the amount of one currency that must be given to buy one unit of another currency. Because U.S. firms have to prepare their financial statements in U.S. dollars, we shall focus on foreign currency exchange rates in terms of U.S. dollars.

Foreign currency exchange rates are quoted daily in the financial press. Two different rates are quoted for each day:

A direct quote, which is the amount in U.S. dollars of one unit of foreign currency:

$$1 \text{ British pound} = \text{US\$1.5505}$$

An indirect quote, which is the amount of foreign currency equivalent to 1 U.S. dollar:

$$\text{US\$1} = 0.6450 \text{ British pound}$$

The above quotes are called *spot rates*, and are rates quoted for transactions to be settled within two business days. For some major currencies, *forward rates* are also quoted, for future delivery (30 days, 60 days, 180 days forward) of the foreign currency.

Currencies are bought and sold like other goods. Under the current system of floating exchange rates, foreign exchange rates, like stock prices, are constantly fluctuating, depending on the forces of supply and demand. Because current exchange rates are both volatile and unpredictable, international business transactions are subject to the additional risk of exchange rate fluctuations.

16.3 ACCOUNTING FOR FOREIGN CURRENCY TRANSACTIONS

International business transactions are cross-border transactions, therefore two national currencies are usually involved: the currency of the buyer and the currency of the seller. For example, when a U.S. corporation sells to a corporation in Germany, the transaction can be settled in U.S. dollars (the seller's currency) or in German marks (the buyer's currency).

TRANSACTIONS DENOMINATED IN U.S. CURRENCY

When the foreign transaction is settled in U.S. dollars, no measurement problems occur for the U.S. corporation. As long as the U.S. corporation receives U.S. dollars, the transaction can be recorded in the same way as a domestic transaction.

EXAMPLE 1   A U.S. firm sells on account equipment worth $100,000 to a German company. If the German company pays the U.S. firm in U.S. dollars, no foreign currency is involved and the transaction is recorded as usual:

Accounts Receivable	100,000	
Sales		100,000
To record sales to German company		

TRANSACTIONS DENOMINATED IN FOREIGN CURRENCY

However, if the transaction above is settled in German marks, the U.S. corporation will receive foreign currency (German marks), which must be translated into U.S. dollars for purposes of recording on the U.S. company's books. Thus, a foreign currency transaction exists when the transaction is settled in a currency other than the company's home currency.

A foreign currency transaction must be recorded in the books of accounts when it is begun (date of transaction), then perhaps at interim reporting dates (reporting date), and finally when it is settled (settlement date). On each of these three dates, the foreign currency transaction must be recorded in U.S. dollars, using the spot rate on that date for translation.

Accounting at transaction date: Before any foreign currency transaction can be recorded, it must first be translated into the domestic currency, using the spot rate on that day. For the U.S. company, this means that any receivable or payable denominated in a foreign currency must be recorded in U.S. dollars.

EXAMPLE 2   Assume that a U.S. firm purchases merchandise on account from a French company on December 1, 20X1. The cost is 50,000 French francs, to be paid in 60 days. The exchange rate for French francs on December 1 is $0.20. Using the exchange rate on December 1, the U.S. firm translates the FFr50,000 into $10,000 and records the following entry:

Dec. 1	Purchases	10,000	
	Accounts Payable		10,000
	To record purchase of merchandise on		
	account (FFr50,000 × $0.20 = $10,000)		

Accounting at interim reporting date: Foreign currency receivables and payables that are not settled at the balance sheet date are adjusted to reflect the exchange rate at that date. Such adjustments will give rise to foreign exchange gains and losses which are to be recognized in the period when exchange rates change.

EXAMPLE 3   Assume that on December 31, 20X1, the exchange rate for the French franc is $0.22. The U.S. firm will make the following adjusting entry:

Dec. 31	Foreign Exchange Loss	1,000	
	Accounts Payable		1,000
	To adjust accounts payable to current		
	exchange rate (FFr50,000 × $0.22		
	= $11,000; $11,000 − $10,000 = $1,000)		

Accounting at settlement date: When the transaction is settled, if the exchange rate changes again, the domestic value of the foreign currency paid on the settlement date will be different from that recorded on the books. This difference gives rise to translation gains and losses which must be recognized in the financial statements.

EXAMPLE 4   To continue our example, assume that on February 1, 20X2, the exchange rate for the French franc is $0.21. The settlement will be recorded as follows:

Feb. 1	Accounts Payable	11,000	
	Cash		10,500
	Foreign Exchange Gain		500

To record payment of accounts payable
(FFr50,000 × $0.21 = $10,500)
and foreign exchange gain

To summarize: In recording foreign currency transactions, *SFAS 52* adopted the two-transaction approach. Under this approach, the foreign currency transaction has two components: the purchase/sale of the asset, and the financing of this purchase/sale. Each component will be treated separately and not netted with the other. The purchase/sale is recorded at the exchange rate on the day of the transaction and is not adjusted for subsequent changes in that rate. Subsequent fluctuations in exchange rates will give rise to foreign exchange gains and losses. They are considered as financing income or expense and are recognized separately in the income statement in the period the foreign exchange fluctuations happen. Thus, exchange gains and losses arising from foreign currency transactions have a direct effect on net income.

16.4   TRANSLATION OF FOREIGN CURRENCY FINANCIAL STATEMENTS

When the U.S. firm owns a controlling interest (more than 50 percent) in another firm in a foreign country, special consolidation problems arise. The subsidiary's financial statements are usually prepared in the language and currency of the country in which it is located, and in accordance with the local accounting principles. Before these foreign currency financial statements can be consolidated with the U.S. parent's financial statements, they must first be adjusted to conform with U.S. Generally Accepted Accounting Principles, and then translated into U.S. dollars.

Two different procedures may be used to translate foreign financial statements into U.S. dollars: (1) translation procedures and (2) remeasurement procedures. Which of these two procedures is to be used depends on the determination of the functional currency for the subsidiary.

THE FUNCTIONAL CURRENCY

SFAS 52 defines the functional currency of the subsidiary as the currency of the primary economic environment in which the subsidiary operates. It is the currency in which the subsidiary realizes its cash flows and conducts its operations. To help management determine the functional currency of its subsidiary, *SFAS 52* provides a list of six salient economic indicators regarding cash flows, sales price, sales market, expenses, financing, and intercompany transactions. Depending on the circumstances:

The functional currency is the local currency. For example, a Japanese subsidiary manufactures and sells its own products in the local market. Its cash flows, revenues, and expenses are primarily in Japanese yen. Thus its functional currency is the local currency (Japanese yen).

The functional currency is the U.S. dollar. For foreign subsidiaries that are operated as an extension of the parent and integrated with it, the functional currency is that of the parent. For example, if the Japanese subsidiary is set up as a sales outlet for its U.S. parent—i.e., it takes orders, bills and collects the invoice price, and remits its cash flows primarily to the parent—then its functional currency is the U.S. dollar.

The functional currency is also the U.S. dollar for foreign subsidiaries that operate in highly inflationary economies (defined as having a cumulative inflation rate of more than 100 percent over a three-year period). The U.S. dollar is deemed the functional currency for translation purposes because it is more stable than the local currency.

Once the functional currency is determined, the specific conversion procedures are selected as follows:

Foreign currency is the functional currency—use translation procedures.

U.S. dollar is the functional currency—use remeasurement procedures.

Translation procedures: If the local currency is the functional currency, the subsidiary's financial statements are translated using the current rate method. Under this method:

All assets and liabilities accounts are translated at the current rate (the rate in effect at the financial statement date).

Capital stock accounts are translated using the historical rate (the rate in effect at the time the stock was issued).

The income statement is translated using the average rate for the year.

All translation gains and losses are reported on the balance sheet, in an account called "Cumulative Translation Adjustments" in the Stockholders' Equity section.

The purpose of these translation procedures is to retain, in the translated financial statements, the financial results and relationships among assets and liabilities that were created by the subsidiary's operations in its foreign environment.

EXAMPLE 5 To illustrate, suppose that the following trial balance, expressed in the local currency (LC) is received from a foreign subsidiary, XYZ Company. The year-end exchange rate is 1 LC = $1.50, and the average exchange rate for the year is 1 LC = $1.25. Under the current rate method, XYZ Company's trial balance would be translated as follows:

(Translation Procedures)
XYZ Company
Trial Balance
December 31, 20X1

	Local Currency Debit	Credit	Exchange Rate	U.S. Dollars Debit	Credit
Cash	LC 5,000		(1 LC = $1.50)	$ 7,500	
Inventory	15,000		"	22,500	
Fixed Assets	30,000		"	45,000	
Payables		LC 40,000	"		$ 60,000
Capital Stock		4,000	Historical rate		5,000
Retained Earnings		6,000	to balance		10,000
Sales		300,000	(1 LC = $1.25)		375,000
Cost of Goods Sold	210,000		"	262,500	
Depreciation Expense	5,000		"	6,250	
Other Expenses	85,000		"	106,250	
	LC350,000	LC350,000		$450,000	$450,000

Note that the translation adjustment is reflected as an adjustment of stockholders' equity in U.S. dollars.

Remeasurement procedures: If the U.S. dollar is considered to be the functional currency, the subsidiary's financial statements are then remeasured into the U.S. dollar by using the temporal method. Under this method:

Monetary accounts such as Cash, Receivables, and Liabilities are remeasured at the current rate on the date of the balance sheet.

Nonmonetary accounts such as Inventory, Fixed Assets, and Capital Stock are remeasured using historical rates.

Revenues and expenses are remeasured using the average rate, except for cost of sales and depreciation expenses, which are remeasured using the historical exchange rates for the related assets.

All remeasurement gains and losses are recognized immediately in the income statement.

The objective of these remeasurement procedures is to produce the same U.S. dollar financial statements as if the foreign entity's accounting records had been initially maintained in the U.S. dollar. The following shows these remeasurement procedures applied to XYZ Company's trial balance. Note that the translation gain/loss is included in the income statement.

(Remeasurement Procedures)
XYZ Company
Trial Balance
December 31, 20X1

	Local Currency		Exchange Rate	U.S. Dollars	
	Debit	Credit		Debit	Credit
Cash	LC 5,000		(1 LC = $1.50)	$ 7,500	
Inventory	15,000		(1 LC = $1.30)	19,500	
Fixed Assets	30,000		(1 LC = $0.95)	28,500	
Payables		LC 40,000	(1 LC = $1.50)		$ 60,000
Capital Stock		4,000	–		5,000
Retained Earnings		6,000			7,000
Sales		300,000	(1 LC = $1.25)		375,000
Cost of Goods Sold	210,000		(1 LC = $1.30)	273,000	
Depreciation Expense	5,000		(1 LC = $0.95)	4,750	
Other Expenses	85,000		(1 LC = $1.25)	106,250	
				$439,500	$447,000
Translation Gain/Loss				7,500	
	LC350,000	LC350,000		$447,000	$447,000

16.5 INTERPRETATION OF FOREIGN FINANCIAL STATEMENTS

To evaluate a foreign corporation, we usually analyze the financial statements of the foreign corporation. However, the analysis of foreign financial statements needs special considerations:

1. We often tend to look at the foreign financial data from a home-country perspective. For example, a U.S. businessperson tends to use U.S. Generally Accepted Accounting Principles (GAAP) to evaluate the foreign financial statements. However, U.S. GAAP are not universally recognized, and many differences exist between U.S. GAAP and the accounting principles of other countries (industrialized or nonindustrialized).

2. Because of the diversity of accounting principles worldwide, we have to overcome the tendency to use our home-country GAAP to evaluate foreign financial statements. Instead, we should try to become familiar with the GAAP used in the preparation of these financial statements and apply them in our financial analysis.

3. Business practices are culturally based. Often they are different from country to country and have a significant impact on accounting measurement and disclosure practices. Therefore, local economic conditions and business practices should be taken into consideration to analyze foreign financial statements correctly.

16.6 HARMONIZATION OF ACCOUNTING STANDARDS

The diversity of accounting systems is an obstacle in the development of international trade and business and the efficiency of the global capital markets. Many concerted efforts have been made to reduce this diversity through the harmonization of accounting standards. Also, as international business expands, there is a great need for international accounting standards that can help investors make decisions on an international scale. The agencies working toward the harmonization of accounting standards are discussed below.

THE INTERNATIONAL ACCOUNTING STANDARDS COMMITTEE (IASC)

The IASC was founded in 1973. At that time, its members consisted of the accountancy bodies of Australia, Canada, France, Japan, Mexico, the Netherlands, the United Kingdom, Ireland, the United States, and West Germany. Since its founding, membership has grown to around 116 accountancy bodies from approximately 85 countries.

The IASC's fundamental goal is the development of international accounting standards. It is also working toward the improvement and harmonization of accounting standards and procedures relating to the presentation and comparability of financial statements (or at least through enhanced disclosure, if differences are present). To date, it has developed a conceptual framework and issued a total of 32 *International Accounting Standards* (IAS) covering a wide range of accounting issues. It is currently working on a project concerned with the core standards in consultation with other international groups, especially the International Organization of Securities Commissions (IOSCO), to develop worldwide standards for all corporations to facilitate multi-listing of foreign corporations on various stock exchanges.

THE INTERNATIONAL FEDERATION OF ACCOUNTANTS (IFAC)

The IFAC was founded in 1977 by 63 accountancy bodies representing 49 countries. By 1990, IFAC membership had grown to 105 accountancy bodies from 78 different countries. Its purpose is to develop "a coordinated worldwide accountancy profession with harmonized standards." It concentrates on establishing auditing guidelines to help promote uniform auditing practices throughout the world. It also promotes general standards for ethics, education, and accounting management.

In addition to the IASC and IFAC, a growing number of regional organizations are involved in accounting harmonization at the regional level. These organizations include, among others, the Inter-American Accounting Association (established in 1949), the ASEAN Federation of Accountants (AFA) (established in 1977), and the Federation des Experts Comptables Européens (FEE), created by the merger in 1986 of the former Union Européenne des Experts Comptables Economiques et Financiers (UEC) and the Groupe d'Etude (GE).

THE EUROPEAN ECONOMIC COMMUNITY (EEC)

The EEC, although it is not an accounting body, has made great strides in harmonizing the accounting standards of its member countries. During the 1970s, it began the slow process of issuing EEC directives to harmonize the national accounting legislation of its member countries. The directives must go through a three-step process before they are finalized. First, they are proposed by the EEC Commission and presented to the national representatives of the EEC members. Second, if the proposal is satisfactory to the nations, it is adopted by the Commission. Finally, it must be issued by the Council of Ministers of the EEC, before it can be enforced on the members.

The most important directives in the harmonization of accounting standards among EEC members are:

The Fourth Directive (1978), regarding the layout and content of annual accounts, valuation methods, annual report, publicity and audit of public and private company accounts

The Seventh Directive (1983), regarding the consolidation of accounts for certain groups of enterprises

The Eighth Directive (1984), regarding the training, qualification and independence of statutory auditors

Summary

(1)   Economic events denominated in a currency other than the U.S. dollar are _____ .

(2)   _____ is the area of accounting that revolves around a subsidiary or parent company operating in a foreign country and using a monetary unit other than the U.S. dollar.

(3)   U.S. Generally Accepted Accounting Principles (GAAP) are followed by all the industrial countries of the world.   T   F

(4)   Foreign exchange rates are constantly changing.   T   F

(5)   Exchange gains and losses arising from foreign transactions affect net income.   T   F

(6)   Adjustments should be made to receivables and payables arising from foreign transactions at the balance sheet date.   T   F

(7)   The International Accounting Standards Committee (IASC) is concerned with the establishment of international auditing standards.   T   F

(8)   The *International Accounting Standards* (IAS) promulgated by the IASC are only guidelines and recommendations for member countries.   T   F

(9)   The directives issued by the European Community are enforceable on member countries.   T   F

(10)   Foreign currency translation is concerned with the restatement of foreign currency financial statements for purposes of consolidation.   T   F

(11)   A foreign currency transaction exists when it is settled in the same currency as the reporting currency of the company.   T   F

(12)   Under *SFAS 52*, gains and losses in foreign currency transactions are netted with the original transaction which was settled in the foreign currency.   T   F

(13)   In the translation procedures using the current rate method, translation gains and losses are recognized in the income statement.   T   F

Answers: (1) foreign currency transactions; (2) foreign currency translation; (3) F; (4) T; (5) T; (6) T; (7) F; (8) T; (9) T; (10) T; (11) F; (12) F; (13) F

Solved Problems

16.1 A Canadian company sold some merchandise to a U.S. company in the amount of $150,000 (U.S. dollars) with credit terms of net 60 days. On the date of sale, the exchange rate was US$0.80, and 60 days later the exchange rate was US$0.70.

What journal entries would the U.S. company make to record the purchase and payment for this transaction?

SOLUTION

Since the transaction is denominated in U.S. dollars, no measurement problem exists for the U.S. company. The payable would be recorded on the date of purchase as follows:

Purchase of Merchandise Inventory	150,000	
Accounts Payable		150,000

When the $150,000 is paid 60 days later, the entry is as follows:

Accounts Payable	150,000	
Cash		150,000

16.2 A Canadian company sold some merchandise to a U.S. company in the amount of $150,000 (Canadian dollars) with credit terms of net 60 days. On the date of sale, the exchange rate was US$0.80, and 60 days later the exchange rate was US$0.70. At the interim reporting date, which was 30 days after the transaction, the exchange rate was US$0.75.

What journal entries would the U.S. company make at the purchase date, at the interim reporting date, and at the settlement date?

SOLUTION

Since the transaction is denominated in Canadian dollars, a measurement problem exists for the U.S. company.

1. At the purchase date, the payable would be recorded in the U.S. dollar equivalent as follows:

Purchase of Merchandise Inventory	120,000	
Accounts Payable		120,000

To record purchase of merchandise inventory on
account (C$150,000 × $0.80 = $120,000)

2. At the interim reporting date, the payable has to be adjusted to reflect the lower exchange rate, resulting in a foreign exchange gain. The journal entry is as follows:

Accounts Payable	7,500	
Foreign Exchange Gain		7,500

To adjust accounts payable to current exchange rate
(C$150,000 × $0.75 = $112,500) and record foreign
exchange gain ($120,000 − $112,500 = $7,500)

3. When the C$150,000 is paid 60 days later, the entry is as follows:

Accounts Payable	112,500	
Foreign Exchange Gain		7,500
Cash		105,000

    To record the payment of account payable
      (C$150,000 × $0.70 = $105,000), and foreign
      exchange gain ($112,500 − $105,000 = $7,500).

16.3 During a highly inflationary period, a foreign subsidiary measures its accounts in the local currency (LC) as follows:

Cash	LC 90,000
Land	80,000
Depreciation Expense	40,000
Office Salaries Expense	20,000
Common Stock	500,000
Retained Earnings	200,000

Assume the following exchange rates of the local currency:

	U.S.
Balance Sheet Date	0.65
Average for Current Year	0.75
Land Purchased	0.80
Depreciable Assets Purchased	0.85
Common Stock Issued	0.90

Assuming a highly inflationary period, what is the U.S. dollar equivalent for the following accounts?

(a) Cash

(b) Land

(c) Depreciation Expense

(d) Office Salary Expense

(e) Common Stock

SOLUTION

    Because of the highly inflationary period, the U.S. dollar is the functional currency and the accounts must be remeasured into U.S. dollars using the temporal method:

(a)	Cash	LC 90,000	×	0.65	=	$ 58,500
(b)	Land	180,000	×	0.80	=	144,000
(c)	Depreciation Expense	40,000	×	0.85	=	34,000
(d)	Office Salary Expense	20,000	×	0.75	=	15,000
(e)	Common Stock	500,000	×	0.90	=	450,000

16.4   The following is the income statement for the current year for the foreign subsidiary of the ABC World Corporation:

ABC World Corporation
Income Statement—FC Subsidiary
Year Ended December 31, 20X2

Sales		FC10,000
Cost of Goods Sold	FC5,000	
Salary Expense	3,000	
Depreciation Expense	1,000	
Other Expenses	500	9,500
Net Profit		FC 500

The relevant exchange rates were as follows:

Average rate for the FC subsidiary during the year: 1 FC = $0.75

Rate for the acquisition of inventory: $0.70

Rate for the purchase of equipment: $0.77

(*a*)   Assuming that the FC is the functional currency, translate the income statement into dollars using *SFAS 52*.

(*b*)   Assuming that the U.S. dollar is the functional currency for this subsidiary, remeasure the statement into dollars.

SOLUTION

(*a*)   Since the FC is the functional currency, the income statement is translated using the current rate method. Under this method, the income statement is translated using the average rate for the year.

ABC World Corporation
Income Statement—FC Subsidiary
Year Ended December 31, 20X2

Sales	FC10,000	×	0.75	=	$ 7,500
Cost of Goods Sold	5,000	×	0.75	=	(3,750)
Salary Expense	3,000	×	0.75	=	(2,250)
Depreciation Expense	1,000	×	0.75	=	(750)
Other Expenses	500	×	0.75	=	(375)
Net Profit	FC 500				$ 375

(*b*)   Since the functional currency is the U.S. dollar, the income statement is remeasured into U.S. dollars, using the temporal method.

ABC World Corporation
Income Statement—FC Subsidiary
Year Ended December 31, 20X2

Sales	FC10,000	×	0.75	=	$ 7,500
Cost of Goods Sold	5,000	×	0.70	=	(3,500)
Salary Expense	3,000	×	0.75	=	(2,250)
Depreciation Expense	1,000	×	0.73	=	(730)
Other Expenses	500	×	0.75	=	(375)
Net Profit	FC 500				$ 645

EXAMINATION V

Chapters 13–16

1. Milich and Saft form a partnership. Milich brings the following into the partnership:

	Ledger Balance	Fair Market Value
Cash	$23,000	$23,000
Accounts Receivable	6,000	6,000
Equipment	8,000	5,200
Accumulated Depreciation, Equipment	3,000	
Accounts Payable	10,000	10,000
Allowance for Uncollectible Accounts	800	800

   Prepare the journal entry for Milich's initial investment.

2. Davis and Peters have capital balances of $100,000 and $150,000, respectively. The net income for the year is $39,000. The net income is distributed as follows: (1) Davis and Peters get salaries of $5,000 and $7,000, respectively; (2) each receives 6 percent interest on capital; and (3) the remainder of the profit is divided based on the capital balances.
   Prepare the journal entry to distribute the net income to the partners.

3. Harris and Baker have capital balances of $30,000 and $20,000, respectively. Net income is shared equally. Ford is admitted to the partnership by contributing $20,000 for a 25 percent interest.
   Prepare the journal entries for Ford's admission.

4. Gard, Klinger, and Lemon decide to liquidate their partnership. All accounts have been adjusted and closed. The post-closing trial balance follows:

Gard, Klinger, and Lemon
Post-closing Trial Balance

Cash	$ 70,000	
Noncash Assets	130,000	
Liabilities		$ 50,000
Gard, Capital		60,000
Klinger, Capital		40,000
Lemon, Capital		50,000
	$200,000	$200,000

The noncash assets are sold for $145,000. The partners share profits and losses equally. Prepare the journal entries for (*a*) the sale of assets, (*b*) the payment to creditors, and (*c*) the cash distribution to partners.

5. Using horizontal analysis, determine the percentage change in the following accounts:

	20X3	20X2
Cash	$50	$40
Accounts Receivable	85	90

6. A condensed income statement for Smart Company follows:

Gross Sales	$340,000
Sales Returns	40,000
Net Sales	$300,000
Cost of Goods Sold	230,000
Gross Profit	$ 70,000
Operating Expenses	25,000
Net Income	$ 45,000

Prepare the income statement using vertical analysis.

7. Charles Corporation reports the following for 20X1:

Accounts Receivable—1/1	$100,000
Accounts Receivable—12/31	150,000
Inventory—1/1	40,000
Inventory—12/31	55,000
Net Credit Sales	800,000
Cost of Goods Sold	450,000

Compute (*a*) accounts receivable turnover, (*b*) collection period, (*c*) inventory turnover, (*d*) age of inventory, and (*e*) operating cycle.

8. Column A lists the name of a ratio and column B indicates how the ratio is computed. For each ratio given in column A indicate the appropriate answer from column B.

Column A		Column B
(1) Profit margin	(*a*)	$\dfrac{\text{Net income}}{\text{Common stock outstanding}}$
(2) Dividend payout	(*b*)	$\dfrac{\text{Market price per share}}{\text{Earnings per share}}$
(3) Earnings per share	(*c*)	$\dfrac{\text{Net income}}{\text{Sales}}$
(4) Dividend yield	(*d*)	$\dfrac{\text{Dividends per share}}{\text{Earnings per share}}$
(5) Quick ratio	(*e*)	$\dfrac{\text{Current assets}}{\text{Current liabilities}}$

(6)	Interest coverage	(*f*)	$\dfrac{\text{Cash} + \text{Marketable securities} + \text{Accounts receivable}}{\text{Current liabilities}}$
(7)	Current ratio	(*g*)	$\dfrac{\text{Dividends per share}}{\text{Market price per share}}$
(8)	Price earnings ratio	(*h*)	$\dfrac{\text{Income before interest and taxes}}{\text{Interest expense}}$

9. Why does the acquisition of land in exchange for common stock qualify as a noncash investing and financing transaction?

10. Indicate on the blanks below the letter of the type of activity (O = operating activity, F = financing activity, I = investing activity, N = noncash transaction) each of the following transactions represents:

_____ (*a*) Sold 2,000 shares of a company's own common stock for cash
_____ (*b*) Sold $120,000 worth of products
_____ (*c*) Paid $250,000 dividend
_____ (*d*) Received $2,250 in interest income
_____ (*e*) Exchanged 10,000 shares of common stock for 15-year bonds
_____ (*f*) Paid $75,000 to the Internal Revenue Service

11. Olsen Company prepares its statement of cash flows using the indirect method. Indicate whether each of the items below would be added to (+) or deducted from (−) net income to determine net cash flows from operating activities.

(*a*) Decrease in Inventory
(*b*) Decrease in Accounts Payable
(*c*) Depreciation
(*d*) Loss on Disposal of Equipment
(*e*) Increase in Accounts Receivable
(*f*) Increase in Salaries Payable
(*g*) Uncollectible Accounts Expense
(*h*) Increase in Prepaid Insurance
(*i*) Gain on Sale of Land
(*j*) Increase in Income Tax Payable

12. A Canadian company sold some merchandise to a U.S. company in the amount of $150,000 (Canadian dollars) with credit terms of net 60 days. On the date of sale, the exchange rates were $2.00 Canadian and $0.80 U.S., and 60 days later the exchange rates were $1.75 Canadian and $0.70 U.S. What journal entries would the U.S. company make to record the purchase and payment for this transaction?

Answers to Examination V

1.

Cash	23,000	
Accounts Receivable	6,000	
Equipment	5,200	
Allowance for Uncollectible Accounts		800
Accounts Payable		10,000
Milich, Capital		23,400

2.

	Davis	Peters	Total
Salary	$ 5,000	$ 7,000	$12,000
Interest	6,000	9,000	15,000
Balance	4,800	7,200	12,000
Total	$15,800	$23,200	$39,000

Income Summary	39,000	
Davis, Capital		15,800
Peters, Capital		23,200

3.

Goodwill	10,000	
Harris, Capital		5,000
Baker, Capital		5,000
Cash	20,000	
Ford, Capital		20,000

4. (a)

Cash	145,000	
Noncash Assets		130,000
Gard, Capital		5,000
Klinger, Capital		5,000
Lemon, Capital		5,000

(b)

Liabilities	50,000	
Cash		50,000

(c)

Gard, Capital	65,000	
Klinger, Capital	45,000	
Lemon, Capital	55,000	
Cash		165,000

5.

	20X3	20X2	Percentage of Increase or (Decrease)
Cash	$50	$40	25.0
Accounts Receivable	85	90	(5.6)

6.

	Amount	Percent
Sales	$340,000	113.3
Sales Returns	40,000	13.3
Net Sales	$300,000	100.0
Cost of Goods Sold	230,000	76.7
Gross Profit	$ 70,000	23.3
Operating Expenses	25,000	8.3
Net Income	$ 45,000	15.0

7. (a) Accounts receivable turnover $= \dfrac{\text{Net credit sales}}{\text{Average accounts receivable}} = \dfrac{\$800,000}{\$125,000} = 6.4$ times

(b) Collection period $= \dfrac{365 \text{ days}}{\text{Accounts receivable turnover}} = \dfrac{365}{6.4} = 57$ days

(c) Inventory turnover $= \dfrac{\text{Cost of goods sold}}{\text{Average inventory}} = \dfrac{\$450,000}{\$47,500} = 9.47$ times

(d) Age of inventory $= \dfrac{365 \text{ days}}{\text{Inventory turnover}} = \dfrac{365}{9.47} = 38.5$ days

(e) Operating cycle:

Collection period	59.0 days
Age of inventory	38.5 days
Operating cycle	95.5 days

8. 1 (c); 2 (d); 3 (a); 4 (g); 5 (f); 6 (h); 7 (e); 8 (b)

9. By purchasing land in exchange for shares of common stock, a company has altered its balance sheet with a transaction that would normally involve cash appearing on the statement of cash flows. Although cash is not involved in this transaction, the balance sheet changes are significant occurrences that should be disclosed on a schedule of significant noncash activities in conjunction with the statement of cash flows.

10. (a) F; (b) O; (c) F; (d) O; (e) N; (f) O

11. (a) +; (b) −; (c) +; (d) +; (e) −; (f) +; (g) +; (h) −; (i) −; (j) +

12. Since the transaction is denominated in Canadian dollars, a measurement problem exists for the U.S. company. The payable would be recorded in the U.S. dollar equivalent on the date of purchase as follows:

Purchase of Merchandise Inventory	120,000	
Accounts Payable		120,000

To record the purchase of goods in the amount of $120,000C when the exchange rate is $0.80US

When the $150,000C is paid 60 days later, the entry is as follows:

Accounts Payable	120,000	
Foreign Exchange Gain		15,000
Cash		105,000

To record the payment of $150,000C when the exchange rate is $0.70US ($150,000C × $0.70US =$105,000US).

INDEX